QUE Bee

From Doubts to **Distinction**
Your ICSE 2026 Exams Partner

GIST OF THE TEXTBOOK
Crisp & Complete Theory - No need to go back to bulky textbooks!

ALL TYPES OF LATEST PATTERN QUESTIONS
MCQs | Statement Based | Assertion-Reason | Odd One Out All in one place!

KEYWORDS HIGHLIGHTED
Important points and Keywords are neatly highlighted; Never miss what matters

COUNCIL-STYLE ANSWERS
Write responses like an examiner expects

SAMPLE QUESTION PAPER
Practice in real-exam mode. Perfect your timing, strategy, and confidence.

arihant

SUCCESS AND NOTHING LESS

ARIHANT PRAKASHAN

(School Division Series)

卐 **ADMINISTRATIVE & PRODUCTION OFFICES**

Regd. Office

'Ramchhaya' 4577/15, Agarwal Road, Darya Ganj, New Delhi -110002
Tele: 011- 47630600, 43518550; Fax: 011- 23280316

卐 **Head Office**

Kalindi, TP Nagar, Meerut (UP) - 250002, Tel: 0121-7156203, 7156204

卐 **SALES & SUPPORT OFFICES**

Agra, Ahmedabad, Bengaluru, Bareilly, Chennai, Delhi, Guwahati, Hyderabad, Jaipur, Jhansi, Kolkata, Lucknow, Nagpur & Pune.

PO No : TXT-XX-XXXXXXX-X-XX

Published By Arihant Publications (India) Ltd.

For further information about the books published by Arihant, log on to www.arihantbooks.com or e-mail at info@arihantbooks.com

Follow us on

卐 **PRICE** ₹200.00

PRODUCTION TEAM

Publishing Manager
Keshav Mohan

Project Head
Shruti Aggarwal

Cover Designer
Bilal Hashmi

Inner Designer
Ankit Tyagi

Page Layouting
Ravinder Kumar

QUE Bee

ICSE
Computer Applications
Class 9

Types of Questions & their Respective Number

Type of Questions	Total Number
Multiple Choice Questions	246
Statement Based Questions	65
Assertion-Reason Type Questions	70
Odd One Out	49
Very Short Answer Type Questions	64
Short Answer Type Questions (Program Based/Output Based, Rewrite or Convert the Code)	159
Differentiate	44
Long Answer Type Questions	92
TOTAL NO. OF QUESTIONS	**789**

Created by

Mahima Masih

20 Yrs. Experienced

PGT Computer

From Learner to Leader

Step-Into the Spotlight

QUE Bee is more than just a book - it's a platform for young achievers like you to guide future toppers. If you've cracked the code to smart study or have insights that can make learning easier for others, this is your moment to shine!

What Can You Share?

- Your study techniques, time management tips, or motivation hacks
- Feedback or suggestions to make QUE Bee even better
- Real experiences that can guide other students through the exam maze

What's in It for You?

- Your name will be featured in our exclusive Student Panel in the next edition
- Win exciting & surprise rewards for impactful suggestions
- **Get published** - your photo, Ideas-or even interviews can be featured in the book
- **Become a student icon** - recognized and followed by peers across schools

Let your learning become someone else's ladder.
Be remembered. Be featured. Be the guide.

SCAN TO SHARE YOUR IDEA

Index

Latest
Course Structure

*There will be **one** written paper of **two hours** duration carrying 100 marks and Internal Assessment of 100 marks.*

Theory - 100 Marks

1. Introduction to Object Oriented Programming Concepts

(i) Principles of Object Oriented Programming, (Difference between Procedure Oriented and Object oriented).

All the four principles of Object Oriented Programming should be defined and explained using real life examples (Data abstraction, Inheritance, Polymorphism, Encapsulation).

(ii) Introduction to JAVA - Types of java programs – Applets and Applications, Java Compilation process, Java Source code, Byte code, Object code, Java Virtual Machine (JVM), Features of JAVA.

Definition of Java applets and Java applications with examples, steps involved in compilation process, definitions of source code, byte code, object code, JVM, features of JAVA - Simple, Robust, secured, object oriented, platform independent, etc.

2. Elementary Concept of Objects and Classes

Modelling entities and their behaviour by objects, a class as a specification for objects and as an object factory, computation as message passing/method calls between objects (many examples should be done to illustrate this). Objects encapsulate state (attributes) and have behaviour (methods). Class as a user defined data type.

A class may be regarded as a blueprint to create objects. It may be viewed as a factory that produces similar objects. A class may also be considered as a new data type created by the user, that has its own functionality.

3. Values and data types

Character set, ASCII code, Unicode, Escape sequences, Tokens, Constants and Variables, Data types, type conversions.

Escape sequences [\n, \t, \\, \", \'], Tokens and its types [keywords, identifiers, literals, punctuators, operators], primitive types and non-primitive types with examples, Introduce the primitive types with size in bits and bytes, Implicit type conversion and Explicit type conversion.

4. Operators in Java

Forms of operators, Types of operators, Counters, Accumulators, Hierarchy of operators, 'new' operator, dot (.) operator.

Forms of operators (Unary, Binary, Ternary), types of operators (Arithmetic, Relational, Logical, Assignment, Increment, Decrement, Short hand operators), Discuss precedence and associativity of memory by using new operator, invoking members of class using dot operator, Introduce System.out.println() and System.out.print() for simple output.

(Bitwise and shift operators are not included).

5. Input in Java

Initialization, Parameter, introduction to packages, Input streams (Scanner Class), types of errors, types of comments

Initialization – Data before execution, Parameters – at the time of execution, input stream – data entry during execution – using methods of Scanner class [nextShort(), nextInt( ), nextLong( ), nextFloat ( ), nextDouble( ), next( ), nextLine( ), next ( ) .charAt(0)]

Discuss different types of errors occurring during execution and compilation of the program (syntax errors, runtime errors and logical errors).Single line comment (//) and multiline comment (/ ... */)*

6. Mathematical Library Methods

Introduction to package java.lang [default], methods of Math class.

pow(x,y), sqrt(x), cbrt(x), ceil(x), floor(x), round (x), abs(a), max(a, b), min(a,b), random( ).

Java expressions – using all the operators and methods of Math class.

7. Conditional Constructs in Java

Application of if, if else, if else if ladder, switch-case, default, break.

if, if else, if else if, Nested if, switch case, break statement, fall through condition in switch case, Menu driven programs, System.exit(0) - to terminate the program.

8. Iterative constructs in Java

Definition, Types of looping statements, entry controlled loops [for, while], exit controlled loop [do while] , variations in looping statements, and Jump statements.

Syntax of entry and exit controlled loops, break and continue, Simple programs illustrating all three loops, inter conversion from for – while – do while, finite and infinite, delay, multiple counter variables (initializations and updations). Demonstrate break and continue statements with the help of loops. Loops are fundamental to computation and their need should be shown by examples.

9. Nested for loops

Introduce nested loops through some simple examples. Demonstrate break and continue statements with the help of nested loops.

Programs based on nested loops [rectangular, triangular [right angled triangle only] patterns], series involving single variable. (Nested while and nested do while are not included.)

10. Computing and Ethics

Ethical Issues in Computing.

Intellectual property rights; protection of individual's right to privacy; data protection on the internet; protection against Spam; software piracy, cybercrime, hacking, protection against malicious intent and malicious code. The stress should be on good etiquette and ethical practices.

01

INTRODUCTION TO OBJECT ORIENTED PROGRAMMING CONCEPTS

Introduction

- Object-Oriented Programming (OOP) is a programming paradigm that organizes code around objects.
- These objects are created from classes, which are blueprints that define what the object will have (data or attributes) and what it can do (functions or methods).
- OOP helps to organize code in a way that reflects how things work in the real world, making programming more logical and easier to manage.

Difference between Procedure-Oriented Programming and Object-Oriented Programming

Procedure-Oriented Programming (POP)	Object-Oriented Programming (OOP)
Focuses on functions or procedures that perform actions.	Focuses on objects, which combine data and functions.
POP follows top down approach.	OOP follows bottom up approach.
Code is written as a sequence of instructions (procedures).	Code is written around objects, each having its own data and methods.
Data and functions are separate.	Data and functions are grouped together in classes (encapsulation).
A program is divided into functions that operate on data.	A program is divided into objects, which represent real-world entities.
Example A function to calculate the area of a rectangle.	**Example** A class for Rectangle with properties like length and width, and methods to calculate the area.

Principles of Object-Oriented Programming (OOP)

The four major principles of object-oriented programming are discussed below

Encapsulation

- The process of binding data and corresponding methods (behavior) together into a single unit is called **encapsulation** in Java.
- In other words, encapsulation is a programming technique that binds the class members (variables and methods) together and prevents them from being accessed by other classes. Thereby, we can keep variables and methods safes from outside interference and misuse.

```
class
{
  data members
  +
  methods (behavior)
}
```

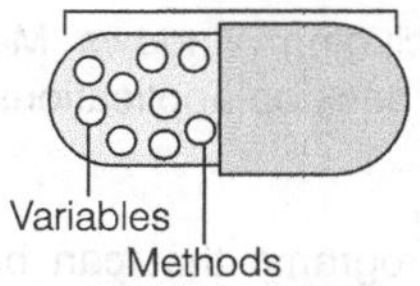

Example The bag contains different stuffs like pen, pencil, notebook etc within it, in order to get any stuff you need to open that bag, similarly in Java an encapsulation unit contains it's data and behavior within it and in order to access them you need an object of that unit.

Data Abstraction

- Abstraction is a process of hiding the internal details or implementations from the user and showing only relevant or abstract(brief or short) information to user.
- Abstractions says that, show only those information to user which is essential or useful for them and hide all other information which is not essential for them.

  Example When we login to any social networking site like Facebook, Linkedin etc, we enter our user id and password and then we get logged in. Here we don't know how they are processing the data or what logic or algorithm they are using for login. Those informations are abstracted/hidden from us, since those are not essential for us. This is basically the abstraction.

Inheritance

- Inheritance means creating new classes based on existing ones. A class that inherits from another class can reuse the methods and fields of that class. In addition, new fields and methods can be added in the current class as well.

  Some important points related to inheritance
  - In the inheritance the class which gives data members and methods is known as **base** or **super** or **parent class**.
  - The class which is taking the data members and methods is known as **derived** or **sub** or **child class**.
  - The concept of inheritance is also known as **re-usability** or **extendable classes** or **sub classing** or **derivation**.

  Example Children inherit properties from their parents, such as the ability to walk, eat and speak.

Polymorphism

- The word polymorphism is made from two words **poly** which means many and **morphism** which means 'forms' or 'types', so the word polymorphism means 'many forms'.
- Polymorphism in Java is a mechanism in which an object or it's behavior can have many different forms, we call such objects as polymorphic object.

  Example An individual can have different relationships with different people. As if a woman can be a mother, a daughter, a sister, and a friend, all at the same time, i.e. she performs different behaviors in different situations.

Introduction to Java

- Java is a high-level object-oriented programming language designed with the principle of **(WORA) "Write Once, Run Anywhere"**.
- **James Gosling** started the Java programming language project in June, 1991 as part of his work on set-top box projects. Initially, the language was named 'Oak,' inspired by an oak tree outside Gosling's office. It was later called 'Green' before finally being renamed 'Java', chosen from a list of random words.
- The first public version, **Java 1.0** was released by Sun Microsystems in 1995.
- On November 13, 2006, Sun Microsystems made a significant move by releasing a large portion of Java as free and open-source software under the **GNU General Public License (GPL)**.
- By May 8, 2007, Sun completed the transition, making all of Java's core code free and open-source, except for a small portion of code that was not under Sun's copyright.
- The Java architecture consists of:
  - a platform-independent representation of a compiled class
  - a pre-defined set of run-time libraries
  - a virtual machine
- Java works on many platforms, including Windows, Mac OS, and different versions of UNIX. Developers use Java to create all kinds of software, like desktop applications, mobile apps, websites, games, and much more.

Types of Java Programs

There are basically two types of programs that can be developed with Java. Java Development Kit (JDK) is a software development environment used for developing Java applications and applets.

1. Java Applications

- A Java application is a standalone program that runs on a computer or device without the need for a web browser.

- It is executed directly by the **Java Runtime Environment** (JRE is a software layer that allows Java Programs to run on a computer) on the machine.
- Java applications are used for a wide variety of purposes, including desktop software, server-side applications, and more.

2. Java Applets

- An applet is a micro application designed to perform a single function or a set of simple functions within an enclosed frame and is typically embedded on a web page in a browser.
- Java applets were commonly used in the past to create interactive content for web pages.
- Applet will have the following stages in its life cycle:
    - **init** method to retrieve the applet
    - **start** method to activate the applet
    - **paint** method to refresh the applet
    - **stop** method to deactivate the applet while keeping it on
    - **destroy** method to fully turn the applet off

Java Compilation Process

The Java compilation process is the series of steps that convert Java source code (written in a .java file) into bytecode (stored in a .class file) that can be executed by the Java Virtual Machine (JVM).

Steps involved in Java Compilation Process

1. Writing the Source Code

The developer writes the Java source code using the Java programming language and saves it in a file with the .java extension (e.g., HelloWorld.java).

2. Compiling the Source Code

The next step is to compile the .java file into bytecode, which is platform-independent.

This is done using the Java Compiler (javac), which reads the .java file and produces a .class file containing the bytecode.

3. Bytecode Generation

The Java compiler (javac) takes the source code and converts it into bytecode, which is a low-level representation of the program. The bytecode is stored in a .class file.

4. Execution by the JVM

When you run the compiled Java program, the Java Virtual Machine (JVM) interprets or just-in-time (JIT) compiles the bytecode into native machine code specific to the system on which it is running.

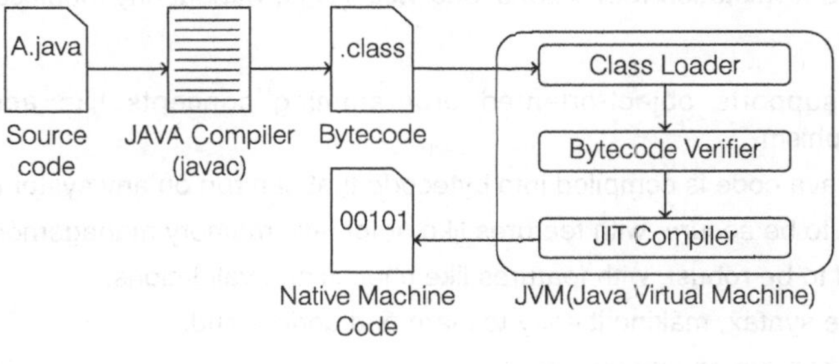

Source Code

- Java source code is the human-readable code that you write when developing a Java program.
- It is written using the Java programming language's syntax, which consists of classes, methods, variables, and other elements that define the logic and structure of the program.
- The source code is created by a developer using a text editor or an **Integrated Development Environment** (IDE) like BlueJ. Java source code files are typically saved with a .java extension.
- It must be compiled into bytecode before execution.
- It is platform-independent, allowing the same code to be run on any device with a Java Virtual Machine (JVM).

ByteCode

- Bytecode is an intermediate, low-level representation of Java source code that is generated by the Java compiler.
- It is platform-independent, meaning it can run on any device or operating system with a Java Virtual Machine (JVM) installed, regardless of the system it was originally compiled on.
- Bytecode is designed to be universal, meaning it doesn't depend on any specific operating system or hardware. As long as the target system has a JVM, it can run the bytecode.
- Bytecode is not directly executable by the hardware. Instead, it is executed by the JVM, which translates the bytecode into machine-specific instructions.
- Bytecode is a set of instructions that are simple for the JVM to interpret or compile into native machine code. These instructions are optimized for portability and efficiency.

Object Code

- Object code is machine-specific, and runs directly on the computer's processor. In Java, the JVM takes the bytecode and further translates it into object code (or native code) at runtime. This object code is specific to the particular hardware and operating system the JVM is running on. This final translation is often done just-in-time (JIT) by the JVM.
- Object code or native code or machine code is the final output. It is platform-dependent and is written in binary language (0s and 1s).

Java Virtual Machine (JVM)

- Java programs are executed by a special program called the **Java Virtual Machine** (JVM).
- It is a specification that defines a runtime environment where Java bytecode can be executed.
- It is an abstract concept, with its implementation varying depending on the algorithm used, and it has been provided by Sun Microsystems and other companies.
- The JVM's primary responsibility is to convert Java bytecode into machine-specific code, enabling it to run on different platforms.
- Additionally, the JVM can also run programs written in other languages that are compiled into Java bytecode. The key tasks performed by the JVM are:
  - Loading code
  - Verifying code
  - Executing code
  - Providing the runtime environment
- This setup allows Java programs to run on any computer system that has the JVM installed, regardless of where the program was originally developed. For example, a Java program created on a Windows PC can run seamlessly on a Sun Ultra workstation with Solaris, and *vice-versa*, without any modifications.

Features of Java

- **Object-oriented** Java supports object-oriented programming concepts like abstraction, encapsulation, inheritance, and polymorphism.
- **Platform independent** Java code is compiled into bytecode that can run on any system with a java runtime.
- **Secure** Java is designed to be secure, with features like automatic memory management and exception handling.
- **Robust** Java is designed to be robust, with features like checks and validations.
- **Simple** Java has a simple syntax, making it easy to learn and understand.
- **Portable** Java programs can run on any device.
- **Multithreading** In Java it is a process of executing multiple processes simultaneously.
- **Distributed** Java is distributed because it facilitates users to create distributed applications in Java. This features of Java makes us able to access files by calling the methods from any machine on the Internet.

Note *Garbage collection in Java is a built-in feature that automatically removes unused code and objects from the Java heap. This process frees up memory and makes Java programs more efficient.*

EXAM ORIENTED QUESTIONS

TYPE - 1 01 Mark

Multiple Choice Questions

Q.1 Java's ability to model real-world entities with attributes and behaviors through the use of classes and objects places it firmly within the ________
(a) Procedural programming language
(b) Structured programming language
(c) Object oriented programming language
(d) Machine code

Q.2 Which OOP concept allows grouping data and related methods into one unit. Promoting data security and modularity?
(a) Data abstraction (b) Data encapsulation
(c) Neither (a) nor (b) (d) Both (a) and (b)

Q.3 Name the feature of Java depicted in the below picture.

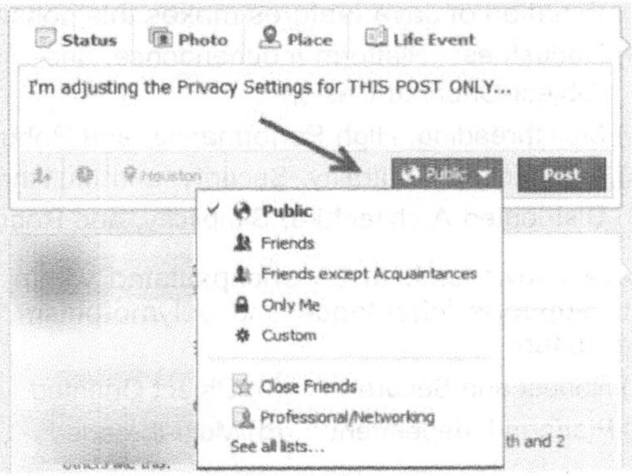

(a) Encapsulation (b) Inheritance
(c) Abstraction (d) Polymorphism

Q.4 OOP principle ensures that internal details of an object are hidden and only relevant information is exposed.
(a) Abstraction (b) Encapsulation
(c) Inheritance (d) Polymorphism

Q.5 Name the feature of Java depicted in the below picture.

(a) Encapsulation (b) Inheritance
(c) Abstraction (d) Polymorphism

Q.6 Name the feature of Java depicted in the given picture.

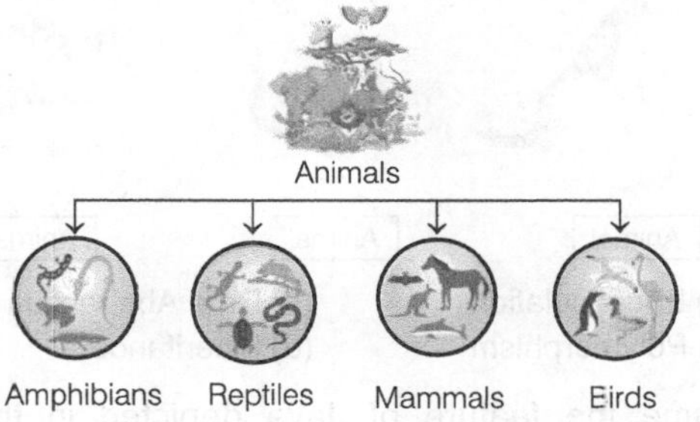

(a) Encapsulation (b) Inheritance
(c) Abstraction (d) Polymorphism

Q.7 Name the feature of Java depicted in the following picture.

(a) Polymorphism (b) Inheritance
(c) Encapsulation (d) Data Abstraction

Q.8 Which of the following real-world examples best represents inheritance?
(a) A driver operating a car without knowing the engine's inner workings
(b) A rectangle class being extended by a square class
(c) A method to calculate a discount behaving differently for regular and premium customers
(d) A bag containing multiple items like a pen and notebook

Q.9 Name the oop's concept that the given picture depicts

$ € £ ¥ ₹

(a) Encapsulation (b) Polymorphism
(c) Inheritance (d) Abstraction

Q.10 A software application needs to ensure that multiple users can log in using different authentication methods, like passwords, fingerprints, or face recognition. Which concept makes this possible?
(a) Encapsulation (b) Abstraction
(c) Inheritance (d) Polymorphism

Q.11 Name the feature of Java depicted in the following picture.

(a) Encapsulation (b) Data Abstraction
(c) Polymorphism (d) Inheritance

Q.12 Name the feature of Java depicted in the given picture.

(a) Encapsulation (b) Inheritance
(c) Polymorphism (d) Data abstraction

Q.13 Which of the following is not a principle of Object-Oriented Programming (OOP)?
(a) Encapsulation (b) Inheritance
(c) Polymorphism (d) Compilation

Q.14 Under which license did Sun Microsystems release most of Java's core code as open-source in 2006?
(a) MIT License (b) GNU General Public License
(c) Apache License (d) BSD License

Q.15 In Java, which file contains the bytecode generated by the compiler?
(a) .java file (b) .class file
(c) .exe file (d) .jar file

Q.16 Which Java program type depends on browser context and follows a distinct life-cycle including methods like init() and destroy()?
(a) Application (b) Applet (c) Module (d) Servlet

Q.17 The Java compiler ....
(a) creates executable
(b) does the packaging
(c) converts Java source code to byte code
(d) produces Java interpreter

Q.18 What is the role of the JVM in Java?
(a) Converts source code to bytecode
(b) Converts byte code to machine code
(c) Provides a platform-specific compiler
(d) Runs Java programs directly from source code

Q.19 View the following figure and answer the question that follows:

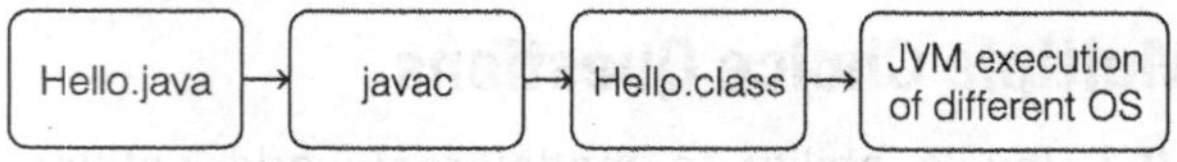

Based on the image, which Java feature does this process represent?
(a) Platform Independence (b) Multithreading
(c) Object-Oriented Design (d) Dynamic Behavior

Q.20 Which feature of Java ensures programs can execute multiple tasks simultaneously?
(a) Platform independence (b) Multithreading
(c) Encapsulation (d) Robustness

Q.21 An e-commerce platform built in Java experiences high traffic during a sale event. The application efficiently handles multiple requests from users, providing quick responses without crashing. Which combination of Java features makes this possible?
(a) Robustness, Platform Independence, and Object-Oriented Design
(b) Multithreading, High Performance, and Robustness
(c) Architecture Neutrality, Security, and Multithreading
(d) Distributed Architecture, Simplicity, and Robustness

Q.22 "Java allows data to be encapsulated within objects and supports inheritance and polymorphism." Name the feature.
(a) Robust and Secure (b) Object Oriented
(c) Platform Independent (d) Multi-threaded

Q.23 "Java programs are less likely to crash because it manages memory and handles exceptions effectively." Name the feature.
(a) Robust and Secure (b) Platform Independent
(c) Object Oriented (d) Architecture Neutral

Q.24 Feature of Java ensures that code written once can run anywhere without modification.
(a) Robust (b) Multithreading
(c) Platform Independence (d) Secure

Answers

1. (c)	**2.** (b)	**3.** (c)	**4.** (a)	**5.** (b)
6. (b)	**7.** (b)	**8.** (b)	**9.** (b)	**10.** (d)
11. (c)	**12.** (c)	**13.** (d)	**14.** (b)	**15.** (b)
16. (b)	**17.** (b)	**18.** (b)	**19.** (a)	**20.** (b)
21. (b)	**22.** (b)	**23.** (a)	**24.** (c)	

TYPE - 2 (01 Mark)

Statement Based Questions

Q.1 Principles of Object-Oriented Programming (Abstraction, Inheritance, Polymorphism, Encapsulation)

Consider the following descriptions of OOP principles, which are jumbled. Choose the correct order of the principles that best match the descriptions.

(i) Hiding the implementation details and showing only essential information.
(ii) Ability of an object to take on many forms.
(iii) Grouping related data and methods into a single unit.
(iv) Deriving new classes from existing classes.

(a) (i), (iv), (ii), (iii) (b) (ii), (iii), (i), (iv)
(c) (iii), (i), (iv), (ii) (d) (iv), (ii), (iii), (i)

Q.2 A software developer is designing a system for managing student records. They want to represent a "Student" object with attributes like name, roll number, and marks. However, they only want to expose the necessary details to the user, hiding the internal implementation details.

They have written the following incorrect statement:

Display all internal attributes of the Student object directly.

What will be the correct approach to manage the student object's information while using data abstraction?

(i) Directly access all attributes of the Student object.
(ii) Create methods to access only necessary details of the Student object.
(iii) Display all attributes without using any methods.

(a) Only (i) (b) Only (ii)
(c) Both (iii) and (i) (d) None of these

Q.3 A Java developer writes a program named "AppletDemo.java" and wants to run it as an applet in a web browser. They have compiled the program using the javac command, but the browser is not executing the code. They have written the following incorrect statement about the execution:

The browser directly executes AppletDemo.java

What will be the correct statement regarding the execution of the applet in a browser?

(i) The browser executes AppletDemo.exe.
(ii) The browser executes AppletDemo.class.
(iii) The browser executes AppletDemo.obj.

(a) Only (i) (b) Only (ii)
(c) All (i), (ii) and (iii) (d) None of these

Q.4 Arrange the following lifecycle stages of a Java Applet in the correct order of execution:

(i) Initialization (init)
(ii) Starting (start)
(iii) Painting (paint)
(iv) Stopping (stop)
(v) Destroying (destroy)

(a) (i), (ii), (iii), (iv), (v) (b) (i), (ii), (iii), (v), (iv)
(c) (ii), (i), (iii), (iv), (v) (d) (iii), (i), (ii), (iv), (v)

Q.5 Arrange the following steps of Java program execution in the correct order:

(i) Bytecode is generated.
(ii) Java source code is written.
(iii) JVM executes the bytecode.
(iv) Source code is compiled by the Java compiler.

(a) (ii), (iv), (i), (iii)
(b) (ii), (i), (iv), (iii)
(c) (iv), (ii), (i), (iii)
(d) (i), (ii), (iv), (iii)

Answers

1. (a) **2.** (b) **3.** (b) **4.** (a) **5.** (a)

TYPE - 3 (01 Mark)

Assertion-Reason Type Questions

Directions (Q. Nos. 1-5) The following questions are Assertion-Reason based questions. Choose the answer based on the code given below

(a) Both Assertion (A) and Reason (R) are true and Reason (R) is a correct explanation of Assertion (A).
(b) Both Assertion (A) and Reason (R) are true and Reason (R) is not a correct explanation of Assertion (A).
(c) Assertion (A) is true and Reason (R) is false.
(d) Assertion (A) is false and Reason (R) is true.

Q.1 Assertion (A) Java supports encapsulation to protect data from unauthorized access.

Reason (R) Encapsulation allows methods and data to be accessed directly without restrictions.

Ans. (c) Encapsulation in Java does protect data from unauthorized access, but it achieves this by restricting direct access to data members through methods, not by allowing direct access without restrictions. Hence, Assertion (A) is true and Reason (R) is false.

Q.2 Assertion (A) Inheritance promotes code reusability in Java.

Reason (R) Inheritance allows child classes to reuse the data members and methods of parent classes.

Ans. (a) Assertion (A) is true, inheritance does promote code reusability in Java. Reason (R) is also true, it accurately describes how inheritance enables child classes to reuse the data members and methods of parent classes.

Q.3 Assertion (A) Polymorphism allows objects to take multiple forms in Java.

Reason (R) Polymorphism is achieved through method overloading and overriding.

Ans. (a) Assertion (A) is true, polymorphism allows objects to take on multiple forms, meaning the same method call can behave differently depending on the object's type. Reason (R) is also true, polymorphism in Java is primarily achieved through method overloading and method overriding.

Q.4 Assertion (A) Java is a platform-independent language.

Reason (R) Java source code is directly executed by the operating system.

Ans. (c) Java achieves platform independence through bytecode execution by the JVM, not direct execution of source code. Hence, Assertion (A) is true and Reason (R) is false.

Q.5 Assertion (A) JVM is a Java interpreter loaded in the computer memory as soon as Java is loaded.

Reason (R) JVM is different for different platforms.

Ans. (b) Assertion (A) is partially true, while the Reason (R) is true but not a direct explanation of the assertion. The JVM does interpret Java bytecode and is loaded into memory, but it's not immediately loaded as soon as Java is loaded. The JVM is a runtime environment that facilitates the execution of Java programs, and its loading is a process that occurs when a Java application is launched, not just when the language is "loaded".

TYPE - 4 — 01 Mark

Odd One Out

Q.1 Choose the odd one out.

(a) Encapsulation (b) Abstraction
(c) Inheritance (d) Looping

Ans. (d) Looping (as it's a procedural concept, not specific to OOP).

Q.2 Choose the odd one out.

(a) Class (b) Object
(c) Polymorphism (d) Algorithm

Ans. (d) Algorithm (it's a general programming concept, not exclusive to OOP).

Q.3 Choose the odd one out.

(a) init() (b) start() (c) stop() (d) main()

Ans. (d) main() (Applets do not use a main() method; they rely on lifecycle methods).

Q.4 Choose the odd one out.

(a) Compilation (b) Interpretation
(c) Inheritance (d) SQL Query

Ans. (d) SQL Query (SQL is used for database operations, not a core Java application concept).

Q.5 Choose the odd one out.

(a) Robust (b) Platform independent
(c) Inheritance (d) Multithreading

Ans. (c) Inheritance (It is a key concept in OOP, not a feature of Java).

TYPE - 5 — 02 Marks

Short Answer Type Questions

Q.1 Mention two limitations of:
(a) **procedure oriented programming**
(b) **object oriented programming**

Ans. (a) Two limitations of procedure oriented programming approach are:
- No restriction on data values.
- Limited and difficult code reusability.

(b) Two limitations of object oriented programming approach are:
- Higher complexity and learning curve.
- Increased memory and processing overhead.

Q.2 In Java, what concept allows combining data and methods within a class while restricting external access, thus ensuring security, control, and modularity?

Ans. Encapsulation is the binding of data and methods into a single unit (class) and restricting direct access to them. Encapsulation is important because it helps secure the data, ensures better control over the program's functionality, and promotes modularity by keeping data and behavior together.

Q.3 Describe the abstraction principle with a real-world example.

Ans. Abstraction hides unnecessary implementation details and shows only essential features.

For example, when logging into a website, the user only interacts with the login interface, not the internal algorithms.

Q.4 Which of the object oriented programming principles explain the following illustrations?

(a) **The variables and methods are put together in a Class.**

(b) **A man withdrawing money from ATM.**

Ans. (a) **Encapsulation** This helps in data hiding by restricting direct access to variables and ensuring they are accessed only through methods.

(b) **Abstraction** When withdrawing money from an ATM, the user interacts with a simple interface (pressing buttons), but the internal banking processes (authentication, balance checking, transaction processing, etc.) remain hidden.

Q.5 State the Java concept that is implemented through
(i) a super class and a sub class
(ii) the act of representing essential features without including background details.

Ans. (i) Inheritance (ii) Abstraction

Q.6 Which OOP concept enables a new class to build upon the features of an existing class, reducing code repetition?

Ans. Inheritance allows a class (child) to reuse and extend the properties and methods of another class (parent), promoting code reusability.

Q.7 Which Object-Oriented Programming principle explains the following illustration?
(a) Creating a "SportsCar" that automatically inherits the "Car" blueprint's properties and actions, but also adds a "turboBoost()" action.
(b) A "Shape" class has a "draw()" method, and both "Circle" and "Square" use the same method to draw themselves in their own way.

Ans. (a) **Inheritance** The "SportsCar" inherits properties and actions from "Car" and adds its own unique features.

(b) **Polymorphism** The "draw()" method is used by both "Circle" and "Square" to draw themselves in different ways.

Q.8 What is meant by 'Base' class and 'Derived' class?

Ans. The class from which other classes are derived through the process of inheritance is called **base class** or **super class**. The class that inherits properties from a base class is called a **derived class**.

Q.9 What is polymorphism in object-oriented programming? Provide a real-life example.

Ans. Polymorphism is the ability of an object or behavior to take many forms. It allows methods to perform different tasks based on the object or context they are used with.

Example A woman can be a mother, daughter, sister, and friend, performing different roles and behaviors in each context, illustrating the concept of polymorphism.

Q.10 Why is bytecode considered platform-independent, while object code is not? Explain with reference to Java's execution model.

Ans. Bytecode is platform-independent because it is executed by the Java Virtual Machine (JVM), which is available on various operating systems. The same bytecode can run on any system with a JVM.

In contrast, object code is machine-specific and depends on the underlying hardware and OS, which makes it platform-dependent.

Q.11 What does JVM stand for? Briefly describe the role of the Java Virtual Machine (JVM) in achieving platform independence for Java programs.

Ans. JVM stand for Java Virtual Machine .The JVM enables platform independence by interpreting Java bytecode into native machine code specific to the operating system.

This allows Java programs to run on any platform with a JVM installed, which ensures the same code works across different systems without modification.

Q.12 The Java compilation process involves converting source code written in Java into bytecode that can be executed by the Java Virtual Machine (JVM).

Draw a diagram to illustrate the Java compilation process, including the steps from writing source code to execution by the JVM.

Ans. **Write Source Code** You write the Java source code in .java files.

Compilation (javac) The Java compiler (javac) takes the source code and converts it into bytecode, stored in .class files.

Bytecode The .class file contains the bytecode, which is platform-independent.

Execution by JVM The Java Virtual Machine (JVM) loads and interprets the bytecode, or just-in-time (JIT) compiles it to native machine code for execution on the specific platform.

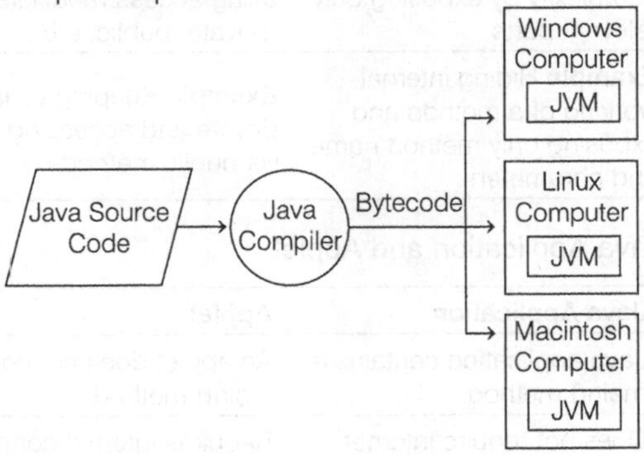

Q.13 Define the following terms of Java:
(a) Robustness (b) Portability

Ans. (a) **Robustness** Robustness in Java means the ability to handle errors and exceptions without crashing. It is achieved through:

- Automatic memory management through garbage collection and exception handling for runtime errors.
- Strict type checking at both compile-time and runtime to prevent errors.

(b) **Portability** Portability in Java means Java programs can run on any platform without modification, thanks to the Write Once, Run Anywhere (WORA) principle:

- Java programs are compiled into bytecode (.class files).
- The JVM interprets bytecode, making it platform-independent.

Q.14 Explain the concept of platform independence in Java.

Ans. Java is platform-independence because its code is compiled into bytecode, which can be executed on any system with a Java Virtual Machine (JVM). This means the same Java program can run on different operating systems without modification.

TYPE - 6 02 Marks

Differentiate

Q.1 Abstraction and Encapsulation

Ans.

Abstraction	Encapsulation
Abstraction is the process of hiding unnecessary details and showing only essential features.	Encapsulation is the process of bundling data and methods that operate on the data into a single unit (class).
It is focused on the interface level, i.e., what to show.	It is focused on the implementation level, i.e., how data is hidden.
Helps in managing complexity by exposing only relevant parts.	Helps in data protection by using access modifiers (private, public, etc.).
Example Hiding internal working of a method and exposing only method name and parameters.	**Example** Keeping variables private and accessing them *via* public methods.

Q.2 Java Application and Applet

Ans.

Java Application	Applet
Java application contains a main() method.	An applet does not contain a main() method.
Does not require internet conncetion to execute.	Requires internet connection to execute.
Is stand alone application.	Is a part of web page.
Can be run without a browser.	Requires a Java compatible browser.
Generally used for console programs.	Generally used for GUI interfaces.

Q.3 Compiler and Interpreter

Ans.

Compiler	Interpreter
Translates the entire source code into machine code before execution.	Translates and executes the source code line-by-line or statement-by-statement.
Generally, it is faster execution after compilation because the code is directly translated to machine code.	Slower execution compared to compiled code, as translation occurs during execution.
Errors are detected and must be corrected after the entire program is compiled.	Errors are detected and must be corrected line-by-line during execution.
Typically, it requires more memory initially to store the executable code.	Uses less memory as it directly executes the instructions without creating an executable file.

Q.4 JDK, JRE and JVM

Ans.

JDK	JRE	JVM
Used to develop Java applications	Used to run Java applications	Responsible for running Java code
Platform-dependent	Platform-dependent	Platform-Independent
It includes development tools like (compiler) + JRE	It includes libraries to run Java application + JVM	It runs the Java byte code and make Java application to work on any platform.
Writing and compiling Java code	Running a Java application on a system	Convert bytecode into native machine code

Q.5 Source code and Object code

Ans.

Source code	Object code
Source code is generated by human or programmer.	Object code is generated by compiler or other translator.
Source code is high level code.	Object code is low level code.
Source code is written in plain text by using some high level programming language.	Object code is translated code of source code. It is in binary format.
Source code is human understandable.	Object code is not human understandable.
Source code is not directly understandable by machine.	Object code is machine understandable and executable.

02

ELEMENTARY CONCEPT OF OBJECTS AND CLASSES

Java Classes

A **Java class** is a blueprint for creating objects or, more simply, a user-defined data type for object-oriented programming. In Java, classes and objects form the foundation of the language. Each class defines specific **attributes** (data) and **methods** (behavior) that its objects can have or perform.

For example, if you want to model students, you would create a Student class. Each individual student record (e.g., student1, student2) would then be an object of the Student class.

A class can also be thought of as a factory that defines a template for producing objects.

Properties of Java Classes

- **No Memory Allocation for the Class Itself** A class itself does not occupy memory until objects are created from it.
- **Blueprint, Not a Real Entity** A class represents a conceptual design or structure but is not a real-world entity on its own.
- **Contains Methods and Data Members** A class primarily consists of **methods** (functions that define behavior) and **data members** (variables that hold state).
- **Supports Nested Classes** Classes can include other classes within them, known as nested classes.
- **Adheres to OOP Principles** Java classes follow object-oriented programming concepts like:
  - **Inheritance** Sharing and reusing code between classes.
  - **Encapsulation** Wrapping up of data and functions in one single unit
  - **Abstraction** Hiding complex implementation details.
  - **Polymorphism** Allowing methods to perform different tasks based on context.

Java Objects

An **object** is a variable of a class type and a fundamental building block of object-oriented programming (OOP). It represents an **instance of a class**. A class defines the structure and behavior, while an object holds the specific data and performs actions defined by the class.

Objects allow access to a class's methods and attributes (data members). This makes objects the key to working with the class's functionality.

Modelling Real-World Entities and Their Behaviour

Modelling in programming means creating a representation of real-world entities (things, objects) using objects in software. These real-world things have two main characteristics:

1. **State** What the thing contains (its properties or data).
2. **Behaviour** What the thing can do (its actions or functions).

In Object-Oriented Programming (OOP), we model these entities as objects, which combine both state and behaviour.

Example A Fan is a physical object, and in OOP, we can model it as an object. Let's break it down:

- **State** These are the attributes of the Fan.

REVISION NOTES

  - **Speed** How fast the fan is rotating (e.g., low, medium, high).
  - **Color** The color of the fan (e.g., white, black, etc.).
  - **Number of Blades** The number of blades the fan has.
- **Behaviour** These are the actions the Fan can perform.
  - **rotate()** The fan starts spinning.
  - **increaseSpeed()** Increases the speed of the fan.
  - **stop()** Stops the fan.

Objects Encapsulate State (Attributes) and Have Behavior (Methods)

In **Object-Oriented Programming (OOP)**, an **object** is a fundamental building block that represents a real-world entity. Each object encapsulates:

State (Attributes)

The **state** of an object is defined by its attributes, which are stored as fields (variables) in the object. The state represents the object's data at any given time. Attributes are usually **private** to prevent direct access and are exposed via getter and setter methods.

For example, in a Car object: [**State** brand, color, speed]

Behavior (Methods)

The **behavior** of an object is defined by its methods. Methods operate on the object's state and perform tasks such as modifying attributes, interacting with other objects, or returning information.

For example, in a Car object: [**Behavior** start(), accelerate(), stop()]

Encapsulation

Encapsulation is the bundling of an object's state and behavior within the object, restricting direct access to the internal state. Instead:

State is accessed and modified through methods (getters and setters).

This ensures data integrity and provides controlled interaction with the object.

In the above example, the **speed** attribute is private and accessed through the getSpeed() method.

Behavior like starting, accelerating, and stopping is encapsulated within the methods start(), accelerate(), and stop().

Computation as Message Passing/Method Calls Between Objects

In Object-Oriented Programming (OOP), computation is achieved by message passing or method calls between objects. Each object encapsulates its state (attributes) and behavior (methods), and objects communicate by invoking each other's methods to share data or perform actions. This process resembles a conversation where one object requests another to perform a task by "sending a message."

Example

Suppose there are two objects: Student and Library.

- The Student object wants to borrow a book.
- Instead of directly accessing the book list inside the Library object, the Student sends a message by calling a method like: library.issueBook("Python Basics")

Class as a User-Defined Data Type

Java uses pre defined data types like int, char etc to provide some basic facilities in Java programming. A user can create a data type and declare certain characteristics and behaviour within it this can be done by using a class. This is the reason why class is referred to as user defined data type.

A Class as a Specification for Objects and as an Object Factory

An Object Factory

A class acts as a factory to produce objects. Using the class as a template, multiple objects can be created with the same structure and behavior but having their own distinct data (state). A class is also a "factory" that produces objects. When you use the new keyword in Java, the class acts as a factory to create an object in memory.

Each object produced by the factory has the same structure (as defined by the class) but can have different states.

Example Using the Car class as a factory, you can create multiple car objects. **car1** and **car2** are two objects created by the **Car** class.

They share the same structure (defined by the class) but have independent states and behavior.

A **class** is both a **specification** that defines the structure and behavior of objects and a **factory** that produces objects adhering to that specification. This dual role of classes makes them a cornerstone of Object-Oriented Programming, enabling the creation of complex systems with reusable, modular, and consistent designs.

Creating Objects of a Class

An object is an instance of a class creating an object of a class is called **instantiation**.

Syntax `<class name> <object name> = new <class name> ();`

e.g. `Car Honda = new Car();`

The keyword **new** is used for allocating space in the dynamic memory for storage of an object. The new operator also invokes the class constructor.

Note *Every class in Java has a constructor if no constructor is defined, the compiler automatically provides a default no-argument constructor.*

EXAM ORIENTED QUESTIONS

TYPE - 1 01 Mark

Multiple Choice Questions

Q.1 ________ is a template to create similar objects that share common characteristics and behavior.
(a) A class (b) An attribute
(c) A procedure (d) A function

Q.2

In the context of object-oriented programming, what does the blueprint of the "Car" represent?
(a) An object (b) A class
(c) A method (d) An attribute

Q.3 Which of the following best describes a class in object-oriented programming?
(a) A variable that stores values
(b) A blueprint or template for creating objects
(c) A method that processes data
(d) A function that defines object behavior

Q.4 What is the main purpose of a Java class in object-oriented programming?
(a) To allocate memory for objects
(b) To act as a template for creating objects
(c) To perform computations directly
(d) To replace primitive data types

Q.5 What does the new keyword do in Java?
(a) Declares a variable (b) Creates an object of a class
(c) Calls a method (d) Deletes an object

Q.6

Dog Class

Name, Breed, Age

Pug Object

Buddy, Pug, 3

What is the relationship between the "Dog" class and the "Pug" object?
(a) The object is a method of the class
(b) The class is an attribute of the object
(c) The object is an instance of the class
(d) The object is a different class

Q.7 In the context of Java objects, which of the following represents the "state" of an object?
(a) The methods defined in the class
(b) The attributes or fields of the object
(c) The constructors used to create the object
(d) The memory allocated to the object

Q.8

Student Class

Name, Roll Number, Marks

Student Object

Nitin,123,85

What is the purpose of defining attributes within a class?
(a) To define the behavior of the class
(b) To define the data that the objects of the class will hold
(c) To create new objects
(d) To define the methods of the class

Q.9 What does the following line represent in OOP?
```
obj.sayHello();
```
(a) Class definition
(b) Object creation
(c) Message passing / Method call
(d) Variable declaration

Q.10 In Java, what does the static keyword indicate in a method declaration?
(a) The method belongs to the class
(b) The method is private
(c) The method requires an object
(d) The method is final

Q.11 Which of these is an example of encapsulation in term of object?
(a) Declaring all variables as public
(b) Using methods to access private variables
(c) Writing global variables
(d) None of the above

Q.12 Rectangle Class Rectangle Object

Rectangle Class	Rectangle Object
Width	10
Height	5

Which of the following is a method that could be defined within a class for the "Rectangle" object?

(a) Name (b) CalculateArea
(c) Width (d) Height

Q.13 In Java, what is created when a class is instantiated to represent a real world entity?

(a) A variable of primitive type
(b) A method within a class
(c) An instance of a class
(d) A package

Q.14 In object-oriented programming, how are objects created from a class?

(a) By directly modifying the class
(b) By using new keyword
(c) By assigning values to attributes
(d) By using message passing between classes

Q.15

Radius	7

What would be the correct way to create an object of the "Circle" class?

(a) `Circle object = new Circle;`
(b) `Circle object = new Circle(7);`
(c) `new Circle object;`
(d) `Object circle = new Circle;`

Q.16 How do objects in OOP typically interact with one another?

(a) By directly accessing each other's attributes
(b) By invoking each other's methods through message passing
(c) By sharing memory allocated by their respective classes
(d) By using a static context to manage shared behavior

Q.17 Which of the following examples best illustrates the use of a class as a "factory" for objects?

(a) A Car class creating multiple car objects like car1 and car2
(b) A HelloWorld class printing "Hello, World!"
(c) A Light class turning a single light on and off
(d) A Dog_Fetch class allowing a dog to fetch a ball

Q.18 How does the concept of object encapsulation benefit object-oriented programming?

(a) By providing a direct way to access object attributes
(b) By bundling data and behavior while restricting direct access to the internal state
(c) By enabling multiple inheritance
(d) By allowing memory allocation for multiple objects

Q.19 What does the following code snippet represent?

```
public void greet(Person other)
{
    System.out.println(name + " says: Hello, " +
                       other.name + "!");
}
```

(a) Encapsulation (b) Message passing
(c) Polymorphism (d) Abstraction

Q.20 What does the System class in Java represent?

(a) The JVM
(b) A predefined class for system-related features
(c) A user-defined class
(d) A class for file handling

Q.21 In the "HelloWorld" Java program, what is the role of the main method?

(a) To compile the Java code into bytecode
(b) To print the output to the console
(c) To serve as the entry point for program execution
(d) To declare global variables

Q.22 In the example of the "Person" class, what does the method Simran.greet(Rohan) demonstrate?

(a) Data encapsulation
(b) Message passing between objects
(c) Method overloading
(d) Object inheritance

Q.23 In the "Car_Details" example, which concept is demonstrated by making the speed attribute private and accessing it through the getSpeed method?

(a) Inheritance (b) Polymorphism
(c) Encapsulation (d) Abstraction

Answers

1. (a)	2. (b)	3. (b)	4. (b)	5. (b)
6. (c)	7. (b)	8. (b)	9. (c)	10. (a)
11. (b)	12. (b)	13. (c)	14. (b)	15. (b)
16. (b)	17. (a)	18. (b)	19. (b)	20. (b)
21. (c)	22. (b)	23. (c)		

TYPE - 2 01 Mark

Statement Based Questions

Q.1 A programmer is creating a "Car" class with a "color" attribute. They want to set the color of a specific car object. They have written the following incorrect statement:

> Access the "color" attribute directly from outside the Car class.

What is the correct way to set the car's color using methods?

A. Directly change the color attribute.

B. Use a method like setColor() to change the color.

C. Do not use any methods to set the color.

(a) Only A (b) Only B

(c) Both A and C (d) None of these

Q.2 A developer is creating a "Shape" class and wants to make a "Circle" shape using it. They have written the following incorrect statement:

Create a Circle object without using the Shape class as a template.

What is the correct way to use the "Shape" class as a blueprint to create a "Circle" object?

A. Create a Circle object without using the Shape class.

B. Use the Shape class to define the Circle object's properties.

C. Ignore the Shape class when creating the Circle object.

(a) Only A (b) Only B

(c) Both A and C (d) None of these

Q.3 A program has a "Message" class to send messages. They want to send a message using a method. They have written the following incorrect statement:

Send the message by directly changing its content from another part of the program.

What is the correct way to send a message using a method?

A. Directly change the message content.

B. Use a method like sendMessage() to send the message.

C. Do not use any method to send the message.

(a) Only A

(b) Only B

(c) Both A and C

(d) None of the above

Q.4 Consider the following statements related to object creation and method calls, which are jumbled. Choose the correct order of the steps involved:

A. The displayDetails() method is called on the object.

B. A Car object is created using the Car class.

C. The Car class is defined with attributes and methods.

D. The displayDetails() method prints the object's attributes.

(a) C, B, A, D (b) B, C, D, A

(c) A, D, B, C (d) D, A, C, B

Q.5 Consider the following statements related to class as a blueprint, which are jumbled. Choose the correct order of the steps involved:

A. A Book class is defined with attributes like title and author.

B. Multiple Book objects are created with different titles and authors.

C. The Book class serves as a blueprint.

D. Each Book object represents a unique book.

(a) A, C, B, D (b) C, A, D, B

(c) B, D, A, C (d) D, B, C, A

Answers

1. (b) **2.** (b) **3.** (b) **4.** (a) **5.** (a)

TYPE – 3 01 Mark

Assertion-Reason Type Questions

Directions (Q. Nos. 1-5) The following questions are Assertion-Reason based questions. Choose the answer based on the code given below

(a) Both Assertion (A) and Reason (R) are true and Reason (R) is a correct explanation of Assertion (A).

(b) Both Assertion (A) and Reason (R) are true and Reason (R) is not a correct explanation of Assertion (A).

(c) Assertion (A) is true and Reason (R) is false.

(d) Assertion (A) is false and Reason (R) is true.

Q.1 Assertion (A) A Java class does not occupy memory until objects are created from it.

Reason (R) Classes are blueprints, not real entities.

Ans. (a) A class only defines the structure and behavior. Memory is allocated only when an object (instance) is created.

Q.2 Assertion (A) Encapsulation helps protect the internal state of an object.

Reason (R) Encapsulation prevents direct access to private variables.

Ans. (a) Encapsulation uses access modifiers like private to restrict direct access, ensuring data protection and controlled interactions.

Q.3 Assertion (A) A method can modify the state of an object.

Reason (R) Methods define the behavior of an object.

Ans. (a) Methods operate on the attributes (state) of an object, enabling changes in state and defining the object's behavior.

Q.4 Assertion (A) Objects in Java can have multiple states.

Reason (R) Each object is an independent instance of a class.

Ans. (a) Objects can have different states based on their attributes, and each object maintains its own independent data.

Q.5 **Assertion (A)** Inheritance allows reusing code between classes.

Reason (R) Inheritance supports encapsulation by bundling state and behavior.

Ans. (b) Inheritance enables code reuse by allowing derived classes to inherit properties and methods, but it does not directly deal with encapsulation.

TYPE - 4 — 01 Mark

Odd One Out

Q.1 Find the odd one out

(a) Data members

(b) Methods

(c) Properties

(d) Characteristic

Ans. (d) Characteristic (Data members, Methods, and Properties are all technical terms in object-oriented programming (OOP) whereas Characteristic is a general English term and not a specific programming construct.)

Q.2 Find the odd one out:

(a) Object (b) Class

(c) Method (d) Loop

Ans. (d) Loop (Object, Class, and Method are key components of Object-Oriented Programming, while Loop is a general programming control structure not specific to OOP.)

Q.3 Find the odd one out:

(a) Polymorphism

(b) Encapsulation

(c) Debugging

(d) Abstraction

Ans. (c) Debugging (Polymorphism, Encapsulation, and Abstraction are OOP principles, whereas Debugging is the process of finding and fixing errors in code, unrelated to OOP concepts.)

Q.4 Find the odd one out:

(a) new (b) class

(c) object (d) for

Ans. (d) for (new, class, and object are related to Java's object-oriented approach, whereas for is a looping construct used for iteration.)

Q.5 Find the odd one out:

(a) Constructor (b) Method

(c) Attribute (d) Compiler

Ans. (d) Compiler (Constructor, Method, and Attribute are parts of a Java class, whereas Compiler is a separate tool used to convert Java code into bytecode.)

TYPE - 5 — 02 Marks

Short Answer Type Questions

Q.1 Name any two principles of Object-Oriented Programming.

Ans. Encapsulation and Inheritance.

Q.2 What is an object?

Ans. An object is an instance of a class that encapsulates state and behavior.

Q.3 Give an example of state and behavior for a Car object.

Ans. **State** Color, speed. **Behavior** Start, stop.

Q.4 Write the Java statement to create a Smartphone object named myPhone. The Smartphone class constructor takes the brand (String) and storageGB (int) as parameters. Assume the brand is "Samsung" and the storage is 128 GB.

Ans. Smartphone myPhone = new Smartphone("Samsung", 128);

Q.5 What are the key components of a Java class?

Ans. Data members (attributes), methods (behavior), and optionally constructors and nested classes.

Q.6 How does a class act as a factory for objects?

Ans. A class defines the structure and behavior of objects, and using the new keyword, it produces instances (objects) of that structure.

Q.7 What is the purpose of the main method in Java?

Ans. The main method serves as the entry point of a Java program, where execution begins.

Q.8 Given a class Vehicle with attributes like speed and color, and methods accelerate() and applyBrakes():

(a) Explain how Vehicle encapsulates state and behavior.

(b) Describe how objects of type Vehicle can interact with each other.

Ans. (a) **Encapsulation** Vehicle holds data (speed, color) and actions (accelerate, applyBrakes) within a single unit.

(b) **Interaction** Objects can call each other's methods, like car1.accelerate() or car2.applyBrakes().

Q.9 Consider a class BankAccount with methods deposit() and withdraw():

(a) Explain how BankAccount models a real-world entity.

(b) Describe how BankAccount can be considered a user-defined data type.

Ans. (a) **Real-world Model** It represents a bank account with deposit/withdrawal actions.

(b) **User-defined Data Type** It defines a new data type with its own properties and methods.

Q.10 Given a class Product with methods getPrice() and getName(), and subclasses Book and Electronics extending Product:

(a) Explain how Product acts as a factory for creating Book and Electronics objects.

(b) Describe how message passing (method calls) would be used to retrieve the price of a Book object.

Ans. (a) **Factory** Product class provides a base for creating related objects (Book, Electronics).

(b) Message passing occurs when the getPrice() method is called on a Book object.

Q.11 Given a class Employee with attributes like name and salary, and methods calculateBonus() and displayDetails():

(a) Explain how Employee models the behavior of an employee.

(b) Describe how Employee can be considered a blueprint for creating employee objects.

Ans. (a) **Behavior Model** It models employee actions like bonus calculation and detail display.

(b) **Blueprint** It defines the structure for creating multiple employee objects.

Q.12 Identify five possible attributes and three possible behaviours of a Car.

Ans.

Attributes	**Behaviours**
Model	Start Engine
Color	Accelerate
Number of Doors	Brake
Fuel Type	Turn On Headlights
Mileage	Park

Q.13 You want to create a class 'Rectangle'. Choose the elements to be used as characteristics and behaviors from the list given below:

Length, Width, Area, Calculate Area, Color, Draw Rectangle, Perimeter, Change Color, Height.

Ans.

Characteristics	**Behaviours**
Length	Calculate Area
Width	Draw Rectangle
Color	Change Color
Perimeter	
Height	

TYPE – 6 — 02 Marks

Differentiate

Q.1 Java Class and Java Object

Ans.

	Java Class	**Java Object**
Definition	A class is a blueprint or template for creating objects.	An object is an instance of a class, created based on the class template.
Memory Allocation	A class itself does not consume memory until objects are created.	An object occupies memory as it stores data and has a specific state.
Structure	A class defines attributes (variables) and methods (functions).	An object holds actual values for attributes and can invoke methods.
Example	The Car class defines properties like brand, color, and methods like start()	An object like car1 represents a specific car with a brand "Toyota" and color "Red".
Reusability	A class can be used as a blueprint to create multiple objects.	Each object is independent and holds its own unique state.

Q.2 Class as a Specification and Class as an Object Factory

Ans.

	Class as a Specification	**Class as an Object Factory**
Definition	A class serves as a blueprint that defines the attributes and behaviors of objects.	A class acts as a factory that produces multiple instances (objects) with the same structure but different data.
Focus	Defines what an object should have and what it can do.	Creates actual objects using the new keyword.
Example	The Car class specifies that every car will have attributes like color and brand.	Using Car car1 = new Car();, the class generates a car object.
Role in OOP	Helps in designing structured and reusable code.	Enables object creation to work with real-world entities in programs.
Output	Does not produce any object unless instantiated.	Produces multiple objects with different values but the same blueprint.

03

VALUES AND DATA TYPES

Character Set

- A character set in Java is a **set of alphabets**, **letters**, and **some special characters** that are valid in java programming language.
- In other words, characters are the smallest units (elements) of Java language that are used to write Java tokens.
- Java is a programming language it also has a set of characters used in forming tokens, instructions, programs, etc.

Character Sets in Java

Letters	Both lowercase (a, b, c, d, e, etc.) and uppercase (A, B, C, D, E, etc.) letters.
Digits	0, 1, 2, 3, 4, 5, 6, 7, 8, 9.
Special symbols	_, (,), {, }, [,], +, -, *, /, %, !, &, |, ~, ^, <, =, >, $, #, ?, Comma (,), Dot (.), Colon (:), Semi-colon (;), Single quote ('), Double quote ("), Back slash (\\).
White space	Space, Tab, New line.

Java program mostly uses ASCII code and Unicode for variable names, comments etc.

ASCII Character Set

- ASCII code stand for **American Standard Code for Information Interchange**.
- In ASCII format we use alphanumeric numbers.
- In this each character represented in 7 bits.
- It consists of total 128 (from 0 to 127) characters.
- The ASCII table includes:
  - **Control characters** (0–31) → \n (newline), \t (tab), \b (backspace)
  - **Printable characters** (32–126) → Letters (A-Z, a-z), digits (0-9), symbols (!@#$%^&*)
- It is also a small subset of Unicode because it contains 2 bytes while ASCII requires only one byte.

For example,

```
char ch1 = 65;
char ch2 = 97;
char ch3 = 66;
char ch4 = 98;
System.out.println(ch1);  // Output: A
System.out.println(ch2);  // Output: a
System.out.println(ch3);  // Output: B
System.out.println(ch4);  // Output: b
```

Unicode Character Set

In Java programming language, characters are defined by the Unicode character set.Unicode is a universal character encoding standard. This standard includes roughly 100000 characters to represent characters of different languages. Unicode uses 4 bytes to represent characters. Hence, it provides a very wide variety of encoding. It has three types namely UTF-8, UTF-16, UTF-32.

Unicode Encoding in Java

Unicode characters are represented in Java using Unicode escape sequences. These sequences start with \u followed by a 4-digit hexadecimal value that represents the Unicode of the character. This allows Java programs to include any character from the Unicode standard.

For example,

```
char ch1 = 'A';   // Unicode: U+0041
char ch2 = '\u0041';   // Unicode escape sequence for 'A'
char ch3 = '\u0939';   // Unicode for 'ह' (Hindi letter)
char ch4 = '\u20B9';   // Unicode for '₹' (Indian Rupee symbol)
System.out.println(ch1); // Output: A
System.out.println(ch2); // Output: A
System.out.println(ch3); // Output: ह
System.out.println(ch4); // Output: ₹
```

Escape Sequences in Java

Escape sequences in Java are special characters used to perform specific tasks, such as formatting or representing characters that cannot be directly included in a string. They begin with a backslash (\) followed by a specific character to denote their purpose. Escape sequences allow programmers to include special characters in their code, like newline, tab, or even a backslash itself.

List of Common Escape Sequences in Java

Escape Sequence	Meaning	Example Output
\n	New Line	Moves text to the next line
\t	Tab	Adds a tab space
\b	Backspace	Removes the previous character
\r	Carriage Return	Moves the cursor to the beginning of the line
\f	Form Feed	Used for page breaks in printing
\'	Single Quote	Prints ' inside a character or string
\"	Double Quote	Prints " inside a string
\\	Backslash	Prints \ inside a string

Tokens

Tokens are the smallest unit or single element of a Java program, which are identified by the compiler. It can also be defined as a individual character used in a Java program. There are five types of tokens, i.e. **literals**, **keywords**, **identifiers**, **operators** and **separators**.

Literals

These are the fixed values in a Java program. It can be any number, text or other information that represents a value. We can specify any value as a literal such as:

Integer Literals	It represents positive or negative value without decimal point. e.g. 14, – 391, etc.
Floating Literals	Java have two kinds of floating point number: float and double. By default, floating literal is double. e.g. 0.01f is floating point literal and 6.5d is double-precision floating point literal.
Character Literals	These are constant valued character expressions embedded in a Java program. Character literals are expressed in Java within a pair of single quotes. These characters are termed as **ASCII characters**. e.g. 'A', '3', '*', etc.
String Literals	String is a set of alphanumeric characters. String literals are expressed within double quotes. e.g. "Hello", "100 pound", "TAJMAHAL", etc.
Boolean Literals	Boolean literals represent any one of the two values, either true or false and can be applied in a Java program to verify that whether the given condition is satisfied or not. e.g. boolean chosen = true;

Keywords

These are reserved words used within the program to specify a particular task.
Some keywords are as follows:

boolean	else	long	synchronized
break	extends	native	this
byte	final	new	throw
case	float	package	throws
catch	for	private	transient
char	goto	protected	try
class	if	public	void
const	implements	return	volatile
continue	import	short	while
default	instanceof	static	
do	int	super	
double	interface	switch	

Identifiers

This is a name given to a package, class, interface, method or variable. It allows a programmer to refer to the item from other places in the program. In Java, there are several points to remember about identifiers. They are as follows:

- An identifier can be any combination of alphabets (A to Z or a to z), digits (0 to 9), currency character ($) and underscore (_).
- The first character in identifier must be an alphabet, currency character or underscore.
- No commas or blanks are allowed within an identifier.
- Most importantly identifiers are case sensitive. e.g. foo and Foo are two different identifiers.
- A keyword cannot be used as an identifier.

e.g. **Legal identifiers** are : age, $salary, _value, _1_value

Illegal identifiers are : 123abc, -salary, auto

Operators

Operators in Java are symbols that perform operations on variables and values. Java provides different types of operators categorized based on their functionality.

Types of Operators in Java

Type	**Operator**
Arithmetic	+, –, *, /, %
Relational (Comparison)	==, !=, >, <, >=, <=
Logical	&&, || ,!
Bitwise	&, |, ^,~,<,>,>>
Assignment	=
Unary	+, –, ++, – –
Ternary	?:

Separators/Punctuators

It helps to define the structure of a program. Some separators are as follows :

Separator	**Symbol**	**Description**
Parenthesis	( )	It holds method definition.
Braces	{ }	It is used to define block/scope of class, code, methods.

Separator	Symbol	Description
Brackets	[ ]	It is used in array declaration.
Period	.	It separates the package name from sub package.
Comma	,	It separates the consecutive variable of same type when declaration.
Semicolon	;	It is used to terminate the statement in Java.

Variables

- A variable is a container which holds the value while the Java program is executed. A variable is assigned with a data type.
- Variable is a name of memory location.

Constants

A constant value represents a named value that remains fixed throughout an entire program. A constant is declared in similar way as variable but with keyword final.

e.g., `final double TAXRATE = 0.25 ;`

Now , you will be able to use TAXRATE's value in your program but you will never be able to change its value again, because you created it with keyword final, which means that this named value will remain fixed for this name throughout the program where it has been created.

Data Types

It refers to the type of data that can be stored in a variable. Sometimes, Java is called a **strongly typed language** because when you declare a variable, you must specify the variable type.

Data types in Java are classified into two types:

Primitive Data Types

These are the data types defined by the language itself. A primitive data type can have only one value at a time and is the simplest built in form of data within Java. Java supports eight primitive data types, they are as follows :

Type	Size	Range	Default Value	Example	Byte
byte	8-bit	−128 to +127	0	byte x = 90;	1 byte
short	16-bit	−32,768 to +32,767	0	short s = 20000;	2 byte
int	32-bit	−2,147,483,648 to +2,147,483,647	0	int a = 50000;	4 byte
long	64-bit	-2^{63} to $+2^{63} - 1$	0L	int a = 100000L;	8 byte
float	32-bit	−3.4e-38 to +3.4e+38	0.0f	float f = 234.5F;	4 byte
double	64-bit	−1.7e-308 to +1.7e+308	0.0d	double d = 123.4D;	8 byte
boolean	1-bit	True/False	False	Boolean one = true;	1 byte
char	16-bit	0 to 65,535	'\u0000' or 0	char letter = 'n';	2 byte

Non-Primitive Data Types (Composite Data Types)

These are **referenced** data types, which are based on primitive data types. These data types are constructed by using primitive data types, as per user's need. Non-primitive data types store the memory address of an object. Class, interface and array are the examples of reference data types.

Note
- *The default value of any reference variable is null.*
- *Whenever we are passing a non-primitive data type to a method, we are passing the address of that object where the data is stored.*

There are five types of non-primitive data types in Java, which are as follows:

1. A **class** in Java is a user-defined data type, i.e. it is created by the user. It acts a template to the data which consists of member variables and methods.

2. An **object** is the variable of the class, which can access the elements of class, i.e. methods and variables.
3. An **interface** is similar to a class however the only difference is that its methods are abstract by default i.e. they do not have body. An interface has only the final variables and method declarations. It is also called a fully abstract class.
4. A **string** represents a sequence of characters for example "Arihant", "Hello world", etc. String is the class of Java.

   One of the ways to create a string and store a value in it is shown below:

   ```
   String str = "You're the best";
   ```

   Here, String type variable str has the value "You're the best".
5. An **array** is a data type which can store multiple homogenous variables i.e., variables of same type in a sequence.

   They are stored in an indexed manner starting with index 0. The variables can be either primitive or non-primitive data types.

   Following example shows how to declare array of primitive data type

   ```
   int [ ] marks;
   ```

   Following example shows how to declare array of non-primitive data type

   ```
   Student[] students;
   ```

Type Conversion

Type conversion is a technique that is used either by the compiler or a programmer to convert one data type to another in Java. Type conversion is also known as **type casting**. For example, converting int to double, double to int, short to int, etc.

There are two types of type casting allowed in Java programming:

Implicit Type Conversion

In this, a smaller type is converted to a larger type, this work is done automatically by the compiler.

Hierarchy of Implicit Type Conversion

From (Smaller Type) byte, short, char, int, long, float

To (Larger Type) short, int, int, long, float, double

e.g.
```
int a = 5;
float x = a;
```

Explicit Type Conversion

Explicit type conversion which is done by the programmer manually. In this conversion, a larger type can be converted into a smaller type.

When a programmer changes the variable type while writing the code. We can use the cast operator to change the type of the variable. For example, double to int or int to double.

Hierarchy of Explicit Type Conversion

From (Larger Type) double, float, long, int, short, char

To (Smaller Type) float, long, int, short, byte, int

e.g.
```
double a = 5.5;
int x = (int) a;
```

EXAM ORIENTED QUESTIONS

TYPE - 1

01 Mark

Multiple Choice Questions

Q.1 int res= 'A'; What is the value of res?

(a) A (b) 66
(c) 65 (d) 97

Q.2 The ASCII code of B is ....

(a) 67 (b) 66
(c) 98 (d) 99

Q.3 Java characters are based on which character set standard?

(a) ASCII (b) Unicode
(c) EBCDIC (d) ANSI

Q.4 What will be the output of the following code?

```
char ch = '\u0041';
System.out.println(ch);
```

(a) 0041 (b) 65
(c) A (d) Compilation error

Q.5 An image showing a "Text message with special characters and emojis", with code like

What does \u263A represent in the output?

(a) A tab space (b) A newline
(c) A smiley face (d) A backslash

Q.6 Which of the following statements about Java character set is true?

(a) Java uses 8-bit characters like ASCII.
(b) Java uses 16-bit characters based on Unicode.
(c) Java characters can only store English letters.
(d) Java does not support escape sequences.

Q.7 Which of the following is not a valid escape sequence in Java?

(a) \n (b) \t
(c) \c (d) \u1234

Q.8 Which of the following is not a valid Java token?

(a) Keywords (b) Operators
(c) Identifiers (d) Packages

Q.9 Which of the following is a valid Java literal?

(a) 10 (b) "Hello"
(c) 3.14 (d) All of these

Q.10 The keyword used to call package in the program

(a) extends (b) export
(c) import (d) package

Q.11 Which of the following keyword is used to create symbolic constants in Java?

(a) final (b) Final
(c) Constant (d) Const

Q.12 An image of a "Recipe Card" that includes a Java snippet

What is the token type of int highlighted in the image?

(a) Identifier (b) Literal
(c) Operator (d) Keyword

Q.13 Which of the following keyword is used to create an instance of a class?

(a) new (b) public
(c) class (d) None of these

Q.14 Which of the following is a valid identifier in Java?

(a) 123name (b) _myVariable
(c) class (d) @token

Q.15 Identify the type of operator &&

(a) ternary (b) unary
(c) logical (d) relational

Q.16 Which of the following is a separator in Java?

(a) ; (b) { }
(c) () (d) All of these

Q.17 How many primitive data types are there in Java?

(a) 6 (b) 7
(c) 8 (d) 9

Q.18 A data type which contains integer as well as fractional part and occupies 32 bits space is

(a) float (b) char
(c) double (d) byte

Q.19

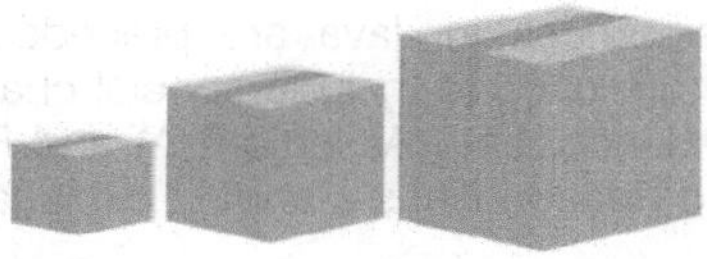

Which box stores the largest data based on the image?

(a) byte (b) int
(c) double (d) short

Q.20 The number of bytes occupied by char data type is .... byte/s.

(a) 4 (b) 8
(c) 2 (d) None

Q.21 What is the range of a byte data type in Java?

(a) -128 to 127
(b) 0 to 255
(c) -32,768 to 32,767
(d) -2,147,483,648 to 2,147,483,647

Q.22 What is the default value of a char variable in Java?

(a) ' ' (space) (b) '\u0000' (null character)
(c) 0 (d) null

Q.23 Which of the following is an example of implicit type conversion?

(a) int → byte (b) double → float
(c) char → int (d) float → long

Q.24 int x=(int) 32.8; is an example of .... typecasting.

(a) implicit (b) automatic
(c) explicit (d) coercion

Q.25

Why does spillage occur in explicit conversion?

(a) Value increases during conversion
(b) Target type is smaller causing data loss
(c) Automatic widening happens
(d) Conversion fails due to syntax error

Q.26 It represents positive or negative value without decimal point.

(a) Integer Literals (b) Float Variables
(c) String Literals (d) Boolean

Q.27 Which data type can have only one value at a time and is the simplest built in form of data within Java?

(a) Primitive data type (b) Composite data type
(c) Reference data type (d) Polymorphic data type

Answers

1. (c)	2. (b)	3. (b)	4. (c)	5. (c)
6. (b)	7. (c)	8. (d)	9. (d)	10. (c)
11. (b)	12. (d)	13. (a)	14. (b)	15. (c)
16. (d)	17. (c)	18. (a)	19. (c)	20. (c)
21. (a)	22. (b)	23. (c)	24. (c)	25. (b)
26. (a)	27. (a)			

TYPE - 2 01 Mark

Statement Based Questions

Q.1 A programmer is working with text data and wants to insert a tab space between two words in a string. They have written the following incorrect statement:

Directly insert the literal characters "t" and "a" between the words.

What is the correct way to insert a tab space using an escape sequence?

A. Use the literal characters "ta".
B. Use the escape sequence "\t".
C. Use the escape sequence "\n".
D. Directly insert a space character.

(a) Only A (b) Only B
(c) Only C (d) Both D and A

Q.2 A developer needs to store a whole number that can range from -128 to 127. They have written the following incorrect statement:

Use the int data type, as it can store any whole number.

What is the most efficient primitive data type to use for this range, considering memory usage?

A. int B. long
C. short D. byte

(a) Only A (b) Only B
(c) Both C and A (d) Only D

Q.3 A programmer is working with a string literal that contains a double quote character. They have written the following incorrect statement:

Directly include the double quote character within the string literal.

What is the correct way to include a double quote character within a string literal?

A. Use a single quote character instead.
B. Use the escape sequence "\"".
C. Use the escape sequence "\".
D. Use the escape sequence "\n".

(a) Only A (b) Only B
(c) Only C (d) Only D

Q.4 Consider the following statements related to tokens in Java, which are jumbled. Choose the correct order of the steps involved:

A. A line of Java code is written with keywords, identifiers, and literals.

B. The compiler breaks the line into individual tokens.

C. The tokens are identified as keywords, identifiers, or literals.

D. The compiler uses the tokens for further processing.

(a) A, B, C, D (b) C, A, D, B
(c) B, D, A, C (d) D, C, B, A

Q.5 Consider the following statements related to primitive data types and type conversion, which are jumbled. Choose the correct order of the steps involved:

A. A byte variable is declared and assigned a value.

B. The byte value is implicitly converted to an int.

C. An int variable is declared.

D. The int variable is assigned the converted value.

(a) A, B, C, D (b) C, A, D, B
(c) B, D, A, C (d) D, C, B, A

Answers

1. (b) **2.** (d) **3.** (b) **4.** (a) **5.** (a)

TYPE - 3

01 Mark

Assertion-Reason Type Questions

Directions (Q. Nos. 1-9) The following questions are Assertion-Reason based questions. Choose the answer based on the code given below

(a) Both Assertion (A) and Reason (R) are true and Reason (R) is a correct explanation of Assertion (A).
(b) Both Assertion (A) and Reason (R) are true and Reason (R) is not a correct explanation of Assertion (A).
(c) Assertion (A) is true and Reason (R) is false.
(d) Assertion (A) is false and Reason (R) is true.

Q.1 Assertion (A) Unicode is preferred over ASCII for character representation in Java.

Reason (R) Unicode can represent a broader range of characters, including those used in various languages and symbols.

Ans. (a) Unicode supports all global characters, which explains why it is preferred over ASCII for broader character representation. Hence, both Assertion (A) and Reason (R) are true and Reason (R) is a correct explanation of Assertion (A).

Q.2 Assertion (A) In Java, escape sequences always start with a backslash (\).

Reason (R) Escape sequences are used to represent characters that cannot be directly typed in a program.

Ans. (a) Escape sequences in Java are preceded by a backslash and are used to include special characters in a program. Hence, both Assertion (A) and Reason (R) are true and Reason (R) is a correct explanation of Assertion (A).

Q.3 Assertion (A) An escape sequence like \n is considered a Java token.

Reason (R) Escape sequences are predefined character representations in Java.

Ans. (d) \n is part of a string/character literal, not a standalone token like keywords.

Hence, Assertion (A) is false and Reason (R) is true.

Q.4 Assertion (A) The default value of a boolean literals in Java is true.

Reason (R) Java initializes all variables with default values when they are declared.

Ans. (d) The default value of a boolean literals in Java is false, not true, though Java does initialize variables with default values. Hence, Assertion (A) is false and Reason (R) is true.

Q.5 Assertion (A) Keywords are case-sensitive in Java.

Reason (R) Java is a case-sensitive programming language.

Ans. (a) Java is case-sensitive, so keywords like int and INT are treated as different identifiers. Hence, both Assertion (A) and Reason (R) are true and Reason (R) is a correct explanation of Assertion (A).

Q.6 Assertion (A) The final keyword in Java allows the value of a variable to be modified later in the program.

Reason (R) Constants in Java are declared using the final keyword to ensure their values remain unchanged.

Ans. (d) The final keyword is used to declare constants whose values cannot be modified once assigned. Hence, Assertion (A) is false and Reason (R) is true.

Q.7 Assertion (A) The identifier my_Variable1 is valid in Java.

Reason (R) Identifiers in Java can contain letters, underscores (_), and dollar signs ($), but cannot start with a digit.

Ans. (a) Java identifiers must begin with a letter, underscore (_), or dollar sign ($) but cannot start with a digit. Since my_Variable1 follows these rules, it is a valid identifier. Hence, both Assertion (A) and Reason (R) are true and Reason (R) is a correct explanation of Assertion (A).

Q.8 Assertion (A) Local variables in Java must be explicitly initialized before use.

Reason (R) Java does not provide default values for local variables.

Ans. (a) Local variables lack default values in Java, so they must be initialized before being used. Hence, both Assertion (A) and Reason (R) are true and Reason (R) is a correct explanation of Assertion (A).

Q.9 Assertion (A) Java allows implicit type casting from double to int.

Reason (R) Implicit type casting in Java always converts from a smaller data type to a larger one.

Ans. (d) Implicit type casting only works from smaller to larger types; double to int requires explicit casting. Hence, Assertion (A) is false and Reason (R) is true.

TYPE - 4 — 01 Mark

Odd One Out

Q.1 Choose the odd one out:

(a) "Java" (b) "J" (c) true (d) "Hello"

Ans. (c) true ("Java", "J", and "Hello" are string literals while true is a boolean literal.)

Q.2 Choose the odd one out:

(a) for (b) while (c) switch (d) loop

Ans. (d) loop (for, while, and switch are control flow statements in Java, while loop is not a Java keyword.)

Q.3 Choose the odd one out:

(a) my_123 (b) totalAmount
(c) 123Value (d) score

Ans. (c) 123Value (my_123, totalAmount, and score are valid identifiers, while 123Value is not because it begins with a digit.)

Q.4 Choose the odd one out:

(a) int (b) float (c) double (d) public

Ans. (d) public (int, float, and double are primitive data types, while public is an access modifier.)

Q.5 Choose the odd one out:

(a) float to double (b) int to long
(c) short to byte (d) long to float

Ans. (c) short to byte (float to double, int to long, and long to float are all implicit type conversion while short to byte is a explicit type conversion.)

TYPE - 5 — 02 Marks

Short Answer Type Questions

Q.1 `int res = 'A';`

What is the value of res?

Ans. The value of res is 65.

Q.2 Identify and name the following tokens

(i) public (ii) 'a' (iii) = = (iv) { }

Ans. (i) Keyword (ii) Character literal
(iii) Operator (iv) Separator

Q.3 Name any four tokens of Java.

Ans. Four tokens in Java are

1. Keywords 2. Literals
3. Identifiers 4. Operators

Q.4 Which term refer to a fixed values like number or text used in Java?

Ans. These are called literals, which represent constant values in the code.

Q.5 Identify the literals listed below

(i) 0.5 (ii) 'A' (iii) false (iv) "a"

Ans. (i) **0.5** is a double precision floating point literal.
(ii) **'A'** is a character literal.
(iii) **false** is a boolean literal.
(iv) **"a"** is a string literal.

Q.6 Name the keyword which

(i) indicates that a method has no return type.
(ii) Represent a true/false value in Java.

Ans. (i) void (ii) Boolean

Q.7 Name the following

(i) Uses 7 bits and include 128 characters.
(ii) Any one reference data type.

Ans. (i) ASCII (ii) class

Q.8 What do we call the reserved words in Java that can't be used as variable names? Give an example.

Ans. They are called keywords and have special meaning in Java. e.g. final, int, new etc.

Q.9 Name the Java keyword that indicates a method has no return type.

Ans. The void keyword, it allows us to create functions that either do not require any parameters or do not return a value.

Q.10 What is an identifier?

Ans. This is a name given to a package, class, interface, method or variable. It allows a programmer to refer to the item from other places in the program.

Q.11 Write the memory capacity (storage size) of short and float data type in bytes.

Ans. Short - 2 bytes
Float - 4 bytes

Q.12 List the variables from those given below that are composite data types

(i) static int x; (ii) arr [i] = 10;
(iii) obj.display( ); (iv) boolean b;
(v) private char chr; (vi) String str;

Ans. Composite data types are as:
(i) arr[i] = 10;
(ii) obj.display( );
(vi) String str;

Q.13 **Give one example each of primitive data type and composite data type.**

Ans. Primitive data type : char

Composite data type : class

Q.14 **Assign the value of pie (i.e. 3.142) to a variable with requisite data type.**

Ans. `double pie = 3.142;`

Here, for pie (3.142) the suitable data type is double because it can hold 64-bit floating point.

Q.15 **Classify the following as primitive or non-primitive data types**

(i) char (ii) arrays

(iii) int (iv) classes

Ans. Primitive data types

(i) char (iii) int

Non-primitive datatypes

(ii) arrays (iv) classes

Q.16 **State the number of bytes occupied by char and int data types.**

Ans. Number of bytes occupied by

char $\rightarrow$ 2 bytes

Number of bytes occupied by

int $\rightarrow$ 4 bytes

Q.17 **Arrange the following primitive data types in an ascending order of their size:**

(i) char (ii) byte

(iii) double (iv) int

Ans. Ascending order of primitive data types with their size

byte < char < int < double

Q.18 **Name the primitive data type in Java that is**

(i) **a 64-bit integer and is used when you need a range of values under than those provided by int.**

(ii) **a single 16-bit unicode character whose default value is '\u0000'.**

Ans. (i) long, because it contain eight byte (64-bit) and it belongs to the int data type.

(ii) char, because firstly it assume a size of 2 byte (16-bits) and another is that unicode characters are of char data type.

Q.19 **State the two kinds of data types.**

Ans. There are two types of data type:

(i) **Primitive Data Types** byte, float, char, boolean, int.

(ii) **Composite Data Types** class, array, interface.

Q.20 **What do you mean by type conversion?**

Ans. Type conversion is changing a value from one data type to another type. Data type conversions are either implicit or explicit, it depends on the data capacities of the data type involved.

Q.21 **What are the types of casting shown by the following examples?**

(i) char c =(char) 120;

(ii) int x = 't';

Ans. (i) Explicit Type Casting

(ii) Implicit Type Casting

Q.22 **What are the types of casting shown by the following examples?**

(i) double x = 15.2;

int y = (int)x;

(ii) int x = 12;

long y = x;

Ans. (i) Explicit type casting

(ii) Implicit type casting

Q.23 **State the escape sequence for horizontal tab and new line feed.**

Ans. The escape sequence for a horizontal tab is \t and for a new line feed is \n .

e.g.

```
printf("This is a line\twith a tab.\nThis is a new line.");
```

Where, \t inserts some whitespace to the left of the cursor and moves the cursor accordingly. \n moves the cursor to the start of the next line.

Output This is a line with a tab.

This is a new line.

Q.24 **Why can a keyword not be used as a variable name?**

Ans. Keywords are reserved words that have a special meaning to the Java compiler.

As Java compiler reserves these words for its own use so they are not available as names for variables or methods.

Q.25 **In what way is float initialization different from double initialization java ?**

Ans. Key points about float *versus* double initialization:

- A double generally has higher precision than a float, meaning it can represent decimal values with more decimal places accurately.
- A float takes up less memory than a double because it uses fewer bits.

Q.26 **What is the difference between "true" and true?**

Ans. The difference between "true" (with quotation marks) and true (without quotation marks) is that

- "true" is considered a string and is simply a sequence of characters that can be manipulated like any other text.
- true represents a boolean value which is used in conditional statements to indicate a true condition.

Q.27 What is type casting in Java, and when is it required?

Ans. Type casting is the process of converting one data type to another. It is required when you need to assign a value from one type to another, such as from a 'double' to an 'int'.

Q.28 How can you convert a double to a float in Java?

Ans. You can use explicit casting to convert a double to a float, but be aware that it may result in a loss of precision.

For example,

1. double num = 3.14159;
2. float floatValue = (float) num;

Q.29 Predict the output of the following code snippet:

```
public class Main
{
  public static void main(String[] args)
  {
    char c1 = 'A';
    int num = c1 + 5;
    System.out.println((char) num + "\t" + num);
  }
}
```

Ans. Output: F\t70

Q.30 Predict the output of the following code snippet:

```
public class Main
{
  public static void main(String[] args)
  {
    int a = 10;
    double b = a / 3.0;
    System.out.println(b);
  }
}
```

Ans. Output: 3.3333333333333335

Q.31 Predict the output of the following code snippet:

```
public class Main
{
  public static void main(String[] args)
  {
    char newline = '\n';
    String text = "Line 1" + newline + "Line 2";
    System.out.println(text);
  }
}
```

Ans. Output:

Line 1
Line 2

Q.32 Given a string variable message and an integer variable count:

```
String message = "Item: ";
int count = 10;
```

(a) Explain how message and count represent data of different types.

(b) Describe how you would combine message and count into a single string for output.

Ans. (a) message is a String (non-primitive data type), representing a sequence of characters. It's used to store textual data.

count is an int (primitive data type), representing an integer number. It's used to store whole numbers.

(b) You would use string concatenation. In Java, you can use the + operator to combine strings and other data types.

Q.33 Given a float variable value and an int variable integerValue:

```
float value = 3.14f;
int integerValue;
```

(a) Explain the difference between float and int data types.

(b) Describe how you would assign the integer part of value to integerValue, and what data loss might occur.

Ans. (a) float is a primitive data type that stores single-precision floating-point numbers (numbers with decimal points).

int is a primitive data type that stores integer numbers (whole numbers).

(b) You would use explicit type casting: integerValue = (int) value;

Data loss occurs because the decimal part of value is truncated (discarded). In this case, integerValue would become 3.

Q.34 Given the following line of Java code:

```
int total = 10 + 5;
```

(a) List and identify the tokens in this line of code.

(b) Explain the role of each token in the execution of this line.

Ans. (a) Tokens and Identification:

- int → Keyword
- total → Identifier (variable name)
- = → Assignment operator
- 10 → Integer literal
- + → Arithmetic operator
- 5 → Integer literal
- ; → Terminator (end of statement)

(b) Role of each token:

- int → Declares the data type of the variable as integer.
- total → Stores the result of the calculation.
- = → Assigns the calculated value to total.
- 10 + 5 → Adds two numbers (10 and 5) giving 15.
- ; → Marks the end of the statement.

Q.35 Evaluate the given expression when the value of str1 = "Hello" and str2 = "World":

```
String combined = str1 + "\n" + str2;
System.out.println("combined = " + combined);
```

Ans. **Output**

combined = Hello

World

TYPE - 6 — 02 Marks

Differentiate

Q.1 ASCII (American Standard Code for Information Interchange) and UNICODE (Universal Character Set)

Ans.

ASCII (American Standard Code for Information Interchange)	**UNICODE** (Universal Character Set)
Lowercase letters (a-z), uppercase letters (A-Z), numerals (0-9), and symbols like parenthesis, dollars, the ampersand, and others are represented by the ASCII code.	A wider range of characters than ASCII is represented by Unicode, including letters from languages like English, Arabic, Greek, and others, mathematical symbols, historical scripts, and emoji.
7-bit encoding for each character.	Variable length encoding (UTF-8, UTF-16, UTF-32).
ASCII is a proper subset of UNICODE.	UNICODE is a superset of ASCII.

Q.2 Token and Identifier

Ans.

Token	Identifier
It is the smallest element in a program that is meaningful to the compiler.	These are the names of variable, method, class, package, interface, etc.
These define the structure of the language. e.g. keyword, literal etc.	These are used to uniquely identify them to the compiler. e.g. 123ab, __ salary etc.

Q.3 Float Literals and Double Literals

Ans.

Float Literals	Double Literals
The float literal has a limited range to store decimal data item. It can hold 32-bit data.	The double literal has a wider range as compared to float, to store decimal data items. It can hold 64-bit data.

Q.4 Boolean Literal and Character Literal

Ans.

Boolean Literal	Character Literal
Boolean literal consists of the keyword true and false.	Character literal is expressed by a single character.
Boolean literal are never enclosed within quotes. e.g. true, false	A character literal constant enclosed within single quotes. e.g. 'A' ,'d', '*', etc.

Q.5 Variables and Constants

Ans.

	Variables	Constants
Definition	A container for storing data that can change.	A container for storing data that cannot change.
Keyword Used	None	final
Value Change	Can be updated during program execution.	Cannot be updated once assigned.
Usage	For storing dynamic data.	For storing fixed values.
Example	`int age = 25;`	`final int MAX_AGE = 100;`

Q.6 Primitive Data Types and Non-Primitive Data Types

Ans.

	Primitive Data Types	Non-Primitive Data Types
Definition	Basic data types provided by Java.	Reference types created by the user.
Memory	Stores the actual value.	Stores references to the data.
Size	Fixed size.	Size depends on the object.
Example	int, float, char, etc.	String, Array, Class, etc.

Q.7 Implicit Type Conversion and Explicit Type Conversion

Ans.

Implicit Type Conversion	Explicit Type Conversion
When the compiler automatically converts data from a smaller data type to a larger data type. This happens when there is no loss of data. For example, converting an integer to a long.	When the programmer manually converts a value to a specific data type. This happens when there is a possibility of data loss. For example, converting a double to an integer.
An implicit type conversion is performed without programmer's intervention.	An explicit type conversion is specified explicitly by the programmer.
Example: int a, double b, c = a + b	Example: int a, double b, s = (int) a + b

TYPE - 7 15 Marks

Long Answer Type Questions

Q.1 What are the resultant data types if the following implicit conversions are performed?

```
short s;
int i;
double d;
byte b;
```

Expressions:

(a) s + b (b) i / d (c) s * i + d (d) b + s / i

Ans. (a) s + b

- short and byte are both promoted to int before the addition.
- **Resultant data type** int

(b) i / d

- int is promoted to double before the division.
- **Resultant data type** double

(c) s * i + d

- short is promoted to int for the multiplication.
- The result of s * i is int.
- int is promoted to double for the addition with d.
- **Resultant data type** double

(d) b + s / i

- byte and short are promoted to int for the division.
- The result of s / i is int.
- byte is promoted to int for addition.
- **Resultant data type** int

Q.2 Write a Java program that does the following:

1. **Declares a char variable and initializes it with the character 'A'.**
2. **Declares an int variable and assigns it the ASCII value of the character 'a'.**
3. **Declares a String variable and initializes it with the text "Hello\tWorld\nJava".**
4. **Prints the character, the integer ASCII value, and the string to the console.**

Ans.

```
public class Main
{
  public static void main(String[] args)
  {
    char ch = 'A';
    int asciiValue = (int) 'a';
    String text = "Hello\tWorld\nJava";
    System.out.println("Character: " + ch);
    System.out.println("ASCII value of 'a': "
                       + asciiValue);
    System.out.println("String: " + text);
  }
}
```

Q.3 What are the resultant data types if the following implicit conversions are performed?

```
long l;
float f;
char c;
byte b;
```

Expressions:

(a) l + c (b) f - b (c) c * b / l (d) f + l * c

Ans. (a) l + c

- char is promoted to int before the addition.
- int is promoted to long before the addition.
- **Resultant data type** long

(b) f - b

- byte is promoted to int before the subtraction.
- int is promoted to float before the subtraction.
- **Resultant data type** float

(c) c * b / l

- byte and char are promoted to int for the multiplication.
- The result of c * b is int.
- int is promoted to long for the division.
- **Resultant data type** long

(d) f + l * c

- char is promoted to int for the multiplication.
- int is promoted to long for the multiplication.
- long is promoted to float for the addition.
- **Resultant data type** float

Q.4 Write a Java program that does the following:

1. **Declares a double variable and initializes it with the value 12.75.**
2. **Declares an int variable.**
3. **Performs an explicit type conversion to assign the integer part of the double variable to the int variable.**
4. **Prints the original double value and the converted int value to the console, along with a message indicating any potential data loss.**

Ans.

```
public class Main
{
  public static void main(String[] args)
  {
    double num = 12.75;
    int intPart = (int) num;
    System.out.println("Original double value: "
                       + num);
    System.out.println("Converted int value: "
                       + intPart);
    System.out.println("Decimal part is lost
                       during conversion.");
  }
}
```

OPERATORS

There are special symbols which are used to perform mathematical calculations like addition, subtraction, multiplication, less than, greater than and many more operations , all these symbols are called operators and variables on which these operators are applied are called operands.

Example
```
class math
{
    public static void main(String args[])
    {
        int a=4, b=9, c;
        c=a+b;
    }
}
```

In the above example,"=","+" are **operators** which are performing different operations and "a","b","c" are **operands** on which operation is applied.

Forms of Operators

Operators are classified based on the number of operands they work with. The primary forms are unary, binary, and ternary operators.

- **Unary Operator** It is used to perform operation on a single operand such as ++, – –, ~, !, etc.
- **Binary Operator** It is used to perform operation between two operand such as +, –, *,>, <, etc.
- **Ternary Operator** It is used to perform operation between three operand such as ?:.

Types of Operators in Java

We can divide all the Java operators into the following groups:

(Three variables are used further namely A, B, and C and values of these variables are 5, 10 and 7 respectively.)

Arithmetic Operator These operators are used to perform basic mathematical calculations like addition, subtraction, multiplication, division, and finding the remainder.

Operator	Name	Description	Example
+	Addition	It adds the values of operands.	A + B = 15
–	Subtraction	Subtracts the value of right hand operand from left hand operand.	A – B = –5
*	Multiplication	Multiplies the values of operands.	A * B = 50
/	Division	Divides left hand operand by right hand operand.	B / A = 2
%	Modulus	Divides left hand operand by right hand operand and returns remainder.	B % A = 0

Relational Operator These operators compare two values and return a boolean (true or false) result.

Operator	Name	Description	Example
= =	Equal to	Check if the values of two operands are equal or not, if yes, then condition becomes true.	(A == B) is false
! =	Not equal to	Check if the values of two operands are equal or not, if values are not equal, then condition becomes true.	(A ! = B) is true
>	Greater than	Check if the value of left operand is greater than the value of right operand, if yes, then condition becomes true.	(A > B) is false
<	Less than	Check if the value of left operand is less than the value of right operand, if yes, then condition becomes true.	(A < B) is true
>=	Greater than or equal to	Check if the value of left operand is greater than or equal to the value of right operand, if yes, then condition becomes true.	(A >= B) is false
<=	Less than or equal to	Check if the value of left operand is less than or equal to the value of right operand, if yes, then condition becomes true.	(A <= B) is true

Logical Operator These operators are used to combine multiple conditions or boolean expressions in programming.

Operator	Name	Description	Example
&&	Logical AND operator	It returns TRUE, if both the condition are true, otherwise returns FALSE.	((A < B)&&(C < B)) returns false
||	Logical OR operator	It returns TRUE, if any of the two conditions is true.	((A < B)||(C < B)) returns true
!	Logical NOT operator	It works on single operand. It is used to reverse the logical state of its operand. If a condition is true, then logical NOT operator will make it false.	!((A < B)&&(C < B)) returns true

Increment and Decrement Operator Increment operators are used to increase the value of a variable by 1. These operators are commonly used in loops or situations where you need to increase a value by a fixed amount.

Decrement operators are used to decrease a variable's value by 1. These operators are commonly used when you need to reduce the value of a variable, often within loops or mathematical operations.

Operator	Name	Description	Example
A++	Post Increment	Add 1 to the variable after use	int A = 2, B; B= A++; A = 3,B = 2
++A	Pre Increment	Add 1 to the variable before use	int A = 2, B;B= ++A; A = 3, B= 3
A--	Post Decrement	Subtract 1 from a variable after use	int A = 2, B; B=A--; A = 1, B= 2
--A	Pre Decrement	Subtract 1 from a variable before use	int A = 2, B; B= --A; A = 1,B = 1

Assignment Operator This operator is used to assign values to variables in programming. They allow you to store and update values in variables.

Operator	Name	Description	Example
=	Assignment	Simple assignment operator, assigns values from right side operands to left side operands.	C = A+B will assign the value of A + B into C

Shorthand Operators also known as compound assignment operators. These operators help simplify common arithmetic and assignment operations, making code shorter and easier to read. They combine an operation with assignment, so you don't have to repeat the variable name in the expression.

Operator	Name	Description	Example
+=	Add and Assign	Adds a value to a variable and then assigns the result back to that variable.	A += B → A = A + B = 15
−=	Subtract and Assign	This operator subtracts a value from a variable and assigns the result back to the variable.	A −= B → A = A − B = 5
*=	Multiply and Assign	This operator multiplies a variable by a value and assigns the result back to that variable.	A *= B → A = A * B = 50
/=	Divide and Assign	This operator divides a variable by a value and assigns the result back to the variable.	B /= A → B = B/A = 2
%=	Modulus and Assign	This operator finds the remainder when a variable is divided by a value and assigns that remainder back to the variable.	B %= A → B = B % A = 0

Conditional Operator (?:)

This operator is used to find the condition result, which could be either true or false. The goal of this operator is to decide, which value should be assigned to the variable.

Syntax `variable x = (expression) ? value1 (if true) : value2 (if false);`

Operator Precedence/Hierarchy of Operator

In Java, operator precedence (or hierarchy) determines the order in which operators are evaluated in an expression. Operators with higher precedence are evaluated before those with lower precedence. If two operators have the same precedence, the evaluation order is determined by their associativity (left-to-right or right-to-left).

Precedence	Operator	Description	Associativity
1.	( )	Parenthesis	Left to Right
	[ ]	Array subscript	
	•	Access object method	
2.	++	Postfix increment	Left to Right
	−−	Postfix decrement	
3.	++	Prefix increment	Right to Left
	−−	Prefix decrement	
	+, −	Unary plus/minus	
	!	Logical NOT	
	~	Bitwise NOT	
4.	*	Multiplication	Left to Right
	/	Division	
	%	Modulus	
5.	+	Addition	Left to Right
	−	Subtraction	
	+	String concatenation	

Precedence	Operator	Description	Associativity
6.	<<	Bitwise left shift	Left to Right
	>>	Bitwise right shift	
	>>>	Bitwise right shift with zero extension(zero fill)	
7.	<, <=	Less than, less than or equal to	Left to Right
	>, >=	Greater than, greater than or equal to	
8.	==	Equal to	Left to Right
	!=	Not equal to	
9.	&	Bitwise AND	Left to Right
10.	^	Bitwise XOR	Left to Right
11.	|	Bitwise OR	Left to Right
12.	&&	Logical AND	Left to Right
13.	||	Logical OR	Left to Right
14.	? :	Conditional	Right to Left
15.	=	Assignment	Right to Left

Some Other Operators

new Operator

In Java new operator is responsible for the creation of new object or instance of class. It dynamically allocates memory which means that the memory is allocated at the run time of the program.

Creation of Dynamic Memory by Using new Operator

- When we declare a class in java, a new data type is created. A class provides the blueprint for objects.
- We can create an object from a class. However obtaining objects of a class is a two-step process :
  - **Declaration** First, declare a variable of the class type. This variable does not define an object. Instead, it is simply a variable that can refer to an object.

    Syntax `class-name var-name;`
  - **Instantiation and Initialization** Second, acquire an actual, physical copy of the object and assign it to that variable. This can be done by using the new operator.
    The new operator instantiates a class by dynamically allocating (i.e, allocation at run time) memory for a new object and returning a reference to that memory. This reference is then stored in the variable. Thus, in Java, all class objects must be dynamically allocated.

    Syntax `var-name = new class-name();`

dot(.) Operator

- In Java, the "dot operator" (represented by a period ".") is used to access members (like variables and methods) within a class or object; essentially allowing you to call a specific function or retrieve a specific value from an object you've created.
- It allows us to:
  - Access fields (variables) of a class or an object.
  - Invoke methods of a class or an object.
  - Access inner classes and interfaces.
  - The chain method calls for fluent APIs.
- Now, let us understand through an example how to invoke a method using the dot operator.

```
// Java Program to demonstrate dot operator
// Used for Invoking Methods
class Person
{
  String name;
  int age;
  void introduce()
  {
    System.out.println("Hello, my name is " + name + " and I am " + age + " years old.");
  }
}
public class Main
{
  public static void main(String[] args)
  {
    Person person = new Person();
     // Using dot operator
    person.name = "John";
    person.age = 30;
    person.introduce();
  }
}
```

Output

Hello, my name is John and I am 30 years old.

REVISION NOTES

Counter

- A counter variable is a variable that keeps track of the number of times a specific piece of code is executed.
- The counter variable is declared and used in the same way as the normal variables are declared and used. The counter variable can be of numeric type (e.g., int, long, double, short).
- The technique of using the counter variable in Java is as follows:
  - Before the repeating cycle, we have to initialize it to zero or one.
  - After that, we have to increase the counter variable in one within the respective cycle.

Accumulator

Accumulators are variables which are used to calculate the sum of a set of values.

For example, `s=0;`

```
s=s+a;
```

Where, the value of 's' will be updated by the input value of 'a' each time when the statement s=s+a is executed. Hence, 's' is referred to as the **accumulator**.

Simple Output in Java

In Java, we can display output using **System.out.print**, **System.out.println**, and **System.out.printf**.

System.out.print in Java

In Java, System.out.print is a method used to display output on the console without moving to a new line.

Syntax `System.out.print(parameter)`

System.out.println in Java

Java System.out.println() is used to print an argument that is passed to it.

Where,

- **System** It is a final class defined in the java.lang package.
- **out** This is an instance of PrintStream type, which is a public and static member field of the System class.
- **println()** As all instances of the PrintStream class have a public method println(), we can invoke the same on out as well. This is an upgraded version of print(). It prints any argument passed to it and adds a new line to the output. We can assume that System.out represents the Standard Output Stream.

Syntax `System.out.println(parameter)`

Where, parameter might be anything that the user wishes to print on the output screen.

Basic Output with print() and println()

```
public class SimpleOutput
{
   public static void main(String[] args)
   {
      System.out.print("Hello, ");
      System.out.println("Java!");
   }
}
```

Output

Hello, Java!

Note *print() prints text without a new line and println() prints text and moves to a new line.*

REVISION NOTES

EXAM ORIENTED QUESTIONS

TYPE - 1   01 Mark

Multiple Choice Questions

Q.1 An operator taking only single operand for its operation is called ....

(a) A unary operator (b) A binary operator
(c) A ternary operator (d) None of these

Q.2

Which of the following correctly matches the operator forms shown?

(a) -a: Binary, a + b: Unary, a > b ? a : b: Ternary
(b) -a: Unary, a + b: Binary, a > b ? a : b: Ternary ?
(c) -a: Ternary, a + b: Binary, a > b ? a : b: Unary
(d) All are Unary operators

Q.3 What is the output of the following code?

```
int a = 10;
a += 5;
System.out.println(a);
```

(a) 10 (b) 15
(c) 5 (d) Compilation Error

Q.4 What will the following code snippet output?

```
int x = 10;
int y = x--;
System.out.println(x + " " + y);
```

(a) 10 10 (b) 9 10
(c) 10 9 (d) 9 9

Q.5 What will the following code output?

```
int x = 5;
x += 3 * 2;
System.out.println("Value: " + x);
```

(a) Value: 16 (b) Value: 11
(c) Value: 10 (d) Value: 15

Q.6 Give the output of the following.

```
int x = 2, y = 4, z = 1;
int result = (++z) +y + (++x) + (z++);
```

(a) 11 (b) 12
(c) 10 (d) 9

Q.7 Give the output of the following, when x = 5

```
x + = x++ + ++ x + --x + x;
```

(a) 29 (b) 28
(c) 26 (d) 30

Q.8 Which of the following operators is used to find the remainder in Java?

(a) / (b) %
(c) * (d) =

Q.9 The correct if statement for the following ternary operation statement is

```
System.out.println(n%2 == 0? "true":"false");
```

(a)
```
if(n%2==0)
  return true;
else
  return false;
```
(b)
```
if(n%2==0)
  return "true";
else
  return "false";
```
(c)
```
if(n%2==0)
  System.out.println("true");
else
  System.out.println("false");
```
(d)
```
if(n%2==0)
  return false;
else
  return false;
```

Q.10 Identify the type of operator &&

(a) ternary (b) unary
(c) logical (d) relational

Q.11 The logical operator which is an unary operator

(a) && (b) ||
(c) ! (d) >>

Q.12 Which of the following logical operators is used to check if both conditions are true?

(a) || (b) &&
(c) ! (d) ==

Q.13 The statement i = i + 1 is equivalent to ....

(a) i++ (b) i += 1
(c) ++i (d) All of these

Q.14 Subtract 1 from a variable after use.

(a) Pre-decrement (b) Post-decrement
(c) Pre-increment (d) Post-increment

Q.15 This operator finds the remainder when a variable is divided by a value and assigns that remainder back to the variable.

(a) %= (b) !=
(c) /= (d) =

Q.16

In the context of the image, which statement about prefix and postfix is correct?

(a) Both increment after printing
(b) Prefix increments before printing, postfix after
(c) Both increment at the same time
(d) None of the above

Q.17 What is the associativity of the ternary operator (? :) in Java?

(a) Left to Right (b) Right to Left
(c) Undefined (d) None of these

Q.18 Which of the following operators has the highest precedence in Java?

(a) + (b) * (c) () (d) =

Q.19 Operators with higher precedence are evaluated before operators with relatively lower precedence. Arrange the operators given below in order of higher precedence to lower precedence.

(i) && (ii) % (iii) >= (iv) ++

(a) (iv), (i), (iii), (ii) (b) (iv), (iii), (ii), (i)
(c) (iv), (ii), (iii), (i) (d) (i), (ii), (iii), (iv)

Q.20 Which of the following statements is correct regarding operator precedence in Java?

(a) The = (assignment) operator has higher precedence than the + (addition) operator.
(b) The && (logical AND) operator has higher precedence than the || (logical OR) operator.
(c) The * (multiplication) operator has lower precedence than the + (addition) operator.
(d) The ternary operator (?:) has the lowest precedence of all operators.

Q.21 Which operator is used to create an object in Java?

(a) new (b) this
(c) super (d) instanceof

Q.22 How can you print the value of a variable x in Java?

(a) `System.out.print(x);` (b) `System.out.println(x);`
(c) Both (a) and (b) (d) `System.out.print("x");`

Q.23

What does the new operator in the image do?

(a) Declares a new class
(b) Allocates dynamic memory for the object
(c) Deletes an object
(d) Invokes a method

Q.24 The dot (.) operator is used for:

(a) Accessing instance variables
(b) Calling methods
(c) Accessing static members
(d) All of the above

Q.25

What is the role of the dot operator shown in the image?

(a) Used to access class members like variables and methods
(b) Multiplies two values
(c) Creates a new object
(d) None of the above

Q.26 What is the default value of a counter when initialized?

(a) 1 (b) 5
(c) 0 (d) 10

Q.27 What is the primary purpose of an accumulator in Java?

(a) To store a single value
(b) To store multiple values
(c) To accumulate or sum values in a loop or iterative process
(d) To subtract values from a total

Q.28 Variables which are used to calculate the sum of a set of values.

(a) Accumulators
(b) Local variables
(c) Counter variables
(d) Arguments

Q.29

Which action represents an accumulator in programming?

(a) Adding sugar spoon by spoon
(b) Pouring juice while keeping the total
(c) Both are counters
(d) None of the above

Q.30 What is the difference between System.out.print() and System.out.println() in Java?

(a) print() adds a new line after the output, while println() does not.
(b) println() adds a new line after the output, while print() does not.
(c) Both do the same thing.
(d) println() prints to the console, and print() prints to a file.

Answers

1. (a)	2. (b)	3. (b)	4. (b)	5. (b)
6. (a)	7. (a)	8. (b)	9. (c)	10. (c)
11. (c)	12. (b)	13. (d)	14. (b)	15. (a)
16. (b)	17. (b)	18. (c)	19. (c)	20. (b)
21. (a)	22. (c)	23. (b)	24. (d)	25. (a)
26. (c)	27. (c)	28. (a)	29. (b)	30. (b)

TYPE - 2

01 Mark

Statement Based Questions

Q.1 A programmer wants to increment a counter variable by 1. They have written the following incorrect statement:

Directly assign the counter to itself plus one using counter = counter + 1.

What is the most concise way to increment the counter using an increment operator?

A. counter = counter + 1;
B. counter++;
C. counter += 1;
D. All of the above

(a) Only A
(b) Only B
(c) Only C
(d) All of the above

Q.2 A programmer wants to compare two integer variables a and b to check if a is greater than b. They have written the following incorrect statement:

Assign the result of the comparison to an integer variable.

What is the correct data type to store the result of a relational comparison in Java?

A. int
B. String
C. boolean
D. char

(a) Both A and B (b) Only B
(c) Only C (d) Only D

Q.3 A programmer wants to create a new instance of a Car class. They have written the following incorrect statement:

Use the Car class name directly to create an object.

What is the correct way to create a new Car object using the new operator?

(a) Car myCar = new Car();
(b) Car myCar = Car();
(c) new Car myCar = new Car();
(d) Car myCar = new();

Q.4 A programmer is working with a Car class that has an attribute color. They want to invoke a method getColor() from a Car object myCar. They have written the following incorrect statement:

Access the getColor() method directly without using the dot operator.

What is the correct way to invoke the getColor() method using the dot operator?

(a) myCar.getColor();
(b) Car.getColor();
(c) myCar → getColor();
(d) getColor(myCar);

Q.5 Consider the following statements related to arithmetic operations and assignment operators, which are jumbled. Choose the correct order of the steps involved:

A. The value of a is incremented by 1.
B. The value of a is initialized with 5.
C. The value of b is assigned the result of a * 2.
D. The updated value of a is printed.

(a) B, A, C, D (b) C, A, B, D
(c) D, C, B, A (d) A, B, C, D

Q.6 Consider the following statements related to the use of the new operator and object creation, which are jumbled. Choose the correct order of the steps involved:

A. A new Car object is created using the new operator.

B. The Car class is defined with attributes and methods.

C. The Car object calls the method displayDetails().

D. The displayDetails() method prints the object's attributes.

(a) A, B, C, D (b) B, A, C, D
(c) C, A, B, D (d) D, C, B, A

Q.7 Consider the following statements related to operator precedence, which are jumbled. Choose the correct order of the steps involved in evaluating the expression:

A. Perform the logical AND (&&) operation.

B. Perform the relational operation (<).

C. Assign the result to status.

D. Evaluate the expression status = 5 < 10 && 3 > 1;.

(a) C, D, A, B (b) A, B, C, D
(c) D, B, A, C (d) B, A, D, C

Answers

1. (d)	2. (c)	3. (a)	4. (a)	5. (a)
6. (b)	7. (c)			

TYPE - 3

01 Mark

Assertion-Reason Type Questions

Directions (Q. Nos. 1-10) The following questions are Assertion-Reason based questions. Choose the answer based on the code given below

(a) Both Assertion (A) and Reason (R) are true and Reason (R) is a correct explanation of Assertion (A).
(b) Both Assertion (A) and Reason (R) are true and Reason (R) is not a correct explanation of Assertion (A).
(c) Assertion (A) is true and Reason (R) is false.
(d) Assertion (A) is false and Reason (R) is true.

Q.1 Assertion (A) Precedence determines the order in which operators are executed.

Reason (R) Multiplication has a higher precedence than addition.

Ans. (a) Operator precedence determines execution order, and multiplication indeed has higher precedence than addition. So, Both Assertion (A) and Reason (R) are true and Reason (R) is a correct explanation of Assertion (A).

Q.2 Assertion (A) The ! operator reverses a boolean value.

Reason (R) It is used to perform logical AND operations.

Ans. (c) The ! operator inverts a boolean value, but it does not perform logical AND operations. So, Assertion (A) is true and Reason (R) is false.

Q.3 Assertion (A) The ternary operator can be used as a replacement for an if-else statement.

Reason (R) It evaluates multiple conditions simultaneously.

Ans. (c) The ternary operator replaces a simple if-else but does not evaluate multiple conditions at once. So, Assertion (A) is true and Reason (R) is false.

Q.4 Assertion (A) The += operator adds a value to a variable and assigns the result.

Reason (R) This operator is equivalent to x = x + y.

Ans. (a) += is a shorthand for x = x + y, making both statements equivalent. So, Both Assertion (A) and Reason (R) are true and Reason (R) is a correct explanation of Assertion (A).

Q.5 Assertion (A) The || operator evaluates conditions from left to right.

Reason (R) It stops evaluating once the first true condition is found.

Ans. (a) The || operator evaluates from left to right and stops as soon as it finds a true condition (short-circuiting). So, Both Assertion (A) and Reason (R) are true and Reason (R) is a correct explanation of Assertion (A).

Q.6 Assertion (A) A counter is always initialized to 0.

Reason (R) The counter variable is used to count iterations or occurrences.

Ans. (c) A counter is used for counting, but it is not always required to be initialized to 0. So, Assertion (A) is false and Reason (R) is true.

Q.7 Assertion (A) The new operator is used to allocate memory.

Reason (R) Memory for objects is allocated on the stack using the new operator.

Ans. (c) The new operator allocates memory for objects, but it does so on the heap, not the stack. So, Assertion (A) is true and Reason (R) is false.

Q.8 Assertion (A) The prefix operator increments a counter before its value is checked in a loop condition.

Reason (R) The loop condition is evaluated after the counter is incremented in a prefix operation.

Ans. (a) The prefix operator (++i) increments the counter before it is evaluated in the loop condition. So, Both Assertion (A) and Reason (R) are true and Reason (R) is a correct explanation of Assertion (A).

Q.9 Assertion (A) Accumulators are initialized before starting loops.

Reason (R) Accumulators store the cumulative value of an operation performed in a loop.

Ans. (a) Accumulators must be initialized before a loop starts to correctly store cumulative values during iterations. So, Both Assertion (A) and Reason (R) are true and Reason (R) is a correct explanation of Assertion (A).

Q.10 Assertion (A) Using post-increment/decrement operators (like i++ or x--) within a loop's condition can sometimes lead to unexpected behavior if not carefully considered.

Reason (R) Post-increment/decrement operators modify the variable after its value has been used in the current expression, including the comparison in the loop condition.

Ans. (a) Post-increment/decrement operators modify a variable after it's used in an expression, affecting loop conditions and potentially causing unexpected behavior. So, Both Assertion (A) and Reason (R) are true and Reason (R) is a correct explanation of Assertion (A).

TYPE - 4 — 01 Mark

Odd One Out

Q.1 Choose the odd one.
(a) > = (b) % (c) / (d) *

Ans. (a) > = (It is relational operator, while other are arithmetic)

Q.2 Choose the odd one.
(a) > (b) == (c) && (d) <

Ans (c) && (It is logical operator, while other are relational)

Q.3 Choose the odd one.
(a) + (b) % (c) / (d) ||

Ans (d) || (It is logical operator, while other are arithmetic)

Q.4 Choose the odd one.
(a) count++ (b) count += 1
(c) count = count + 1 (d) count--

Ans. (d) count-- (It decrements instead of increments.)

Q.5 Choose the odd one.
(a) System.out.print() (b) System.out.println()
(c) System.out.printf() (d) System.in.read()

Ans. (d) System.in.read() (It is used for input, while others are for output.)

TYPE - 5 — 02 Marks

Short Answer Type Questions

Q.1 What is an operator? On what basis are operators classified in Java?

Ans. An operator is a specialised symbol that performs a specific kind of evaluation on one, two, or three operands, and produces a result.

Operators in Java can be categorized based on two criteria:

- Forms of operators
- Types of operators

Q.2 What are the priority levels of arithmetic operation in Java?

Ans. There are two priority levels of arithmetic operation in java. They are as follows:
High priority * / %
Low priority + −

Q.3 What is the result of relational operator when it is used in looping or branching statement?

Ans. The result of all relational operators is always of a boolean type. It returns always true or false.

Q.4 Consider the following code snippet.

```
int i = 10; int n = i++%5;
```

(i) What are the values of i and n after the code is executed?

(ii) What are the final values of i and n if instead of using the postfix increment operator (i++), you use the prefix version (++i))?

Ans. (i) i=11,n=0

(ii) Using i++ (postfix increment):

```
i = 11     n = 0
```

Using ++i (prefix increment):

```
i = 11    n = 1
```

Q.5 Besides incrementing by 1, how else can you change a variable's value using shorthand operators?

Ans. Besides incrementing (or decrementing) by 1, you can change a variable's value using shorthand operators by adding, subtracting, multiplying, dividing, or finding the modulus of another value and assigning the result back to the original variable using operators like +=, -=, *=, /=, and %=.

Q.6 Explain the following code sample:
result = someCondition ? value1 : value2;

Ans. This code should be read as: "If someCondition is true, assign the value of value1 to result. Otherwise, assign the value of value2 to result.

Q.7 Which operators are used in Java to:
(i) Access class member
(ii) Create objects at runtime

Ans. (i) The dot operator is used to access or invoke individual members of a class.

(ii) The new operator dynamically allocates memory space for an object.

Q.8 What are operands ? Name the forms of operators depending on the operands.

Ans. An operand is a value or variable that an operator acts upon in an expression. Operands can be constants, variables, or expressions that provide data for operations.

Forms of Operators Based on the Number of Operands Operators in Java are categorized based on the number of operands they work with:

Operator Type	Number of Operands	Examples
Unary	1	++x, – – x, !x, ~x
Binary	2	a + b, x * y, a > b, x && y
Ternary	3	condition ? value1 : value2

Q.9 What is the use and syntax of a ternary operator?

Ans. Ternary operator deals with three operands. It is also called conditional assignment statement because the value assigned to a variable depends upon the logical expression. The common use of ternary operator is in checking the condition.

Syntax

```
Variable = (test expression)? Value 1: Value 2
```

Q.10 Name the operators listed below.

(i) < (ii) + + (iii) & & (iv) ? :

Ans. (i) < → Relational operator

(ii) + + → Postfix/Prefix Increment

(iii) & & → Logical AND Operator

(iv) ? : → Conditional Operator/Ternary operator

Q.11 What will be the output of the following code?

```
int k = 5, j = 9;
k+=k++ - ++j+k;
System.out.println("k ="+k);
System.out.println("j ="+j);
```

Ans. k + = (k++) – (++j) + k;

= k + (k++ – ++j + k); [∴ left to right]

= 5 + (5 – 10 + 6);

k = 6

Hence, k = 6, j = 10

Q.12 What will be the output for the following program segment?

```
int a=0, b=30,c=40;
a=--b + c + ++b;
System.out.println("a ="+ a);
```

Ans. int a = 0, b = 30, c = 40;

a = – –b + c + ++ b (∵ left to right)

= 29 + 40 + 30 = 99

Q.13 Find the output of the following program segment, when

(i) val= 500 (ii) val=1600

```
int val, sum, n = 550;
sum = n +val>1750?400:200;
System.out.println(sum);
```

Ans. (i) When, val = 500, n = 550

Sum = n+val > 1750 ? 400 : 200;

= 550 + 500 > 1750 ? 400 : 200;

= 1050 > 1750 ? 400 : 200;

Sum = 200

(ii) When, val = 1600, n = 550

Sum = n + val > 1750 ? 400 : 200;

= 550 + 1600 > 1750 ? 400 : 200;

= 2150 > 1750 ? 400 : 200;

Sum = 400

Q.14 What is the difference between the following two statements? Explain the results.

```
x -= 5;
x =- 5;
```

Ans. The first statement, x -= 5; subtracts 5 from x and assigns the result back to x. It is equivalent to x = x – 5;

The second statement, x =- 5; assigns the value of -5 to x.

Q.15 When an expression in Java contains multiple operator, which concept govern their evaluation order and direction?

Ans. Precedence of operators refers to the order in which the operators are applied to the operands in an expression.

Associativity of operators refers to the direction of execution of operators ("Left to Right" or "Right to Left") when operators in an expression have the same precedence.

Q.16 Explain the purpose of using a 'new' keyword in a Java program.

Ans. 'new' operator is used to create an instance of an object. It is also used to create an instance of a class. Actually, it dynamically allocates memory in the heap with the reference, we define pointed from the stack.

e.g. `Myclass abc = new Myclass();`

Here, an instance of the class Myclass is created.

Q.17 Determine the output of the following program.

```
public class Test
{
    public static void main(String[] args)
    {
        int a = 1, b = 2;
        System.out.println("Output1: " + a + b);
        System.out.println("Output2: " + (a + b));
    }
}
```

Ans. Output

Output1: 12

Output2: 3

Q.18 Given an integer variable count and the following code snippet:

```
int court = 5;
count++
System.out.println(count);
```

(a) Explain the purpose of the ++ operator.

(b) Describe how this code demonstrates the use of a counter and how it relates to increment operators.

Ans. (a) The ++ operator increments the value of count by 1

(b) The code shows a counter increasing from 5 to 6 using ++, which is commonly used in loops or counting logic.

Q.19 Given two integer variables a and b and the following code snippet:

```
int a = 10;
int b = 20;
boolean result = a > b;
System.out.println(result);
```

(a) Explain the purpose of the > operator.

(b) Describe how this code demonstrates the use of relational operators and how the result is stored in a boolean variable.

Ans. (a) The > operator compares if a is greater than b.

(b) It shows how a relational operator checks a condition and stores the result (true or false) in a boolean variable.

Q.20 Given a class Circle with a method calculateArea() and the following code snippet:

```
Circle myCircle = new Circle();
double area = myCircle.calculateArea();
System.out.println("Area: " + area);
```

(a) Explain the purpose of the . operator in this context.

(b) Describe how this code demonstrates the use of the dot operator to invoke a method of a class and how it relates to object-oriented programming.

Ans. (a) The . operator is used to access the method calculateArea() from the myCircle object.

(b) It demonstrates how the dot operator is used in object-oriented programming to invoke methods or access fields of a class object.

Q.21 Write the output of the following Java operator expressions:

```
int a = 5;
int b = 10;
```

(a) System.out.println(++a * b--);

(b) System.out.println(a > b ? "Greater" : "Smaller");

Ans. (a) 60 (b) Smaller

Q.22 Write the output of the following using the dot operator:

```
class Example
{
    int num = 10;
    String text = "Hello";
}
public class Main
{
    public static void main(String[] args)
    {
        Example obj = new Example();
    }
}
```

(a) System.out.println(obj.num);

(b) System.out.println(obj.text.length());

Ans. (a) 10 (b) 5

TYPE - 8 02 Marks

Differentiate

Q.1 Unary operators and binary operators

Ans.

Unary Operator	Binary Operator
It works/operates on single operand or variables. *Or* Holds only one operand	It works/operates on two variables or operands. *Or* Holds more than one operand
e.g. ++, – –, ! etc.	e.g. +, –, *, %, etc.

Q.2 / operator and % operator

Ans.

/ Operator	% Operator
This is a division operator.	This is a modulus operator.
It is used to find the quotient of division of two numbers.	It is used to find the remainder of the division of two numbers.

e.g.
`int x = 10, y = 5, z;`
`x = x/y;`
value of z will be 2.
	e.g.
	`int x = 10, y = 5, z;`
	`z = x%y;`
	value of z will be 0.

Q.3 = operator and = = operator

Ans.

= operator	= = operator
It is assignment operator.	It is relational (binary) operator.
It is used to assign a value to any variable. e.g. `x = 10;`	It compares two object, based on memory reference. e.g. `(A = = B)`

Q.4 Prefix operator and Postfix operator

Ans.

Prefix Operator	Postfix Operator
It works on the principle of CHANGE-THEN-USE.	It works on the principle of USE-THEN-CHANGE.
It is written before the operand.	It is written after the operand.
e.g. `int a = 99;` `int b = ++a;` After the execution of these two statements, both a and b will have the value of 100.	e.g. `int a = 99;` `int b = a++;` After the execution of these two statements, a will have the value of 100 and b will have the value of 99.

Q.5 Counter and Accumulator

Ans.

Counter	Accumulator
Used to count occurrences (e.g., loop iterations, number of elements)	Used to store a running total (sum of values)
Usually starts from 0 or 1	Usually starts from 0
Incremented by a fixed amount (e.g., counter++ or counter += 1)	Updated by adding variable values (accumulator += value)
Counting number of iterations in a loop	Summing numbers in an array

Q.6 System.out.print() and System.out.println()

Ans.

System.out.print()	System.out.println()
It prints data to the console but the cursor remains at the end of the data in the same line.	It prints data to the console and places the cursor in the next line.
e.g. `System.out.print("Hello ");` `System.out.print("World!");` **Output** HelloWorld!	e.g. `System.out.println("Hello");` `System.out.println("World!");` **Output** Hello World!

Q.7 Operator and Expression

Ans.

Operator	Expression
Operators are special symbols used for mathematical or logical function.	An expression is a statement that can convey a value.
Generally, these are used between two operands.	It may be any combination of variables, literals, operators.
e.g. x + y here + is an operator.	e.g. a = b + c is an expression.

TYPE - 9

02 Marks

Programming Based Questions

Q.1 Write a simple program to illustrate the binary operator.

Ans.
```
public class BinaryExample
{
   public static void main(String[] args)
   {
      int a = 20, b = 10, num = 10;
      boolean x = true, y = false;
      System.out.println(a + b); // 30
      System.out.println(a % b); // 0
      System.out.println(a > b); // true
      System.out.println(a == b); // false
      System.out.println(x && y); // false
      System.out.println(x || y); // true
      num += 5; // num = num + 5
      System.out.println(num); // 15
   }
}
```

Q.2 Write a simple program to find the greatest of three numbers.

Ans.
```
// A program to display the greater of the three
number
class Ternary
{
   public static void main(String args[])
   {
      int a=42,b=56,c=88,max;
      max=(a>b)?(a>c?a:c):(b>c?b:c);
      System.out.println("The greatest number
                                    = "+max);
   }
}
```

Q.3 Write a program to input two numbers and display their addition, subtraction, multiplication, division and modulus.

Ans.
```
public class ArithmeticExample
{
   public static void main(String[] args)
   {
      int a = 10, b = 5;
      System.out.println(a + b); // 15
      System.out.println(a - b); // 5
      System.out.println(a * b); // 50
      System.out.println(a / b); // 2
      System.out.println(a % b); // 0
   }
}
```

Q.4 Write a Java program demonstrating the use of arithmetic, relational, and logical operators in a single program.

Ans.
```
public class OperatorExample {
    public static void main(String[] args) {
        int a = 10, b = 5;
        boolean x = true, y = false;
            // Arithmetic Operators
        System.out.println("Addition: " + (a + b));
            // 15
        System.out.println("Subtraction: " + (a - b));
            // 5
            // Relational Operators
        System.out.println("Is a > b? " + (a > b));
            // true
        System.out.println("Is a == b? " + (a == b));
            // false
            // Logical Operators
        System.out.println("Logical AND: " + (x && y));
            // false
        System.out.println("Logical
            OR " (x || y):" + (x || y)); // true
    }
}
```

Q.5 Write a simple program showing the use of new operator.

Ans.
```
public class NewExample1
{
    void display()
    {
        System.out.println("Invoking Method");
    }
    public static void main(String[] args)
    {
        NewExample1 obj=new NewExample1();
        obj.display();
    }
}
```

Q.6 Write a simple program to print your name and your father's name by using system. out.print() and system.out.println().

Ans.
```
public class NamePrinter
{
    public static void main(String[] args)
    {
        // Using System.out.print() to print on the
                                        same line
        System.out.print("My name is John ");
        // Using System.out.println() to print on a
                                        new line
        System.out.println("and my father's name is
                                    Michael.");
    }
}
```

TYPE - 11

02 Marks

Evaluate the Following

Q.1 Evaluate the expression when the value of x = 4

`x * = --x + x++ +x`

Ans. The expression can be written as

x = x * (– – x + x+ + + x)

x = 4 * (3 + 3 + 4)

x = 4 * 10

x = 40

Q.2 Evaluate the expression

`Z += a++ + --b + ++a + --b;`

where a = 10, b = 5, Z = 10

Ans. Z= Z + (a+ + + --b + + +a + --b)

Z = 10 + (10 + 4 + 12 + 3)

Z = 10 + 29

Z = 39

Q.3 What is the value of m after evaluating the following expression?

`m - = 9%++n + ++n/2;`

when int m=10,n=6

Ans. The expression can be written as

m = m – (9 % + +n + + +n / 2)

m = 10 – (9 % 7 + 8 / 2)

m = 10 – (2 + 4)

m = 10 – 6

m = 4

Q.4 Evaluate the following expression if the value of x = 2, y = 3 and z = 1.

`v = x + --z+ y++ +y`

Ans. v=2+--1+3+++4

v=2+0+3+++4

v=2+0+3+4

v=2+0+3+4

v=9

Q.5 What is the value of y after evaluating the expression given below?

y+ = ++y + y– – + – – y; when int y = 8

Ans. y + = + +y+y – – + – – y

= y+[(+ +y)+(y– –) + (– –y)]

= 8 + [9 + 9 + 7]

= 8 + [25]= 33

Q.6 Evaluate the value of n if value of p = 5, q = 19

`int n=(q–p)>(p–q)? (q–p):(p–q);`

Ans.

Step 1 Compute (q - p) and (p - q)

q-p=19-5=14

p-q=5-19=-14

Step 2 Evaluate the Conditional Expression

The condition is:

(q-p)>(p-q)

14>-14

Since 14 is greater than -14, the condition evaluates to true.

Step 3 Assign the True Branch Value

Since the condition is true, n takes the value of (q - p), which is 14.

n=14

Q.7 If a = 5, b = 9 calculate the value of

a+=a++ − ++b+a;

Ans. a+ = a++ − ++b + a (∵ left to right)

= a + (a++ − ++b + a)

= 5 + (5 − 10 + 6) = 5 + 1 = 6

The value of a after execution will be 6.

Q.8 Evaluate the following expressions, if the values of the variables are a = 2, b = 3 and c = 9

(i) a − (b ++) * (− − c)

(ii) a * (+ + b)% c

Ans. (i) 2 − 3 × 8 = 2 − 24 = − 22

(ii) 2 * 4 % 9 = 8 % 9 = 8

Q.9 Evaluate the given expression when the value of p = 8 and q = 4:

```
int output = --p / q++ + p % 3;
System.out.println("p = " + p);
System.out.println("q = " + q);
System.out.println("output = " + output);
```

Ans. p = 7

q = 5

output = 2

Q.10 Evaluate the given expression when the value of x = 5 and y = 2:

```
int result = x++ + --y * x;
System.out.println("x = " + x);
System.out.println("y = " + y);
System.out.println("result = " + result);
```

Ans. x = 6

y = 1

result = 11

TYPE - 12 02 Marks

Rewrite the Following

Q.1 Rewrite the following using ternary operators

```
if( x > y)
   c= 'A';
else
   c = 'a';
```

Ans. c = (x > y)? 'A' : 'a';

Q.2 Rewrite the following using ternary operator

```
if (bill >10000 )
   discount = bill * 10.0/100;
else
   discount = bill * 5.0/100;
```

Ans. Using ternary operator

```
discount = bill >10000? (bill*10.0/100):
(bill*5.0/100);
```

Q.3 Rewrite the following using ternary operator

```
if (x% 2 = = 0)
   System.out.print("EVEN");
else
   System.out.print("ODD");
```

Ans. Using ternary operator

```
System.out.print (x % 2 = = 0) ? (''EVEN''):
                                      ("ODD");
```

Q.4 Rewrite the following using ternary operator

```
if(income<=10000)
   tax=0;
else
   tax=12;
```

Ans. tax=income < = 10000 ? 0 : 12;

Q.5 Rewrite the following statements without using shorthand operators.

(a) p /= q (b) p -= 1

(c) p *= q + r (d) p -= q -r

Ans. (a) p = p / q

(b) p = p - 1

(c) p = p * (q + r)

(d) p = p - (q - r)

TYPE - 13 15 Marks

Long Answer Type Questions

Q.1 A bakery sells cupcakes for $2.50 each and cookies for $1.75 each. Write a program to calculate the total cost if a customer buys 12 cupcakes and 8 cookies. Display the total cost in a user-friendly format.

Ans.
```
public class Bakery
{
   public static void main(String[] args)
   {
      double cupcakePrice = 2.50;
      double cookiePrice = 1.75;
      int cupcakes = 12;
      int cookies = 8;
      double totalCost = (cupcakes * cupcakePrice)
                                + (cookies * cookiePrice);
```

```
    System.out.printf("Total cost for %d cupcakes
        and %d cookies: $%.2f\n", cupcakes, cookies,
                                        totalCost);
  }
}
```

Q.2 A student scored 78 out of 120 on a math test and 92 out of 150 on a science test. Write a program to calculate and display the percentage score for each test.

Ans.
```
public class TestScores
{
  public static void main(String[] args)
  {
    int mathScore = 78;
    int mathTotal = 120;
    int scienceScore = 92;
    int scienceTotal = 150;
    double mathPercentage = (double) mathScore
                              / mathTotal * 100;
    double sciencePercentage = (double)
                  scienceScore / scienceTotal * 100;
    System.out.printf("Math test percentage:
                           %.2f%%\n", mathPercentage);
    System.out.printf("Science test percentage:
                        %.2f%%\n", sciencePercentage);
  }
}
```

Q.3 A company's revenue increased from $500,000 to $575,000 in one year. Write a program to calculate and display the percentage increase in revenue.

Ans.
```
public class RevenueIncrease
{
  public static void main(String[] args)
  {
    double initialRevenue = 500000;
    double finalRevenue = 575000;
    double revenueIncrease = finalRevenue -
                                   initialRevenue;
    double percentageIncrease = (revenueIncrease
                          / initialRevenue) * 100;
    System.out.printf("Percentage increase in
         revenue: %.2f%%\n", percentageIncrease);
  }
}
```

Q.4 A rectangle has a length of 15.5 cm and a width of 8 cm. Write a program to calculate and display the area and perimeter of the rectangle.

Ans.
```
public class Rectangle
{
  public static void main(String[] args)
  {
    double length = 15.5;
    double width = 8;
    double area = length * width;
    double perimeter = 2 * (length + width);
    System.out.printf("Area of the rectangle:
                               %.2f cm²\n", area);
    System.out.printf("Perimeter of the rectangle:
                          %.2f cm\n", perimeter);
  }
}
```

Q.5 A train travels at a speed of 80 km/h for 2.5 hours and then at a speed of 60 km/h for 1.5 hours. Write a program to calculate and display the total distance traveled by the train.

Ans.
```
public class TrainJourney
{
public static void main(String[] args)
{
    double speed1 = 80; // km/h
    double time1 = 2.5; // hours
    double speed2 = 60; // km/h
    double time2 = 1.5; // hours
    double distance1 = speed1 * time1;
    double distance2 = speed2 * time2;
    double totalDistance = distance1 + distance2;
    System.out.printf("Total distance traveled by
            the train: %.2f km\n", totalDistance);
}
}
```

Q.6 A store is offering a 15% discount on all items. Write a program to calculate and display the final price of an item after the discount, given the original price of the item.

Ans.
```
public class DiscountCalculator
{
public static void main(String[] args)
{
    double originalPrice = 100.0;
        // Example original price
    double discountPercentage = 15.0;
    double discountAmount = (discountPercentage
                         / 100.0) * originalPrice;
    double finalPrice = originalPrice -
                                  discountAmount;
    System.out.println("Original Price: $"
                               + originalPrice);
    System.out.println("Discount Amount: $"
                              + discountAmount);
    System.out.println("Final Price: $"
                                 + finalPrice);
}
}
```

05

INPUT IN JAVA

Input is important in Java programs because it helps the program take data from users or other sources. This allows the program to work on different data, perform tasks, and give results based on what the user provides. It makes the program useful and interactive.

Initialization – Data Before Execution in Java

In Java, initialization is the process of assigning starting values to variables, objects, or data structures before they are used in the program. This ensures that the data is valid and ready to use when the program runs. The term "Data before execution" refers to preparing and setting up the required data (through initialization) before the program or method begins its operations.

Example

```
int age = 18;
String name = "Arihant";
```

Note *In Java, if you don't manually initialize instance variables, the system automatically provides default values such as 0* ***for numeric types, false for boolean****, and* ***null for reference types*** *before execution begins.*

Parameters

In Java, parameters are special variables used to pass data into methods. When a method is called, you can send values (called arguments) to it. The method then uses parameters to work with that data.

Defining Methods with Parameters:

In Java, you can add parameters inside the parentheses after the method name while creating a method. These parameters work like named variables that store data passed to the method when it is called.

Each parameter you define requires two things:

- **Data Type** Specifies the type of data it will hold (like text, numbers, etc.).
- **Name** Acts as a label to access the data inside the method.

Example

```
public static void greet(String name)
{
    System.out.println("Hello, " + name);
}
greet("John");
```

Packages in Java

A package in Java is like a folder or directory that helps group related classes, interfaces, and sub-packages together. It provides a simple way to organize your code and makes it easier to manage large projects. Think of packages as similar to folders on your computer, where each file or sub-folder has a specific role or purpose.

Types of Packages in Java

- **Built-in Packages** Java includes several predefined packages for common tasks, such as:
  - **java.util** Contains utility classes like ArrayList, HashMap, and Collections.
  - **java.io** Handles input and output operations, such as reading and writing files.
  - **java.net** Provides tools for networking operations, such as working with URLs and sockets.

- **User-defined Packages** You can create your own custom packages to organize classes based on the needs of your project

Note *By using packages, Java helps developers create clean, modular, and maintainable code, especially in large and complex applications.*

Importing Packages in Java

When you create a package or use a built-in package in Java, you need to import its classes and interfaces into your program to access them. This is done using the import statement. Importing allows you to use the code from the package without writing the full package name every time.

Syntax

The general syntax for importing a class or interface from a package is:

```
import packageName.ClassName;
```

Here's what the syntax means:

- packageName is the name of the package where the class or interface is located.
- ClassName is the specific class or interface you want to use from that package.

If you want to import all the classes and interfaces from a package, you can use an asterisk (*) instead of a class name:

```
import packageName.*;
```

Types of Importing Packages

- **Importing a Specific Class** to use the Scanner class from the java.util package to take user input, the syntax is

  Syntax `import java.util.Scanner;`

- **Importing All Classes from a Package** If you need multiple classes from a package, you can import them all using the wildcard *. For example:

  Syntax `import java.util.*;`

Note ***Key Points About Importing Packages***

- ***No Need to Import Classes from java.lang*** *The java.lang package contains commonly used classes such as String, Math, System, and Object. This package is automatically imported into every Java program, so you don't need to explicitly include it in your code.*
- ***Fully Qualified Name*** *Instead of using the import statement, you can directly refer to a class by its fully qualified name, which includes the package name. This method is particularly useful when there are classes with the same name in different packages, as it avoids ambiguity.*

Input Streams(Scanner class) in Java

Java's Input package offers a powerful framework for managing data input operations. Streams play a key role in this process, enabling interaction with various data types, objects, and files. Two primary classes used for accepting input are BufferedReader and Scanner, each with its own strengths.

1. BufferedReader

- It reads character streams efficiently, either line by line or as character arrays.
- It uses InputStreamReader to convert byte streams into character streams, Which makes it suitable for BufferedReader.

2. Scanner

- A versatile class for parsing input from various sources like the console, files, and strings.
- No need for explicit exception handling and offers direct methods for reading specific data types like nextInt(), nextFloat(), and nextLine().

Java Scanner Class

The Scanner class provides several methods to read different types of input data. These methods are used to capture input from the standard input stream (typically the keyboard) and store the entered data in variables.

To create a scanner object for reading input from keyboard

Syntax `Scanner input = new Scanner(System.in);`

Common Methods of the Scanner Class

1. **nextShort()** This method is used to read a short integer value entered by the user.
2. **nextInt()** This method reads an integer value entered by the user.

3. **nextLong()** This method reads a long integer value entered by the user.
4. **nextFloat()** This method reads a float value entered by the user.
5. **nextDouble()** This method reads a double-precision floating-point value entered by the user.
6. **next()** This method reads a single word (or token) from the user. It stops reading at the first space.
7. **nextLine()** This method reads a full line of text, including spaces.
8. **next().charAt(0)** This combination is used when you want to read a single character input from the user. The next() method gets the next token (word) and charAt(0) extracts the first character of that word.

Here's an example that demonstrates the use of these methods in a program:

```
import java.util.Scanner;
public class UserInputExample
{
  public static void main(String[] args)
   {
     Scanner scanner = new Scanner(System.in);
     // Read a short value
     System.out.print("Enter a short number: ");
     short shortValue = scanner.nextShort();
     System.out.println("You entered: " + shortValue);
     // Read an integer value
     System.out.print("Enter an integer: ");
     int intValue = scanner.nextInt();
     System.out.println("You entered: " + intValue);
     // Read a long value
     System.out.print("Enter a long number: ");
     long longValue = scanner.nextLong();
     System.out.println("You entered: " + longValue);
     // Read a float value
     System.out.print("Enter a float number: ");
     float floatValue = scanner.nextFloat();
     System.out.println("You entered: " + floatValue);
     // Read a double value
     System.out.print("Enter a double number: ");
     double doubleValue = scanner.nextDouble();
     System.out.println("You entered: " + doubleValue);
     // Read a single word
     System.out.print("Enter a word: ");
     String word = scanner.next();
     System.out.println("You entered: " + word);
     // Read a full sentence
     scanner.nextLine(); // Consume the newline character left by nextInt, nextFloat, etc.
     System.out.print("Enter a sentence: ");
     String sentence = scanner.nextLine();
     System.out.println("You entered: " + sentence);
     // Read a single character
     System.out.print("Enter a character: ");
     char character = scanner.next().charAt(0);
     System.out.println("You entered: " + character);
     // Close the scanner
     scanner.close();
   }
}
```

Note *When using methods like nextInt(), nextFloat(), etc., the nextLine() method should be used carefully. This is because methods like nextInt() do not consume the newline character left in the input buffer after reading numerical inputs. As a result, when you try to read a string immediately after reading a number, it may cause unexpected behavior. To avoid this, it's a good practice to use scanner.nextLine() after reading numerical inputs to consume the remaining newline character.*

Streams in Java

1. **Input Streams** Used for reading data into your program (e.g., from a file or keyboard).

   Examples FileInputStream, BufferedInputStream, ByteArrayInputStream.

2. **Output Streams** Used for sending data out of your program (e.g., to a file or screen).

   Examples FileOutputStream, BufferedOutputStream, ByteArrayOutputStream.

Errors in Java

Errors are issues in the code that stop the program from running as expected. These errors can happen for many different reasons, and knowing the different types of errors can help you find and fix them more easily.

In Java (and most programming languages), errors can occur at different stages of the program execution process. These errors can broadly be categorized into three types:

- Syntax Errors
- Runtime Errors
- Logical Errors

Each type of error arises from different issues in the code, and understanding them is crucial to effectively debugging and writing error-free programs.

1. **Syntax Errors** Syntax errors occurs when the code doesn't follow the rules of the Java language. This includes things like missing semicolons, unmatched parentheses, incorrect keywords, or misspelled variable names.These errors are caught by the compiler at the time of compilation, before the program is executed.
2. **Runtime Errors** These errors occur during the execution of the program. The program compiles successfully, but an error happens when you run the code. This can happen when the program tries to perform illegal operations like dividing by zero, accessing a null object, or accessing an array index out of bounds.
3. **Logical Errors** Logical errors are bugs in the program that occur when the program runs without throwing any exceptions, but it produces incorrect results. These errors often occur due to incorrect algorithms, improper conditionals, or wrong assumptions. These errors happen due to flaws in the program's logic and are difficult to detect because the code compiles and runs without throwing exceptions. The program might execute without errors but produce incorrect results.

Note
- ***Syntax errors*** *are detected by the compiler and must be corrected before the program can run.*
- ***Runtime errors*** *occur during execution and cause the program to crash or behave unexpectedly. These errors often require debugging using exception handling or validating inputs.*
- ***Logical errors*** *are the hardest to detect because the program runs normally but produces incorrect results. Debugging these errors requires careful inspection of the program logic and understanding of the desired behavior.*

Comments in Java

In Java, comments are used to add explanatory notes or remarks to your code. These comments are not executed by the program but serve as documentation for anyone reading the code. Java supports two types of comments:

- **Single-line Comments (//)** A single-line comment is used to add comments that span a single line. It is denoted by two forward slashes (//), and everything following the slashes on that line is treated as a comment. Single-line comments are useful for short descriptions or explanations.
- **Multi-line Comments (/* ... */)** A multi-line comment is used when the comment spans more than one line. It begins with /* and ends with */, allowing multiple lines of text between the start and end markers to be treated as comments. Multi-line comments are useful for adding longer explanations, block comments, or commenting out large sections of code.

Note *Both single line and multi-line types of comments improve code readability and help other developers (or your future self) understand the logic behind the code.*

EXAM ORIENTED QUESTIONS

TYPE - 1

01 Mark

Multiple Choice Questions

Q.1

What does the image represent when int a = 10; is written?

(a) Comment writing (b) Variable Declaration
(c) Variable Initialization (d) Compilation process

Q.2 Which of the following is the default value of a boolean variable in Java?

(a) 1 (b) false
(c) 0 (d) true

Q.3 What is the default value of an instance variable of type int in Java?

(a) 0 (b) null
(c) -1 (d) undefined

Q.4 Name the default value of a reference variable in Java.

(a) 0 (b) " "
(c) false (d) null

Q.5

What is happening in the image?

(a) Method returning values
(b) Method receiving parameters
(c) Class execution
(d) Package importing

Q.6 Which of the following is the correct purpose of importing a package in Java?

(a) To declare variables in Java
(b) To use pre-defined classes and methods from the Java API
(c) To compile the Java program
(d) To define custom classes

Q.7 Name the keyword used to create a custom package in Java.

(a) import (b) try
(c) throw (d) package

Q.8

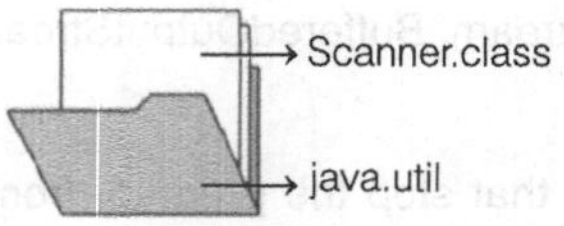

What does the image represent?

(a) Syntax Error
(b) Package structure in Java
(c) Runtime input
(d) Scanner method execution

Q.9 In Java, which method of the Scanner class is used to read a single word from the user input?

(a) next() (b) nextLine()
(c) nextChar() (d) nextString()

Q.10 Which package does the Scanner class belong to in Java?

(a) java.lang (b) java.util
(c) java.io (d) java.net

Q.11

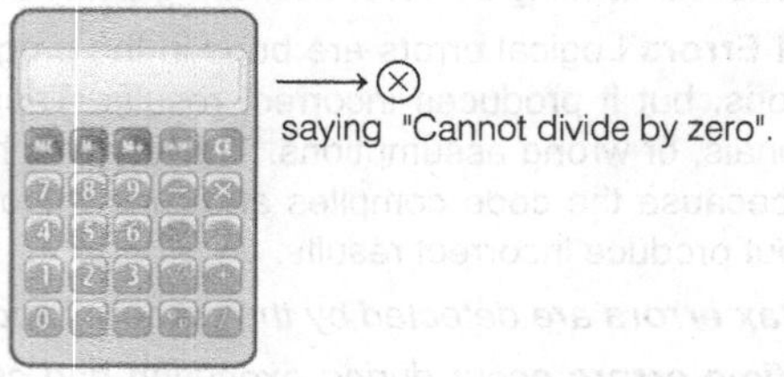

What type of error is shown in the image?

(a) Syntax Error (b) Logical Error
(c) Runtime Error (d) Comment Error

Q.12 What does the nextLine() method of the Scanner class do?

(a) Reads a single character
(b) Reads a full line of text
(c) Reads a token
(d) Reads a float

Q.13 Which of the following is NOT a built-in package in Java?

(a) java.util (b) java.io
(c) java.lang (d) java.user

Q.14 What does the next().charAt(0) method combination do in the Scanner class?

(a) Reads a whole word (b) Reads a single character
(c) Reads a string (d) Reads an integer

Q.15 Name the class used to take input from the user in Java.

(a) ArrayList (b) Scanner
(c) Character (d) Default

Q.16 Name the package that contains the Scanner class.

(a) java.io (b) java.util
(c) java.lang (d) java.net

Q.17 Name the method used to read a full line of text in the Scanner class.

(a) next (b) nextInt
(c) nextFloat (d) nextLine

Q.18 Name the method used to read an integer value in the Scanner class.

(a) next (b) nextLine
(c) nextFloat (d) nextInt

Q.19 What type of error occurs when a program tries to divide by zero?

(a) Syntax error
(b) Runtime error
(c) Logical error
(d) Compilation error

Q.20 Name the error that occurs when trying to divide by zero.

(a) ArrayIndexOutOfBoundsException
(b) NumberFormatException
(c) ArithmeticException
(d) FormatException

Q.21 Name the type of error caused by incorrect logic in the code.

(a) Syntax error
(b) Compilation error
(c) Runtime error
(d) Logical error

Q.22

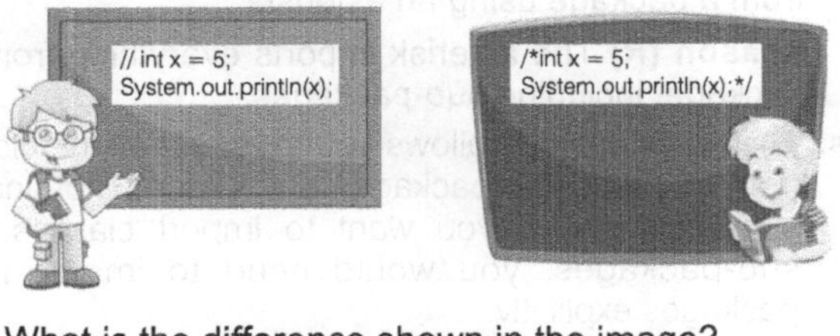

What is the difference shown in the image?

(a) Errors (b) Input methods
(c) Comment Types (d) Packages

Answers

1. (c)	2. (b)	3. (a)	4. (d)	5. (b)
6. (b)	7. (d)	8. (b)	9. (a)	10. (b)
11. (c)	12. (b)	13. (d)	14. (b)	15. (b)
16. (b)	17. (d)	18. (d)	19. (b)	20. (c)
21. (d)	22. (c)			

TYPE - 2 — 01 Mark

Statement Based Questions

Q.1 A developer is trying to read an integer value from the user using the Scanner class. They've written the following code:

```
int userAge = input.nextInt();
```

However, the code throws an error during compilation because input is not declared.

What is the correct way to initialize the Scanner object?

A. `Scanner input = new Scanner();`
B. `Scanner input = new Scanner(System.in);`
C. `Scanner input = new Scanner("10");`
D. `Scanner input = Scanner.read();`

(a) Only A (b) Only B
(c) Only C (d) Both D and A

Q.2 A programmer wants to pass a string "Hello" as a parameter to a method greetUser. They have the following method signature:

```
public static void greetUser(String userName)
{
    // ... code ...
}
```

What is the correct way to call the greetUser method with the string "Hello"?

A. `greetUser("Hello");`
B. `greetUser(Hello);`
C. `String userName = "Hello";`
`greetUser(userName);`
D. Both A and C

(a) Only A (b) Only B
(c) Only C (d) Both A and C

Q.3 A Java program attempts to perform the following operation:

```
int result = 10 / 0;
```

This leads to an error during program execution. What type of error is this?

A. Syntax Error B. Runtime Error
C. Logical Error D. Compilation Error

(a) Only A (b) Only B
(c) Only C (d) Only D

Q.4 A developer wants to add a single-line comment to their Java code explaining the purpose of a variable. They have the following line:

```
int count = 0; // Initialize counter
```

Which of the following describes the correct syntax for a single-line comment?

A. /* Initialize counter */
B. // Initialize counter

C. ' Initialize counter

D. -- Initialize counter

(a) Both A and B (b) Only B
(c) Only C (d) Only D

Q.5 Consider the following steps involved in reading user input using the Scanner class, which are jumbled. Choose the correct order of the steps:

A. The user enters data at the console.

B. The Scanner object is created with System.in as input.

C. The Scanner method (e.g., nextInt()) is called.

D. The entered data is processed or stored.

(a) B, A, C, D (b) A, B, D, C
(c) C, D, A, B (d) D, C, B, A

Q.6 Consider the following actions related to variable initialization and parameter passing in Java, which are jumbled. Choose the correct order of the actions:

A. A method is called with arguments.

B. Variables are declared and assigned values before execution.

C. Values are passed to method parameters during method call.

D. Variables are initialized with default values or specific values.

(a) D, B, C, A (b) C, A, D, B
(c) B, D, A, C (d) A, C, B, D

Q.7 Consider the following steps related to error handling in Java, which are jumbled. Choose the correct order of the steps:

A. The code is compiled and executed.

B. An error occurs during compilation or runtime.

C. The programmer identifies the type of error (syntax, runtime, logical).

D. The programmer corrects the code or implements error handling.

(a) D, A, B, C (b) B, C, D, A
(c) C, D, A, B (d) A, B, C, D

Answers

1. (b) **2.** (d) **3.** (b) **4.** (b) **5.** (a)
6. (c) **7.** (d)

TYPE - 3

01 Mark

Assertion-Reason Type Questions

Directions (Q. Nos. 1-5) The following questions are Assertion-Reason based questions. Choose the answer based on the code given below

(a) Both Assertion (A) and Reason (R) are true and Reason (R) is a correct explanation of Assertion (A).

(b) Both Assertion (A) and Reason (R) are true and Reason (R) is not a correct explanation of Assertion (A).

(c) Assertion (A) is true and Reason (R) is false.

(d) Assertion (A) is false and Reason (R) is true.

Q.1 Assertion (A) **In Java, the next() method of the Scanner class reads a full line of input.**

Reason (R) **The next() method reads only a single token from the input.**

Ans. (d) The next() method of the Scanner class reads only a single token (word) from the input, not the entire line. To read an entire line, the nextLine() method should be used. Therefore, the assertion is false and the reason is true.

Q.2 Assertion (A) **Scanner.nextInt() reads a single integer value from the user input.**

Reason (R) **You should use nextLine() to handle numeric inputs.**

Ans. (c) The nextInt() method reads an integer from the input correctly. The reason provided is false because nextLine() is used to read an entire line of text, not to handle numeric inputs. Therefore, the assertion is true and the reason is false.

Q.3 Assertion (A) **Java classes are automatically imported from the java.lang package.**

Reason (R) **The java.lang package contains essential classes like String, System, and Math.**

Ans. (a) The java.lang package is automatically imported in every Java program, so you don't need to explicitly import classes from it.

This package includes essential classes such as String, System, and Math, making the assertion and the reason both true.

Q.4 Assertion (A) **Java allows the import of all classes from a package using an asterisk.**

Reason (R) **The asterisk imports everything from the package, including sub-packages.**

Ans. (c) The asterisk (*) allows you to import all the classes from a particular package, but it does not include sub-packages. If you want to import classes from sub-packages, you would need to import those packages explicitly.

Q.5 Assertion (A) **An instance variable of type boolean in Java will be initialized to false by default.**

Reason (R) **Java automatically initializes all primitive data types to zero.**

Ans. (c) The default value for an uninitialized boolean variable in Java is false. However, the reason is false because Java does not initialize all primitive types to zero. For example, numeric types like int, float, and double are initialized to 0 or 0.0, but boolean is initialized to false, not 0.

TYPE - 4 — 01 Mark

Odd One Out

Q.1 Choose the odd one out.

(a) int (b) float
(c) char (d) String

Ans. (d) int, float, and char are primitive data types, while String is a reference data type.

Q.2 Choose the odd one out.

(a) Scanner (b) BufferedReader
(c) FileReader (d) Math

Ans. (d) Scanner, BufferedReader, and FileReader are used for input/output operations, while Math is used for mathematical operations.

Q.3 Choose the odd one out.

(a) nextInt() (b) nextFloat()
(c) nextLine() (d) nextDouble()

Ans. (c) nextInt(), nextFloat(), and nextDouble() are methods for reading numerical data, while nextLine() reads a full line of text (including spaces).

Q.4 Which of the following is the odd one out?

(a) java.util.Scanner (b) java.util.ArrayList
(c) java.util.Date (d) java.io.File

Ans. (d) java.util.Scanner, java.util.ArrayList, and java.util.Date are part of the java.util package, whereas java.io.File is part of the java.io package.

TYPE - 5 — 01 Mark

Very Short Answer Type Questions

Q.1 What do we call the process of assigning initial values to variables before using them in Java?

Ans. Initialization.

Q.2 What is the default value of a boolean variable in Java?

Ans. The default value of a boolean variable in Java is false.

Q.3 What happens if you don't initialize instance variables in Java?

Ans. If not initialized, instance variables are given default values like 0 for numeric types and null for reference types.

Q.4 What are formal parameters in Java?

Ans. Formal parameters are variables listed in the method declaration that act as placeholders for actual values.

Q.5 What does the nextInt() method in the Scanner class do?

Ans. The nextInt() method reads an integer value entered by the user.

Q.6 What is the use of the import statement in Java?

Ans. The import statement is used to include classes or entire packages in the program for use.

Q.7 What is the difference between nextLine() and next() methods in the Scanner class?

Ans. nextLine() reads an entire line, while next() reads a single word or token.

Q.8 What does the nextDouble() method of the Scanner class do?

Ans. The nextDouble() method reads a double-precision floating-point number entered by the user.

TYPE - 6 — 02 Marks

Short Answer Type Questions

Q.1 Why might a Java program run without any errors but still give the wrong output?

Ans. Because of a logical error, where the program's logic is incorrect even though there are no syntax or runtime issues.

Q.2 In Java, what value is assigned to a short type instance variable when it is declared but not explicitly initialized? Also, why is this default assignment useful?

Ans. The default value of a short variable in Java is 0. This ensures that instance variables have a valid value even if the programmer forgets to initialize them, which helps avoid unexpected behavior during execution.

Q.3 How does Java handle the initialization of instance variables?

Ans. Java automatically initializes instance variables to default values (e.g., 0 for int, false for boolean, and null for reference types).

Q.4 In programming what is considered to be an Input?

Ans. Programming involves taking in some data, processing it using some instructions and giving some meaningful result. Taking in some data is called Input.

Q.5 Why it is important to initialize before execution.

Ans. Initialization is crucial for the following reasons:

- **Valid Data for Variables** Before using a variable in any expression, condition, or operation, it must be initialized to ensure it holds valid data. This can be done either explicitly or implicitly.
- **Prevents Unpredictable Behavior** If variables are not initialized, they may contain garbage values (in the case of local variables) or default values (for instance variables), leading to unpredictable behavior in the program.
- **Memory Safety** Initializing variables at the time of declaration or within constructors helps prevent the

program from referencing invalid or unallocated memory, ensuring the program operates safely and efficiently.

Q.6 Explain what happens when you use nextInt() followed by nextLine() in a Scanner object.

Ans. nextInt() reads the number but leaves a newline character in the input buffer, which is then consumed by nextLine() to avoid skipping input.

Q.7 Java provides pre-defined classes and interfaces grouped into packages. Can you name one such built-in package and mention its use?

Ans. One built-in package in Java is java.util. It contains utility classes like Scanner for input handling, and ArrayList, HashMap for data structures, making it widely used in Java programs.

Q.8 What is the purpose of the import statement in Java?

Ans. It is used to include classes or entire packages into a Java program to access their functionality.

Q.9 What are comments? Name the different types of comments used in Java.

Ans. A comment is a programmer-readable explanation or annotation in the source code of a computer program. The different types of comments in Java are:

- Single line comment
- Multiline comment

TYPE - 7 — 02 Marks

Differentiate

Q.1 Differentiate between Initialization and Parameter Passing

Feature	Initialization	Parameter Passing
Timing	Occurs before program execution.	Occurs during method call (runtime).
Purpose	Sets initial values for variables.	Passes values to methods for use within the method's scope.
Scope	Typically within the class or block where declared.	Values are local to the method's parameters.
Example	int count = 0; (before execution)	myMethod(10); (during method call)

Q.2 Differentiate between Syntax Errors and Runtime Errors

Feature	Syntax Errors	Runtime Errors
Detection	Detected by the compiler during compilation.	Occur during program execution.
Cause	Violations of Java language rules (e.g., missing semicolon).	Issues during execution (e.g., division by zero).
Impact	Prevents program compilation.	Causes program termination or exceptions.
Example	int x = 10 (missing semicolon)	int result = 10 / 0; (division by zero)

Q.3 Differentiate between next() amd nextLine() (from Scanner Class)

Feature	next()	nextLine()
Input Reading	Reads the next token (word) separated by whitespace.	Reads the entire line up to the newline character.
Behavior	Stops reading at the first whitespace.	Reads until it encounters a newline.
Whitespace Handling	Ignores leading whitespace, stops at next space.	Includes leading whitespace, reads the whole line.
Use Case	Reading individual words or tokens.	Reading full sentences or lines of text.

Q.4 Differentiate between Single-line Comments and Multi-line Comments

Feature	Single-line Comment(//)	Multi-line Comments (/* ... */)
Syntax	// followed by the comment.	/* starts, */ ends the comment block.
Scope	Comments out a single line.	Comments out multiple lines or blocks of code.
Usage	Short, inline explanations.	Longer explanations, documentation, or disabling code blocks.
Readability	Good for quick notes.	Better for detailed explanations or larger sections.

TYPE - 8 — 15 Marks

Long Answer Type Questions

Q.1 The area of a triangle can be calculated using Heron's formula:

Area = v(s(s-a)(s-b)(s-c))

where s is the semi-perimeter of the triangle, calculated as s = (a + b + c) / 2, and a, b, and c are the lengths of the sides.

Write a program in Java to calculate the area of a triangle when the lengths of its three sides are given as input.

Ans.
```
import java.util.Scanner;
public class TriangleArea
{
    public static void main(String[] args)
    {
        Scanner input = new Scanner(System.in);
        System.out.print("Enter the length of side a: ");
        double a = input.nextDouble();
        System.out.print("Enter the length of side b: ");
        double b = input.nextDouble();
        System.out.print("Enter the length of side c: ");
        double c = input.nextDouble();
        double s = (a + b + c) / 2;
        double area = Math.sqrt(s * (s - a) * (s - b) *
                                                    (s - c));
        System.out.println("The area of the triangle
                                              is: " + area);
    }
}
```

Q.2 Write a program in Java that accepts a temperature in Celsius as input and converts it to Fahrenheit. The formula to convert Celsius to Fahrenheit is:

Fahrenheit = (Celsius * 9/5) + 32

Ans.
```
import java.util.Scanner;
public class CelsiusToFahrenheit
{
    public static void main(String[] args)
    {
        Scanner input = new Scanner(System.in);
        System.out.print("Enter the temperature in
                                              Celsius: ");
        double celsius = input.nextDouble();
        double fahrenheit = (celsius * 9 / 5) + 32;
        System.out.println("The temperature in
                                 Fahrenheit is: " + fahrenheit);
    }
}
```

Q.3 A shopkeeper offers a 15% discount on the printed price of a laptop. However, a customer has to pay 8% VAT (Value Added Tax) on the remaining amount. Write a program in Java to calculate the amount to be paid by the customer, taking the printed price as input.

Ans.
```
import java.util.Scanner;
public class LaptopPrice
{
    public static void main(String[] args)
    {
        Scanner scanner = new Scanner(System.in);
        System.out.print("Enter the printed price
                                        of the laptop: ");
        double printedPrice = scanner.nextDouble();
        double discount = 0.15 * printedPrice;
        double priceAfterDiscount = printedPrice
                                              - discount;
        double vat = 0.08 * priceAfterDiscount;
        double finalPrice = priceAfterDiscount + vat;
        System.out.println("Amount to be paid by
                           the customer: " + finalPrice);
        scanner.close();
    }
}
```

06

MATHEMATICAL LIBRARY METHODS

Introduction to Package (java.lang)

In Java, the java.lang package is automatically imported in every Java program. This means you don't need to explicitly import it, and the classes within this package are readily available for use. The java.lang package provides essential classes and methods that are fundamental to the Java programming language.

Key Classes in java.lang

- **Object** Root of all classes.
- **String** Text manipulation.
- **Math** Mathematical functions.
- **System** System-related operations.
- **Wrapper classes (e.g., Integer, Double)** Primitive type objects.
- **Thread** Multithreading.
- **Exception** Error handling.

A method is a named block of code within a class. It executes a defined set of instructions. Some methods are defined by the user itself. These types of methods are user-defined methods. Methods which are defined by the Java System developers are known as Library Methods or built-in methods.

Methods of Math class

All mathematical functions are included in a class called "Math" that is part of the java.lang package. The java.lang is default package. This package is automatically included in every Java program.

Syntax `Math.MethodName(arguments);`

Some of the basic methods of the Math class are

1. pow()

This method returns the value of the first argument raised to the power of second argument provided.

Syntax `double result = Math.pow(x, y);`

Parameters **x** is the base number.
y is the exponent.

Returns The pow() method always returns a double value, even if the result is a whole number.

2. sqrt(x)

The sqrt(x) method is used to calculate the square root of a given number x.

Syntax `double result = Math.sqrt(double x);`

Parameters **(x)** A non-negative number (a double value) whose square root is to be calculated. If x is negative, the method will return NaN (Not a Number).

Returns The square root of the given number x as a double.

Note *If the input value x is negative, Math.sqrt() will return NaN because the square root of a negative number is not defined for real numbers.*

Example

```
System.out.println(Math.sqrt(-4)); // Output: NaN
```

3. cbrt(x)

The cbrt(x) method is used to calculate the cube root of a given number x.

Syntax `double result = Math.cbrt(double x);`

Parameters (x) A number (a double value) whose cube root is to be calculated. It can be positive, negative, or zero.

Returns The cube root of the input value x as a double.

4. ceil(x)

The ceil(x) method in Java is used to return the smallest integer value that is greater than or equal to the given number x. It effectively rounds the number up to the nearest whole number.

Syntax `double result = Math.ceil(double x);`

Parameters (x) A number (a double value) for which the ceiling value is to be calculated.

Returns A double value representing the smallest integer greater than or equal to x.

Note *The behavior of the ceil() method is given below as:*

- *For positive numbers with a fractional part, it rounds up to the next integer.*
- *For negative numbers with a fractional part, it rounds up towards zero (less negative).*
- *For integers, it returns the same number as a double.*

5. floor(x)

The floor(x) method in Java is used to return the largest integer value that is less than or equal to the given number x. It effectively rounds the number down to the nearest whole number.

Syntax `double result = Math.floor(double x);`

Parameters (x) A number (a double value) for which the floor value is to be calculated.

Returns A double value representing the largest integer less than or equal to x.

Note *The behavior of the floor() method is given below as:*

- *For positive numbers with a fractional part, it rounds down to the integer below.*
- *For negative numbers with a fractional part, it rounds down further away from zero (more negative).*
- *For integers, it returns the same number as a double.*

6. round(x)

The round(x) method is used to round a floating-point number to the nearest integer.

For fractional values, if the fractional part is **less** than **0.5**, the value is rounded **down**.
if the fractional part is **0.5 or greater**, the value is rounded **up**.

Syntax

```
long result = Math.round(float x);   // For a float value
long result = Math.round(double x);  // For a double value
```

Parameters (x) A floating-point value (float or double) that you want to round.

Returns If the input is a float or double, the return type is long, representing the rounded value.

Note *The behavior of the round() method is given below as:*

- *Rounds up or down based on the fractional part.*
- *Works with both positive and negative numbers.*
- *For numbers ending in .5, it rounds away from zero (e.g., 2.5→ 3, -2.5→ -3).*

7. abs(a)

The abs(a) method in Java is used to calculate the absolute value of a number. It removes the sign of the number and always returns a non-negative value.

Syntax

```
int result = Math.abs(int a);          // For integer input
long result = Math.abs(long a);        // For long input
float result = Math.abs(float a);      // For float input
double result = Math.abs(double a);    // For double input
```

Parameters **(a)** The number whose absolute value is to be calculated. It can be of type int, long, float, or double.

Returns The absolute value of the a. The return type depends on the data type of the input:

int → Returns an int
long → Returns a long
float → Returns a float
double → Returns a double

Note *The behavior of the abs() method is given below as:*

- *It converts negative numbers to positive.*
- *Does nothing to positive numbers (absolute value of a positive number is the number itself).*

8. max(a, b)

The max(a, b) method in Java is used to find and return the larger of two values. It compares two numbers and determines which one is greater.

Syntax
```
int result = Math.max(int a, int b);          // For integer inputs
long result = Math.max(long a, long b);       // For long inputs
float result = Math.max(float a, float b);    // For float inputs
double result = Math.max(double a, double b); // For double inputs
```

Parameters **a** The first number to compare.
b The second number to compare.

Returns The larger value of the two inputs, a and b. The return type depends on the data type of the inputs:

int → Returns an int
long → Returns a long
float → Returns a float
double → Returns a double

Note *The behavior of the max() method is given below as:*

- *If the two numbers are equal, the method returns the same number.*
- *For floating-point numbers (float and double), if one number is NaN (Not-a-Number), the result will also be NaN.*

9. min(a, b)

The min(a, b) method in Java is used to find and return the smaller of two values. It compares the inputs and determines which one is lesser.

Syntax
```
int result = Math.min(int a, int b);          // For integer inputs
long result = Math.min(long a, long b);       // For long inputs
float result = Math.min(float a, float b);    // For float inputs
double result = Math.min(double a, double b); // For double inputs
```

Parameters **a** The first number to compare.
b The second number to compare.

Returns The smaller value between the two inputs. The return type depends on the data type of the inputs:

int → Returns an int
long → Returns a long
float → Returns a float
double → Returns a double

10. random()

The random() method in Java generates a random floating-point number between 0.0 (inclusive) and 1.0 (exclusive).

Syntax
```
double randomValue = Math.random();
```

Returns A random value of type double in the range [0.0, 1.0). This means it can generate any value starting from 0.0 up to but not including 1.0.

Expressions

An expression in Java is any valid combination of operators, constants, and variables i.e., a legal combination of Java tokens. An expression is made up of operands and operators. The objects of the operation(s) are referred to as operands and the operations are represented through operators. The expressions in Java can be of any type:

Arithmetic Expressions

Expression that use arithmetic operators are called Arithmetic expressions. Arithmetic expressions containing all integer type operands are pure integer expressions. An expression containing only real numbers is called real expression. Sometimes a mixed expression can also be formed which is a mixture of real and integer expressions.

For example, expression $\frac{-b+\sqrt{b^2-4ac}}{2a}$ will be written in Java as:

```
(- b + Math.sqrt(b * b - 4 * a * c))/(2 *a)
```

Similarly, expression $\frac{ax^2+b}{cx+d}$ will be written in Java as

```
(a * Math.pow(x, 2) + b)/(c * x + d)
```

Relational Expressions

Expressions that establish the relation of two or more variables/values using relational operators are called relational expressions.

For example, x > y, a ! = b, p = = r etc. are relational expressions.

Logical Expressions

Expressions that use logical operators (&&, || and !) to combine relational expressions to make a complex expression are called Logical expressions.

For example, (x > y) && (y > z) is a logical expression.

Logical expressions are sometimes also referred to as boolean expression as these result into true or false values which are Boolean values.

Boolean Expressions

The expressions results into false or true are called Boolean expressions. The Boolean expressions are combination of constant, variables and logical and relational operators.

For example, following are examples of some valid Boolean expressions.

```
          x > y               (x + z) > = (x/z)
(a + b) > = c && (c < = d)    (y – x) < (z – y)
```

EXAM ORIENTED QUESTIONS

TYPE - 1 01 Mark

Multiple Choice Questions

Q.1 What value will Math.sqrt(Math.ceil(15.3)) return?

(a) 16.0 (b) 16
(c) 4.0 (d) 5.0

Q.2 `System.out.println(Math.sqrt(24-25));`

Name the type of error that occurs for the above statement.

(a) Syntax error (b) Runtime error
(c) Logical error (d) No error

Q.3 Which method is used to find the absolute value of a number in Java?

(a) Math.abs() (b) Math.min()
(c) Math.pow() (d) Math.random()

Q.4

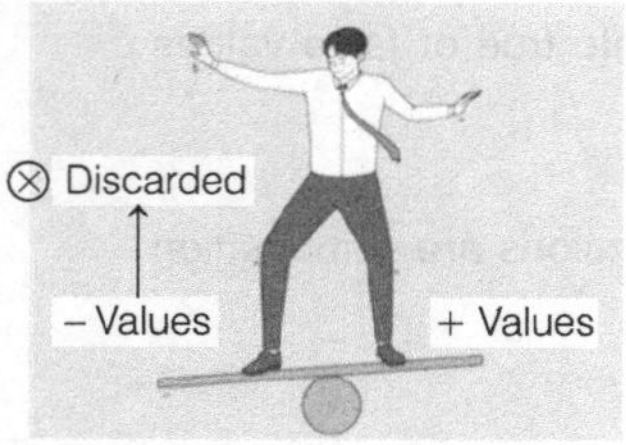

How does the image represent Math.abs(-10)?

(a) Ignoring negative values and converting them to positive
(b) Finding the sum of values
(c) Subtracting values
(d) Finding the maximum value

Q.5 Which method could return the same value for both Math.abs(-0.0) and Math.abs(0.0)?

(a) Math.random() (b) Math.ceil()
(c) Math.abs() (d) Math.floor()

Q.6 `Math.pow(625, 3/2) + Math.sqrt(144);`

Give the output of the following statement.

(a) 17.0 (b) 13.0
(c) 37.0 (d) 13

Q.7 What is the value of y after the following code executes?

```
double x = 16.0;
double y = Math.sqrt(Math.sqrt(x));
```

(a) 2.0 (b) 4.0
(c) 8.0 (d) 16.0

Q.8

What does the image represent when Math.pow(5, 3) is written?

(a) Finding the cube root
(b) Exponentiation of base to exponent
(c) Square root calculation
(d) Rounding the number

Q.9

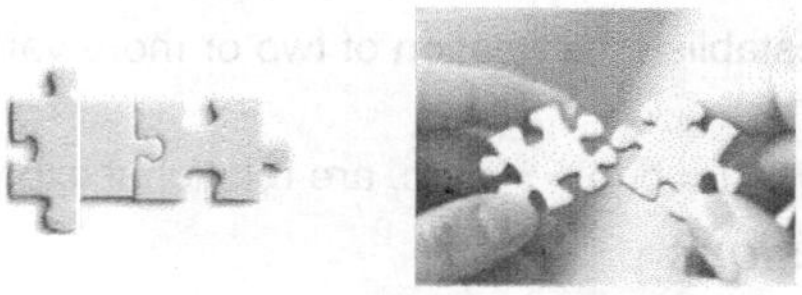

How does the image represent the operation Math.sqrt(49)?

(a) Finding the factor of 49
(b) Rounding off the number
(c) Finding the square root of 49
(d) Exponentiation of the number

Q.10 Which method returns NaN if given a negative argument?

(a) Math.abs() (b) Math.ceil()
(c) Math.sqrt() (d) Math.cbrt()

Q.11 What is the final value stored in variable x?

```
double x = Math.ceil(Math.abs(-7.3));
```

(a) 7.0 (b) 8.0 (c) 6.0 (d) 9.0

Q.12

How does the image represent Math.ceil(4.2)?

(a) Rounding down to the nearest integer
(b) Rounding up to the nearest integer
(c) Finding the square of the number
(d) Finding the factor of the number

Q.13 Which method ensures Math.ceil(-4.7) returns -4 instead of -5?

(a) Math.floor() (b) Math.random()
(c) Math.abs() (d) Math.ceil()

Q.14 What is the final value stored in variable x?

```
double a = -8.35;
double x = Math.abs(Math.floor(a));
```

(a) 9.0 (b) 7.0 (c) 6 (d) 7

Q.15 Which of the following statements correctly calculates and returns the cube root of a given number x in Java?

(a) Math.sqrt(x) (b) Math.cbrt(x)
(c) Math.abs(x) / 3 (d) Math.pow(x, 1/3)

Q.16 Which method correctly computes the cube root of -27?

(a) Math.sqrt() (b) Math.cbrt()
(c) Math.ceil() (d) Math.abs()

Q.17 Consider the following Java statement:

```
int a = 45, b = 78;
System.out.println(Math.max(a, b));
```

What will be the output of the above statement?

(a) 45 (b) 78
(c) 123 (d) Compilation error

Q.18 Which of the following best describes the functionality of the Math.floor(double x) method in Java?

(a) It rounds a floating-point number up to the nearest integer.
(b) It returns the smallest integer that is greater than or equal to x.
(c) It rounds a floating-point number down to the nearest integer.
(d) It always returns a positive integer.

Q.19 Which of the following method calls will correctly compute the square root of a given number y using Java's Math class?

(a) Math.pow(y, 0.5) (b) Math.sqrt(y)
(c) Math.root(y) (d) Both (a) and (b)

Q.20 What will be the output of the following Java statement?

```
System.out.println(Math.abs(-25.9));
```

(a) -25.9 (b) 25.9
(c) 26 (d) Compilation error

Q.21 What will be the result of the following expression?

```
Math.max(Math.min(20, 30), Math.max(10, 5));
```

(a) 5 (b) 10 (c) 20 (d) 30

Q.22 Which of the following methods correctly computes the square root of a positive number z?

(a) Math.pow(z, 2) (b) Math.sqrt(z)
(c) Math.cubeRoot(z) (d) Math.exponent(z, 0.5)

Q.23 Which of the following best describes the behavior of the Math.random() method in Java?

(a) It returns a random integer between 0 and 100.
(b) It returns a random floating-point number between 0.0 (inclusive) and 1.0 (exclusive).
(c) It returns a random integer between 0 and 1.
(d) It returns a random floating-point number between 1 and 10.

Q.24

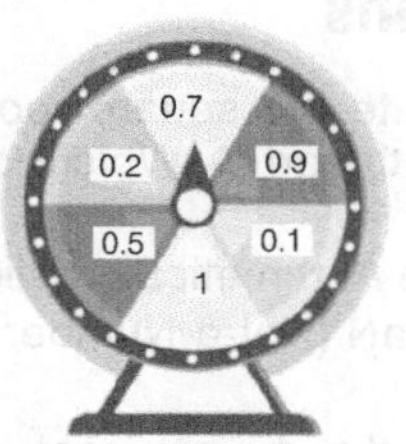

How does the image represent Math.random()?

(a) Generating a random number between 0 and 1
(b) Rolling a dice to get a random number between 1 and 6
(c) Finding the minimum value
(d) Squaring a number randomly

Q.25 Which method generates a number that will never be exactly 1.0?

(a) Math.ceil() (b) Math.random()
(c) Math.floor() (d) Math.abs()

Q.26 What is the final value stored in variable z?

```
double a = 2.7;
int b = 5;
double z = Math.round(a * b) / b;
```

(a) 2.5 (b) 3.0 (c) 2.0 (d) 2.7

Q.27 What will be the return type of the following Java statement?

```
System.out.println(Math.round(5.8));
```

(a) int (b) double (c) long (d) float

Q.28 Which method in the Math class ensures that a given floating-point number is always rounded up to the nearest integer?

(a) Math.floor(x) (b) Math.ceil(x)
(c) Math.round(x) (d) Math.abs(x)

Q.29 What will be the result of the following Java expression?

```
Math.round(6.7) + Math.floor(4.9);
```

(a) 9 (b) 10 (c) 11 (d) 12

Q.30 What will be the output of the following Java statement?

```
System.out.println(Math.max(34, Math.min(20, 50)));
```

(a) 20 (b) 34 (c) 50 (d) 40

Answers

1. (c)	**2.** (c)	**3.** (a)	**4.** (a)	**5.** (c)
6. (b)	**7.** (a)	**8.** (b)	**9.** (c)	**10.** (c)
11. (b)	**12.** (b)	**13.** (d)	**14.** (a)	**15.** (b)
16. (b)	**17.** (b)	**18.** (c)	**19.** (d)	**20.** (b)
21. (c)	**22.** (b)	**23.** (b)	**24.** (a)	**25.** (b)
26. (c)	**27.** (c)	**28.** (b)	**29.** (c)	**30.** (b)

TYPE - 2 01 Mark

Statement Based Questions

Q.1 A developer wants to calculate the square root of a negative number using Math.sqrt(). Which of the following will occur?

A. The program will throw an ArithmeticException.

B. The program will return NaN (Not-a-Number).

C. The program will return 0.

D. The program will return the square root of the absolute value.

(a) Only A (b) Only B
(c) Only C (d) Only D

Q.2 A developer needs to round a double value 3.75 to the nearest integer. Which method should they use?

A. Math.ceil()

B. Math.floor()

C. Math.round()

D. Math.abs()

(a) Only A (b) Only B
(c) Only C (d) Only D

Q.3 Which of the following methods returns a pseudo-random double value in the range [0.0, 1.0)?

A. Math.randomInt()

B. Math.rand()

C. Math.random()

D. Math.generateRandom()

(a) Only A (b) Only B
(c) Only C (d) Only D

Q.4 A developer wants to find the smallest integer that is greater than or equal to a given double value x. Which method should they use?

A. Math.round(x)

B. Math.floor(x)

C. Math.ceil(x)

D. Math.min(x)

(a) Only A (b) Only B
(c) Only C (d) Only D

Q.5 Consider the following steps involved in calculating the square root of a number and rounding it to the nearest integer using the Math class. Choose the correct order of the steps:

A. The Math.sqrt() method is called with the number as an argument.

B. The Math.round() method is called with the result of the square root as an argument.

C. The number is provided as input.

D. The rounded result is stored or displayed.

(a) C, A, B, D (b) A, C, D, B
(c) B, D, A, C (d) D, C, B, A

Q.6 A developer is writing a program that needs to calculate the hypotenuse of a right-angled triangle given the lengths of the two other sides (a and b). They know the formula is: hypotenuse = $\sqrt{(a^2 + b^2)}$. They want to use the Math class methods to perform this calculation. Which of the following code snippets correctly calculates the hypotenuse?

A. `double hypotenuse = Math.sqrt(a * a + b * b);`

B. `double hypotenuse = Math.pow(a, 2) + Math.pow(b, 2);`

C. `double hypotenuse = Math.sqrt(Math.pow(a, b));`

D. `double hypotenuse = Math.cbrt(a * a + b * b);`

(a) Only A (b) Only B
(c) Only C (d) Only D

Q.7 Consider the following steps involved in generating a random number between a specified range (e.g., 10 to 20) using Math.random() and scaling it. Choose the correct order of the steps:

A. Calculate the range (difference between maximum and minimum values).

B. Generate a random double between 0.0 (inclusive) and 1.0 (exclusive) using Math.random().

C. Multiply the random double by the range and add the minimum value to shift it to the desired range.

D. Store or display the final random number.

(a) A, B, C, D (b) B, A, C, D
(c) C, D, A, B (d) D, C, B, A

Answers

1. (b) **2.** (c) **3.** (c) **4.** (c) **5.** (a)
6. (a) **7.** (a)

TYPE - 3 01 Mark

Assertion-Reason Type Questions

Directions (Q. Nos. 1-8) The following questions are Assertion-Reason based questions. Choose the answer based on the code given below

(a) Both Assertion (A) and Reason (R) are true and Reason (R) is a correct explanation of Assertion (A).

(b) Both Assertion (A) and Reason (R) are true and Reason (R) is not a correct explanation of Assertion (A).

(c) Assertion (A) is true and Reason (R) is false.

(d) Assertion (A) is false and Reason (R) is true.

Q.1 Assertion (A) The Math.abs(x) method can only be used for integer values.

Reason (R) The Math.abs(x) method can take arguments of type int, long, float, or double and returns the absolute value.

Ans. (d) The assertion is false because Math.abs(x) works with int, long, float, and double. The reason is true, as it correctly describes how the method works with different data types.

Q.2 Assertion (A) Math.ceil(x) returns the largest integer less than or equal to x.

Reason (R) Math.ceil(x) rounds the number up to the nearest integer greater than or equal to x.

Ans. (d) The assertion is false because Math.ceil(x) rounds a number up, not down. The reason is true, as it describes the rounding behavior correctly.

Q.3 Assertion (A) The Math.max(x, y) method returns the minimum of x and y.

Reason (R) The Math.max(x, y) method compares two numbers and returns the larger value.

Ans. (d) The assertion is false because Math.max(x, y) returns the larger of the two numbers, not the smaller. The reason is true, as it correctly describes the method's functionality.

Q.4 Assertion (A) The Math.round(x) method rounds x to the nearest integer.

Reason (R) If the fractional part of x is 0.5 or greater, the number is rounded up.

Ans. (a) The assertion and the reason are both true. The Math.round(x) method rounds the floating-point value x to the nearest integer, and the reason correctly explains this rounding behavior.

Q.5 Assertion (A) Math.sqrt(x) returns the square root of a negative number.

Reason (R) The method Math.sqrt(x) returns NaN (Not a Number) for negative inputs.

Ans. (d) Assertion is false, Reson is true.

Q.6 Assertion (A) Math.random() can generate a value greater than or equal to 1.

Reason (R) The value generated by Math.random() is always between 0.0 and 1.0 (exclusive).

Ans. (d) The assertion is false because Math.random() never generates a value greater than or equal to 1. The reason is true, as it explains the valid range for Math.random().

Q.7 Assertion (A) The Math.cbrt(x) method returns the cube root of x.

Reason (R) The Math.cbrt(x) method can be used for both positive and negative numbers.

Ans. (a) Both the assertion and the reason are correct. The Math.cbrt(x) method returns the cube root, and it works for both positive and negative values of x.

Q.8 Assertion (A) Math.floor(x) rounds the value of x to the nearest integer.

Reason (R) The Math.floor(x) method always rounds the number down to the nearest whole integer.

Ans. (a) The assertion and reason are both correct. Math.floor(x) always rounds a number down, regardless of whether the fractional part is less than or greater than 0.5.

TYPE - 4 — 01 Mark

Odd One Out

Q.1 Choose the odd one out.

(a) Math.sqrt() (b) Math.pow()
(c) Math.abs() (d) Math.random()

Ans. (d) Math.random() (Math.random() generates a new random number, while the others modify an existing number.)

Q.2 Choose the odd one out.

(a) Math.cbrt()
(b) Math.round()
(c) Math.max()
(d) Math.ceil()

Ans. (c) Math.max() (Math.max() finds the greater value, while the others modify numbers by rounding or approximation.)

Q.3 Choose the odd one out.

(a) Math.ceil() (b) Math.abs()
(c) Math.floor() (d) Math.pow()

Ans. (d) Math.pow() (Math.pow() raises a number to a power, whereas the others modify a number's magnitude.)

Q.4 Choose the odd one out.

(a) Math.abs() (b) Math.max()
(c) Math.min() (d) Math.round()

Ans. (d) Math.round() (Math.round() rounds a number, while the others deal with comparisons.)

TYPE - 5 — 01 Mark

Very Short Answer Type Questions

Q.1 What will `Math.sqrt(49) - Math.sqrt(25)` return?

Ans. 2.0

Q.2 What is the output of `Math.pow(4, Math.pow(2, 1))`?

Ans. 16.0

Q.3 What is the range of values that `Math.random() * 10` can return?

Ans. 0.0 (inclusive) to 10.0 (exclusive)

Q.4 What is the result of `Math.round(4.6) + Math.round(4.4)`?

Ans. 9

Q.5 If x = -15.7, what does `Math.abs(Math.floor(x))` return?

Ans. 16.0

Q.6 Given a = 12 and b = 25, what is the result of `Math.max(Math.min(a, b), Math.sqrt(144))`?

Ans. 12.0

Q.7 If x = 5.8, what does `Math.floor(x) + Math.ceil(x)` return?

Ans. 11.0

Q.8 What is the result of `Math.cbrt(125) + Math.pow(2, 3)`?

Ans. 13.0

Q.9 What will `Math.min(Math.ceil(7.2), Math.floor(8.9))` return?

Ans. 8

Q.10 What is the result of `Math.ceil(Math.random() * 6)`?

Ans. A random integer between 1 and 6

Q.11 Write a statement in Java for

$\sqrt{((a+b)^3/|a-b|)}$

Ans.
```
System.out.println(Math.sqrt(Math.pow((a + b), 3)
                                / Math.abs(a - b)));
```

Q.12 Write a Java expression for the following: $|x^2 + 2xy|$

Ans. `Math.abs(Math.pow(x, 2) + 2 * x * y);`

Q.13 Round 3.14159 to the nearest integer using a Math method.

Ans. `Math.round(3.14159)`

Q.14 What's the value of `Math.ceil(7.0)`?

Ans. 7.0 (It's a double, not an int).

Q.15 Give a Math method call to find the absolute value of -15.

Ans. `Math.abs(-15)`

Q.16 Write a Java expression to calculate the roots of a quadratic equation given the coefficients a, b, and c.:

$x = (-b \pm \sqrt{(b^2 - 4ac)}) / 2a$

Ans. double x = (-b + Math.sqrt(b * b - 4 * a * c)) / (2 * a);

Q.17 Write a Java expression to calculate the area of a triangle using Heron's formula, given the sides a, b, and c:

Area = $\sqrt{(s(s-a)(s-b)(s-c))}$, where s = (a + b + c) / 2.

Ans. double s = (a + b + c) / 2;
double area = Math.sqrt(s * (s - a) * (s - b) * (s - c));

Q.18 Write a Java expression to calculate the volume of a cylinder given radius (r) and height (h):

Volumn = $\pi r^2 h$

Ans. double volume = Math.PI * Math.pow(*r*, 2) * *h*;

TYPE - 6 — 2 Marks

Short Answer Type Questions

Q.1 How does Math.abs() behave when applied to a NaN value or Double.NaN in Java?

Ans. Math.abs() returns NaN when applied to NaN. This is because NaN represents "Not-a-Number," and absolute values are undefined for it.

Q.2 What would Math.pow(2, -3) return, and why is this behavior significant in programming?

Ans. Math.pow(2, -3) returns 0.125 because raising a number to a negative exponent is equivalent to calculating the reciprocal of the number raised to the positive exponent (i.e., $1 / 2^3 = 1 / 8 = 0.125$). This is essential for dealing with inverse relationships in math-based algorithms.

Q.3 What is the result of Math.floor(-5.3) and how does it differ from Math.ceil(-5.3)?

Ans. Math.floor(-5.3) returns -6, while Math.ceil(-5.3) returns -5. This illustrates that Math.floor() rounds down towards negative infinity, and Math.ceil() rounds up towards zero.

Q.4 Given a scenario where you need to generate a random number between 50 and 100, how would you use Math.random() to achieve that?

Ans. To generate a random number between 50 and 100 using Math.random(), you can scale and shift the result as follows:
```
int randomNumber = 50 + (int)(Math.random() * 51);
```

Q.5 How would you use Math.max() and Math.min() to find the middle value among three given numbers, a, b, and c?

Ans. To find the middle value of a, b, and c, you can combine Math.max() and Math.min() like this:
```
int middle = Math.max(Math.min(a, b),
Math.min(Math.max(a, b), c));
```

Q.6 How would you compute the square root of the absolute value of a number x that could potentially be negative?

Ans. You can use Math.sqrt(Math.abs(x)) to first convert the number into its absolute value and then compute its square root. If x is negative, Math.abs(x) ensures no error or domain exception occurs.

Q.7 What is the behavior of Math.cbrt() when applied to Double.NaN, and how can this behavior be used in handling error cases?

Ans. Math.cbrt(Double.NaN) returns NaN, which allows developers to handle invalid or undefined numbers effectively in scenarios like calculations with incomplete or erroneous data. This behavior is consistent with other Math methods dealing with NaN.

Q.8 If x = 7.6, what would Math.round(Math.pow(x, 2)) return, and why is this important in numerical approximations?

Ans. Math.pow(7.6, 2) gives 57.76, and Math.round(57.76) rounds this to 58. Rounding is often used in numerical approximations to limit decimal precision or to adjust for floating-point inaccuracies.

Q.9 What will the following code snippet return, and why?

```
Math.max(Math.min(7, Math.pow(3, 2)), Math.sqrt(25))
```

Ans. It will return 7. Here's the breakdown:

Math.pow(3, 2) is 9.
Math.sqrt(25) is 5.
Math.min(7, 9) is 7.
Math.max(7, 5) is 7.

Q.10 How does Math.ceil() behave when applied to a negative floating-point number, and how can this property be used in certain algorithm optimizations?

Ans. Math.ceil() always rounds up towards positive infinity, even for negative numbers, for example
Math. ceil (–3.7) returns –3.0
This behavior can be used in algorithms where upward rounding is necessary but must take into account the direction of rounding for negative numbers.

Q.11 Write a program to print:

(i) p to the power q (ii) the square root of p

The values of p and q are 64 and 2 respectively.

Ans.

```
public class KboatNumber
{
  public static void main(String args[])
  {
    int p = 64;
    int q = 2;
    double r1 = Math.pow(p, q);
    System.out.println("p to the power of q = " + r1);
    double r2 = Math.sqrt(p);
    System.out.println("Square root of p = " + r2);
  }
}
```

Q.12 Write a program to generate random integers in the range 10 to 20.

Ans.

```
public class KboatRandom
{
  public static void main(String args[])
  {
    int min = 10, max = 20;
    int range = max - min + 1;
    int num = (int)(range * Math.random() + min);
    System.out.println("Random number in the
                           range 10 to 20: " + num);
  }
}
```

Q.13 A Java program that calculates the area of a circle using Math.PI and Math.pow():

(a) Explain how Math.PI provides a precise value for pi and why it's preferable to defining your own constant.

(b) Describe how Math.pow() is used to calculate the square of the radius, and discuss the advantages of using Math.pow() over direct multiplication (e.g., radius * radius).

Ans. (a) Math.PI provides a precise value for pi, which is preferred over defining your own constant because it's accurate and part of Java's standard library.

(b) Math.pow(radius, 2) calculates the square of the radius. While multiplication works, Math.pow() is more flexible for handling different powers.

Q.14 Consider a scenario where you need to generate a random number within a specific range using Math.random():

(a) Explain how Math.random() generates a pseudo-random double between 0.0 (inclusive) and 1.0 (exclusive).

(b) Write a Java code snippet that demonstrates how to scale and shift the output of Math.random() to generate a random integer between 10 and 50 (inclusive).

Ans. (a) Math.random() produces a double value greater than or equal to 0.0 and less than 1.0. It uses an algorithm to generate these numbers, which makes them "pseudo-random".

(b)

```
int min = 10;
int max = 50;
int randomNum = (int) (Math.random() *
                    (max - min + 1)) + min;
System.out.println(randomNum);
```

Q.15 Suppose you have a collection of numerical measurements (e.g., temperatures) and need to find the minimum and maximum values within that collection:

(a) Describe how Math.min() and Math.max() can be used iteratively to efficiently determine the minimum and maximum values from the given measurements.

(b) Discuss the efficiency implications of using Math.min() and Math.max() compared to writing your own custom logic to find the minimum and maximum values within the collection.

Ans. (a) Initialize min and max with the first value. In each iteration, use Math.min(current, min) to update min if the current value is smaller, and Math.max(current, max) to update max if the current value is larger.

(b) Math.min() and Math.max() are highly optimized, typically implemented in native code. They are generally more efficient than custom logic (especially for large collections) due to reduced overhead and optimized comparisons.

Q.16 **Predict the output of the following code snippet:**

```
public class MathPrediction1
{
  public static void main(String[] args)
  {
    double num1 = 16.3;
    double num2 = -8.7;
    int rounded1 = (int) Math.round(num1);
    int absolute2 = (int) Math.abs(num2);
    System.out.println("Rounded num1: " + rounded1);
    System.out.println("Absolute num2: " + absolute2);
  }
}
```

Ans. **Output**

Rounded num1: 16
Absolute num2: 8

Q.17 **Predict the output of the following code snippet:**

```
public class MathPrediction2
{
  public static void main(String[] args)
  {
    double base = 2.0;
    double exponent = 3.0;
    double powerResult = Math.pow(base, exponent);
    double sqrtResult = Math.sqrt(powerResult);
    System.out.println("Power result: " +
                                    powerResult);
    System.out.println("Square root of power
                         result: " + sqrtResult);
  }
}
```

Ans. **Output**

Power result: 8.0
Square root of power result: 2.8284271247461903

Q.18 **Predict the output of the following code snippet:**

```
public class MathPrediction3
{
  public static void main(String[] args)
  {
    double value = 12.6;
    int ceilValue = (int) Math.ceil(value);
    int floorValue = (int) Math.floor(value);
    System.out.println("Ceil: " + ceilValue);
    System.out.println("Floor: " + floorValue);
  }
}
```

Ans. Output

Ceil: 13
Floor: 12

TYPE - 7 — 2 Marks

Differentiate

Q.1 Math.floor(x) and Math.ceil(x)

Ans.

Math.floor(x)	Math.ceil(x)
It rounds the number down to the largest integer less than or equal to the value of x.	It rounds the number up to the smallest integer greater than or equal to x.
Useful when you want to round down, e.g., when determining the maximum index in an array.	Useful when you need to round up, e.g., calculating the number of items that can fit in a fixed-sized container.
e.g. Math.floor(3.7) returns 3.	e.g. Math.ceil(3.7) returns 4.

Q.2 Math.abs(x) and Math.round(x)

Ans.

Math.abs(x)	Math.round(x)
It returns the absolute value of x, effectively removing any negative sign (if present).	It rounds the floating-point number x to the nearest integer. If the decimal part is 0.5 or greater, it rounds up, otherwise it rounds down.
Commonly used when you need the magnitude of a number, regardless of its sign.	Typically used when you want to convert a floating-point value to the nearest integer.
e.g. Math.abs(-5) returns 5, and Math.abs(5) returns 5.	e.g. Math.round(2.3) returns 2, and Math.round(2.7) returns 3.

Q.3 Math.min(a, b) and Math.max(a, b)

Ans.

Math.min(a, b)	Math.max(a, b)
It returns the smaller of two values.	It returns the larger of two values.
Used when you need to find the lower boundary or smaller value between two options.	Used to determine the upper boundary or larger value between two options.
e.g. Math.min(4, 7) returns 4.	e.g. Math.max(4, 7) returns 7.

Q.4 Math.sqrt(x) and Math.cbrt(x)

Ans.

Math.sqrt(x)	Math.cbrt(x)
It returns the square root of x.	It returns the cube root of x.
Typically used when calculating the square root in geometric and mathematical operations.	Used when you need the cube root, such as in problems involving volumes or cubic equations.
e.g. Math.sqrt(16) returns 4.	e.g. Math.cbrt(27) returns 3.

Q.5 Math.pow(a, b) and Math.random()

Ans.

Math.pow(a, b)	Math.random()
It returns a raised to the power of b, i.e., calculates a^b.	It generates a random double value between 0.0 (inclusive) and 1.0 (exclusive).

Math.pow(a, b)	Math.random()
Used in mathematical computations that require exponentiation, such as growth formulas or compound interest calculations.	Commonly used in simulations, games, or when generating random values for non-deterministic applications.
e.g. Math.pow(2, 3) returns 8.	e.g. Math.random() could return any value like 0.4235 or 0.9837.

TYPE - 11 — 15 Marks

Long Answer Type Questions

Q.1 The Math class in Java provides functions for trigonometry, exponentiation, rounding, and other mathematical operations.

Write a Java program that demonstrates the use of the following methods: Math.sqrt() Math.pow() Math.abs() Math.floor() Math.random().

Ans. Below is a Java program demonstrating the use of Math.sqrt(), Math.pow(), Math.abs(), Math.floor(), and Math.random():

```
public class MathFunctionsDemo
{
  public static void main(String[] args)
  {
    # Math.sqrt()
    double num1 = 25.0;
    double sqrtResult = Math.sqrt(num1);
    System.out.println("Square root of " + num1
                       + " is: " + sqrtResult);
    # Math.pow()
    double base = 2.0, exponent = 3.0;
    double powerResult = Math.pow(base, exponent);
    System.out.println(base + " raised to the
        power " + exponent + " is: " + powerResult);
    # Math.abs()
    int negativeNum = -10;
    int absResult = Math.abs(negativeNum);
    System.out.println("Absolute value of "
              + negativeNum + " is: " + absResult);
    # Math.floor()
    double decimalNum = 7.9;
    double floorResult = Math.floor(decimalNum);
            System.out.println("Floor value of "
            + decimalNum + " is: " + floorResult);
    # Math.random()
    double randomNumber = Math.random();
    System.out.println("A random number between
                   0.0 and 1.0: " + randomNumber);
  }
}
```

Q.2 Write a program to calculate the compound interest given the principal amount, rate of interest, time period, and the number of times interest is compounded per year.

Ans.

```
import java.util.Scanner;
public class CompoundInterest
{
  public static void main(String[] args)
  {
    Scanner scanner = new Scanner(System.in);
    System.out.print("Enter principal amount: ");
    double principal = scanner.nextDouble();
    System.out.print("Enter annual interest rate
                          (in percentage): ");
    double rate = scanner.nextDouble() / 100;
       // Convert percentage to decimal
    System.out.print("Enter time period in years: ");
    double time = scanner.nextDouble();
    System.out.print("Enter number of times
          interest is compounded per year: ");
    int n = scanner.nextInt();
    double amount = principal * Math.pow(1 +
                         (rate / n), n * time);
    double compoundInterest = amount - principal;
    System.out.println("Compound Interest: "
                         + compoundInterest);
  }
}
```

Q.3 Write a program in Java to calculate and display the hypotenuse of a right-angled triangle by taking perpendicular and base as inputs.
Hint: $h = \sqrt{p^2 + b^2}$

Ans.

```
import java.util.Scanner;
class Main
{
  public static void main(String args[])
  {
    Scanner in = new Scanner(System.in);
    System.out.print("Enter Perpendicular: ");
    double p = in.nextDouble();
    System.out.print("Enter Base: ");
    double b = in.nextDouble();
    double h = Math.sqrt(Math.pow(p, 2)
                          + Math.pow(b, 2));
    System.out.println("Hypotenuse = " + h);
  }
}
```

Q.4 Write a program that accepts a number x and then prints: $x^0, x^1, x^2, x^3, x^4, x^5$

Ans.

```
import java.util.Scanner;
public class KboatXPower
{
  public static void main(String args[])
```

```
{
    Scanner in = new Scanner(System.in);
    System.out.print("Enter x: ");
    int x = in.nextInt();
    System.out.print(Math.pow(x, 0) + ", ");
    System.out.print(Math.pow(x, 1) + ", ");
    System.out.print(Math.pow(x, 2) + ", ");
    System.out.print(Math.pow(x, 3) + ", ");
    System.out.print(Math.pow(x, 4) + ", ");
    System.out.print(Math.pow(x, 5));
  }
}
```

Q.5 For every natural number m>1; 2m, m^2 - 1and m^2 + 1 form a Pythagorean triplet. Write a program to input the value of 'm' through console to display a 'Pythagorean Triplet'.

Sample Input: 3

Then 2m = 6, $m^2 - 1 = 8$ and $m^2 + 1 = 10$

Thus 6, 8, 10 form a 'Pythagorean Triplet'.

Ans.
```
import java.util.*;
public class Q2
{
  public static void main(String args[])
  {
    Scanner in = new Scanner(System.in);
    int m, x, y, z;
    System.out.println("Enter a natural number");
    m = in.nextInt();
    x=2*m;
    y=m*m-1;
    z=m*m+1;
    System.out.println(x+ "," +y+ "and" +z+ "are
                                  Pythagorean Triplet");
  }
}
```

Q.6 Write a program to input a number.Calculate its square root and cube root.Finally,display the result by rounding it off.

Sample Input:5

Square root of 5=2.2360679

Rounded form = 2

Cube root of 5 = 1.7099759

Rounded form = 2

Ans.
```
import java.util.*;
public class Q3
{
  public static void main(String args[])
  {
    Scanner in = new Scanner(System.in);
    long x, cb, sq;
    System.out.println("Enter a number");
    x = in.nextInt();
    sq = Math.round(Math.sqrt(x));
    cb = Math.round(Math.cbrt(x));
    System.out.println ("Square root =" + sq);
    System.out.println("Cube root 11 =" + cb);
  }
}
```

Q.7 The volume of a sphere is calculated by using formula $v = \frac{4}{3} * \frac{22}{7} * r^3$

Write a program to calculate the radius of a sphere by taking its volume as an input.

Hint : radius = $\sqrt[3]{volume * \frac{3}{4} * \frac{7}{22}}$

Ans.
```
import java.util.*;
public class Q4
{
  public static void main(String args[])
  {
    Scanner in = new Scanner(System.in);
    double vol, r;
    System.out.println("Enter the volume of the
                                            sphere");
    vol = in.nextDouble();
    r = Math.cbrt(vol * 3/4 * 7/22);
    System.out.println("Radius=" +r);
  }
}
```

Q.8 The sum of first n odd natural numbers can be calculated as n², where n is the number of odd natural.

For example,

Sum=1+3+5+7; number of odd natural = 4

Therefore, Sum = 42 = 16

Write a program to input number of odd natural terms and display sum of the given series:

a. 1+3+5+.......+29+31

b. 1+3+5+7+....... +47 +49

Ans.
```
import java.util.*;
public class KboatCalculateSum
{
  public static void main(String args[])
  {
    Scanner in = new Scanner(System.in);
    System.out.print("Enter the number of odd
                                  natural terms: ");
    int num = in.nextInt();
    System.out.println("Number of odd natural
                                    terms =" + num);
    double sum = Math.pow(num, 2);
    System.out.println("Sum = "+ sum);
  }
}
```

07

CONDITIONAL CONSTRUCTS IN JAVA

Conditional constructs are used in programming languages to cause the flow of execution in advance. These statements are the branch based statements, where branches are depend on the state of a program.

In Java, conditional constructs can be divided under the following three categories:

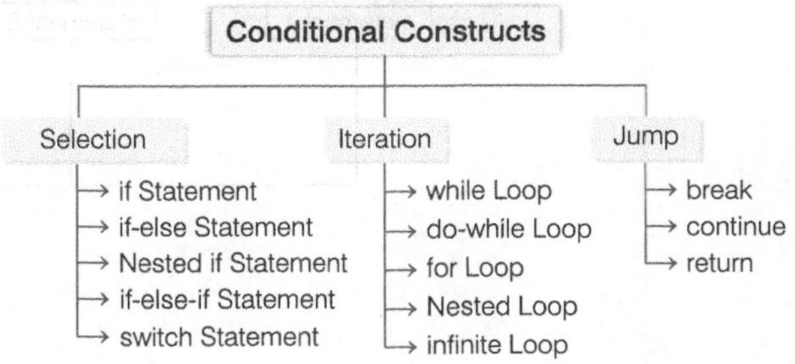

In this chapter, we will discuss only selection statement. Other two statements are discuss in next chapter.

Selection Statements

Selection statements are used in a program to choose different paths of execution based upon the outcome of an expression or the state of a variable.

if Statement

The if statement is a powerful decision making statement and is used to control the flow of execution of statement. Its simplest form is:

```
if(condition)
{
    statement;
}
```

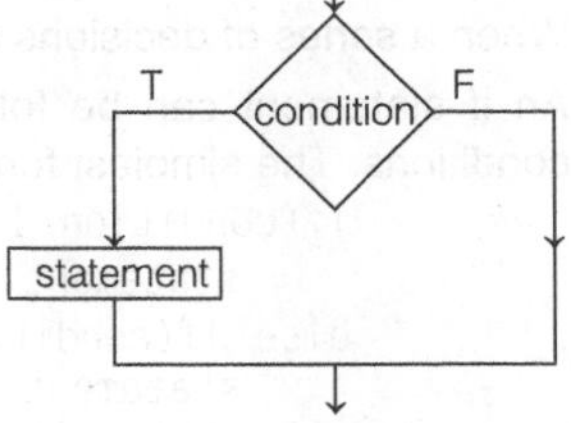

Here,

- condition is a boolean expression.
- if condition is true, then the statement will be executed.
- if condition is false, then the statement will be passed.

if-else Statement

The if-else statement can be used to route program execution through two different paths. The simplest form of if-else statement is:

```
if(condition)
{
    statement 1;   // if condition is true
}
else
{
    statement 2;  // if condition is false
}
```

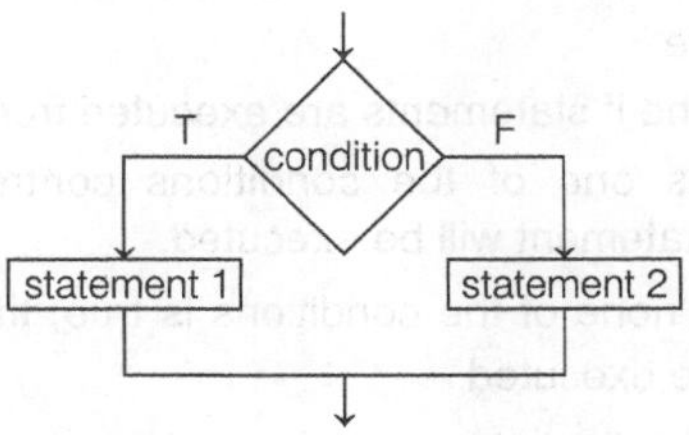

Here,

- condition is a boolean expression.
- if condition is true, statement 1 or if block will be executed.
- if condition is false, statement 2 or else block will be executed.

Nested if Statement

The if statement can be nested in Java, which means one if or if-else statement inside another if or if-else statement can be used. The simplest form of nested if statement is:

```
if(condition 1)
{
     if(condition 2)
     {
          statement 1;
     }
     else
     {
          statement 2;
     }
}
else
{
     if(condition 3)
     {
          statement 3;
     }
     else
     {
          statement 4;
     }
}
```

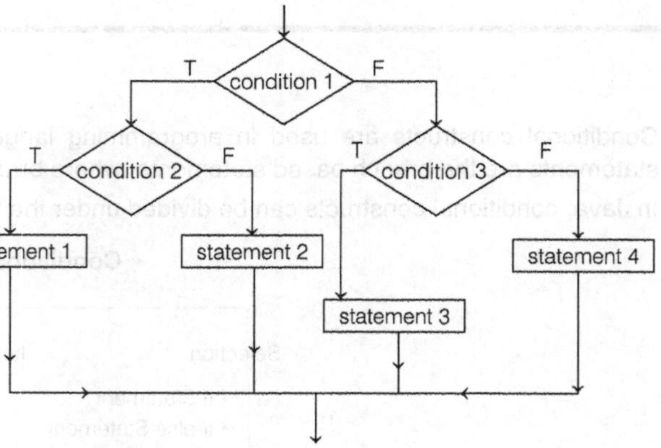

Here,

- if condition 1 is true, then condition 2 will be evaluated.
- if condition 2 is true, then statement 1 will execute.
- if condition 2 is false, then statement 2 will execute.
- if condition 1 is false, then in else block, condition 3 will be evaluated.
- if condition 3 is true, then statement 3 will execute.
- if condition 3 is false, then statement 4 will execute.

if else if Ladder

When a series of decisions are involved, we have to use more than one if else statement.

An if statement can be followed by an optional else if...... else statement, which is very useful to test various conditions. The simplest form is:

```
if(condition 1)
     statement 1;
else if(condition 2)
     statement 2;
else if(condition 3)
     statement 3;
:
else
     statement n+1;
```

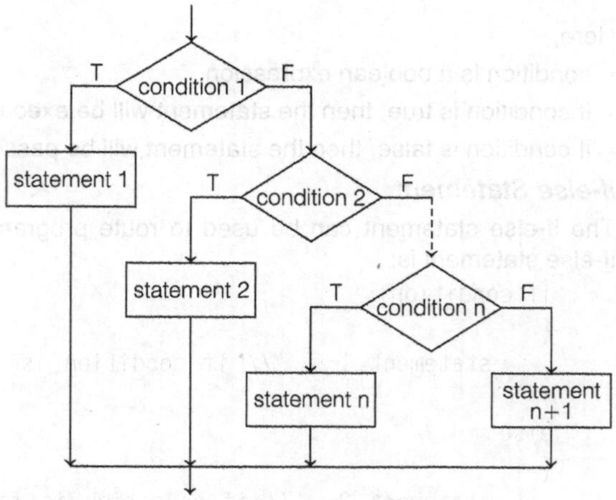

Here,

- The if statements are executed from the top.
- As one of the conditions controlling the if is true, the statement will be executed.
- If none of the conditions is true, the final else statement will be executed.
- The final else acts as a default condition, if all the conditions become false, then it will be executed.

switch Statement

In Java, the switch statement is another selection statement that defines different paths of execution for a program. It can be used in place of chain of else statements. The simplest form of switch statement is:

```
switch(expression)
{
     case value 1:     // statement sequence
     break;
     case value 2:     // statement sequence
     break;
     :
     case value N: // statement sequence
     break;
     default:   // default statement sequence
}
```

Here,

- The expression must be of type byte, short, int or char.
- Each case value must be a unique literal (that is, it must be a constant not a variable).
- The break statement is used inside the switch to terminate a statement sequence.
- If none of the constants matches with the value of the expression, then the default statement will be executed.

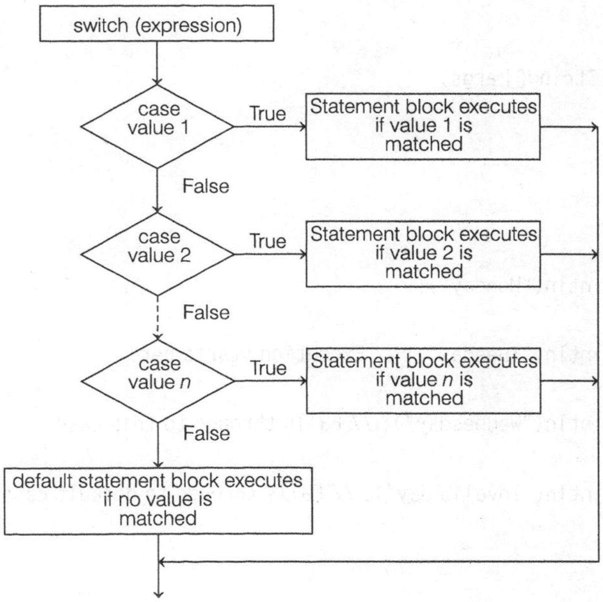

Fall-Through Condition

In Java, a fall-through condition occurs when a case in a switch statement does not include a break statement, causing execution to continue into the next case.

Without Fall-Through (Using break) Usually, break is used to prevent fall-through:

```
public class SwitchExample
{
  public static void main(String[] args)
   {
      int day = 2;
      switch (day)
      {
         case 1:
```

```
            System.out.println("Monday");
            break; // Stops execution
        case 2:
            System.out.println("Tuesday");
            break; // Stops execution
        case 3:
            System.out.println("Wednesday");
            break;
        default:
            System.out.println("Invalid day");
      }
   }
}
```

Output

Tuesday

With Fall-Through (Without break) If we remove the break, execution will continue to the next case(s):

```
public class SwitchExample
{
   public static void main(String[] args)
   {
      int day = 2;
      switch (day)
      {
        case 1:
            System.out.println("Monday");
        case 2:
            System.out.println("Tuesday"); // Execution starts here
        case 3:
            System.out.println("Wednesday"); // Falls through to this case
        default:
            System.out.println("Invalid day"); // Falls through to default case
      }
   }
}
```

Output

Tuesday
Wednesday
Invalid day

System.exit(0) in Java

System.exit(0) is a method used to terminate a Java program immediately. It stops the execution and shuts down the Java Virtual Machine (JVM)

Syntax `System.exit(0);`

Note *0 → Indicates normal termination (successful execution).*

Non-zero values (e.g., System.exit(1), System.exit(-1)) → Indicate abnormal termination (error).

Using System.exit(0) in a Simple Program

```
public class ExitExample
{
    public static void main(String[] args)
    {
        System.out.println("Program started...");
            // Terminate the program
        System.exit(0);
            // This line will NOT execute
        System.out.println("This will never print.");
    }
}
```

Output Program started...

Using System.exit(0) in a Menu-Driven Program

```
import java.util.Scanner;
public class MenuExitExample
{
    public static void main(String[] args)
    {
        Scanner scanner = new Scanner(System.in);
        int choice;
        while (true)
        {
            System.out.println("\n1. Say Hello");
            System.out.println("2. Exit");
            System.out.print("Enter choice: ");
            choice = scanner.nextInt();
            switch (choice)
            {
                case 1:
                    System.out.println("Hello, User!");
                break;
                case 2:
                    System.out.println("Exiting program...");
                    System.exit(0);  // Terminates the program
                default:
                    System.out.println("Invalid choice! Try again.");
            }
        }
    }
}
```

Output

1. Say Hello
2. Exit

Enter choice: 1

Hello, User!

1. Say Hello
2. Exit

Enter choice: 2

Exiting program...

EXAM ORIENTED QUESTIONS

TYPE - 1 — 01 Mark

Multiple Choice Questions

Q.1 Which of the following is used to check a condition and execute a block of code if the condition is true?

(a) switch statement (b) if statement
(c) while loop (d) for loop

Q.2 What will happen if you omit the parentheses () in the if condition?

(a) Compilation error
(b) The code will still work
(c) It will execute the else block
(d) It will cause a runtime exception

Q.3 Predict the output of the following code snippet:

```
int a = 1;
int b = 2;
if (a == b)
  System.out.println ("Both values are equal");
else
  System.out.println ("Values are not equal");
```

(a) Both values are equal
(b) Incorrect use of the == operator
(c) Values are not equal
(d) No output

Q.4 What is the output of the following code?

```
int x = 10, y = 5;
if (x > y)
{
  System.out.println("X is greater");
}
else
{
  System.out.println("Y is greater");
}
```

(a) X is greater (b) Y is greater
(c) Error (d) No output

Q.5 Consider the following code snippet:

```
if ( c > d)
  x = c;
else
  x = d;
```

Choose the correct option if the code mentioned above is rewritten using the ternary operator:

(a) x = (c >d) ? c : d; (b) x = (c >d) ? d : c;
(c) x = (c >d) ? c : c; (d) x = (c >d) ? d : d;

Q.6

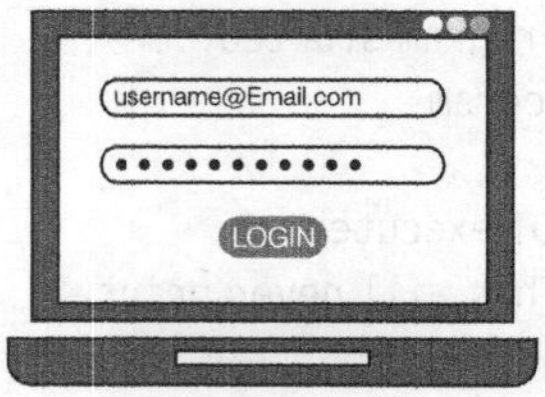

What is the most appropriate conditional construct to check if both the username and password match the stored credentials?

(a) switch-case (b) if-else
(c) do-while (d) for

Q.7

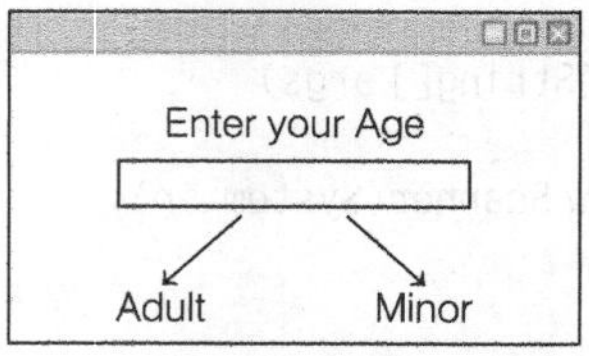

Which conditional structure is best suited for determining the output of a program that has two possible outcomes?

(a) if (b) if-else
(c) switch (d) nested if

Q.8

Which conditional structure is best for checking if someone is both a senior citizen and a member?

(a) if (b) if-else
(c) switch (d) nested if

Q.9 What is the correct syntax for an if-else if statement in Java?

(a)
```
if (condition)
{
  // Code
}
else if (condition)
{
  // Code
}
```

(b)
```
if (condition)
  // Code
else if (condition)
  // Code
```

(c)
```
if cordition
{
   // Code
}
else if condition
{
   // Code
}
```
(d)
```
if (condition)
{
   // Code
}
else if (condition);
{  // Code
}
```

Q.10 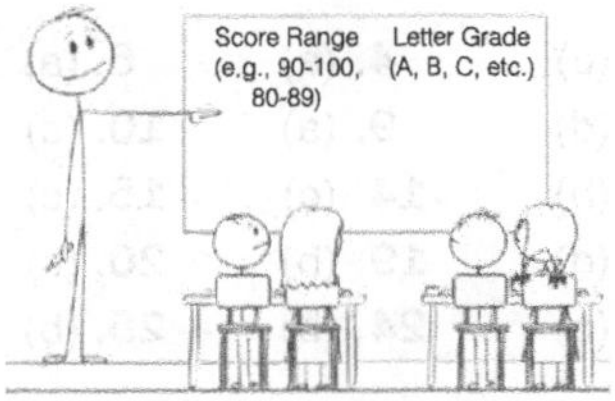

Which conditional construct is best suited for assigning a letter grade based on a student's numerical score?
(a) if only (b) switch-case
(c) if-else-if ladder (d) Nested if

Q.11 How many conditions can you check using else if in a single if-else chain?
(a) Only two conditions
(b) Unlimited number of conditions
(c) Up to 10 conditions
(d) One condition only

Q.12 What is the error in the following code?
```
int x = 5;
if (x > 0);
   System.out.println("Positive");
else if (x == 0)
   System.out.println("Zero");
else
   System.out.println("Negative");
```
(a) Missing else block
(b) Extra semicolon ; after if condition
(c) No error
(d) Syntax error in else if

Q.13 What is the output of the following code?
```
int x = 10;
if (x < 10)
   System.out.println("Less than 10");
else if (x == 10)
   System.out.println("Equal to 10");
else
   System.out.println("Greater than 10");
```
(a) Less than 10 (b) Equal to 10
(c) Greater than 10 (d) Compilation Error

Q.14 What will happen if the default case is not included in a switch statement?
(a) Compilation error
(b) Program will crash
(c) No error, but if no case matches, nothing happens
(d) JVM will throw an exception

Q.15 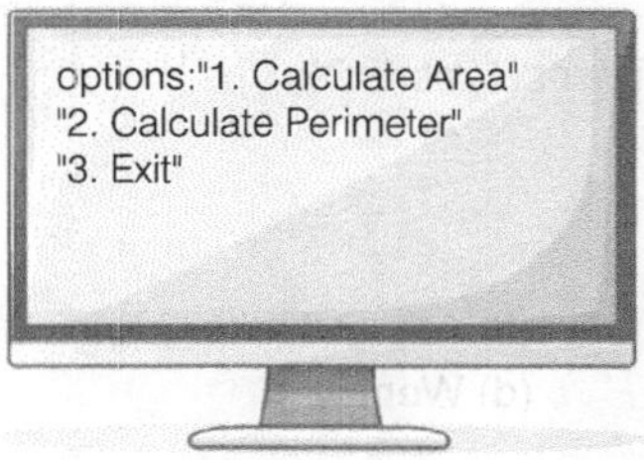

What conditional construct is most efficient for handling user input from a menu with multiple options?
(a) if-else (b) if-else-if ladder
(c) switch-case (d) Nested if

Q.16 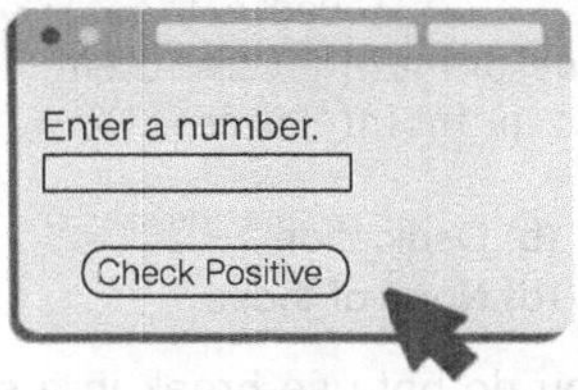

What conditional statement would you use to check if a variable 'num' is greater than 0?
(a) switch(num) (b) if (num > 0)
(c) while (num > 0) (d) for (num > 0)

Q.17 Consider the following program segment and select the output of the same when n=10 :
```
switch(n)
{
   case 10 : System.out.println(n*2);
   case 4 : System.out.println(n*4);break;
   default: System.out.println(n);
}
```
(a) 20
40
(b) 10
4
(c) 20, 40
(d) 10
10

Q.18 Multiple branching statement of Java is
(a) for (b) while
(c) do ... while (d) switch

Q.19 Give the output of the following.
```
switch(x)
{
   case 'M':
      System.out.print("Microsoft Teams");
      break;
   case 'G':
      System.out.print("Google Meet");
   default:
      System.out.print("Any software");
      break;
```

```
case 'W':
    System.out.print("Web Ex");
    break;
}
```

When x='g'

(a) Google Meet (b) Any software
(c) Google Meet Any software (d) WebEx

Q.20 Give the output of the following

```
switch(x)
{
  case 'a' : System.out.println ("Discipline");
  case 'b' : System.out.println
                      ("Dedication"); break;
  case 'c' : System.out.println ("Commitment");
  default : System.out.println("Success");
} when x='A'
```

(a) Discipline (b) Dedication
(c) Success (d) None of these

Q.21 What will happen if you do not use break in a switch statement?

(a) Only the matched case executes
(b) Compilation error occurs
(c) Fall-through occurs (execution continues to the next case)
(d) The program terminates immediately

Q.22 The absence of which statement leads to fall through situation in switch case statement?

(a) continue (b) break
(c) return (d) System.exit(0)

Q.23 The jump statement that is used inside a switch case construct to terminate a statement sequence.

(a) continue (b) break
(c) return (d) goto

Q.24 Which statement is true about System.exit(0); in Java?

(a) It continues the execution of the program
(b) It terminates the program immediately
(c) It throws an exception
(d) It does nothing

Q.25 What will be the output of the following program?

```
public class TestExit
{
   public static void main(String[] args)
   {
     System.out.println("Hello");
     System.exit(0);
     System.out.println("World");
   }
}
```

(a) Hello World (b) Hello
(c) World (d) No output

Q.26 What happens if System.exit(1); is used instead of System.exit(0);?

(a) The program terminates normally
(b) The program terminates with an error
(c) The program enters an infinite loop
(d) Nothing happens

Answers

1. (b)	**2.** (a)	**3.** (c)	**4.** (a)	**5.** (a)
6. (b)	**7.** (b)	**8.** (d)	**9.** (a)	**10.** (c)
11. (b)	**12.** (b)	**13.** (b)	**14.** (c)	**15.** (c)
16. (b)	**17.** (a)	**18.** (d)	**19.** (b)	**20.** (c)
21. (c)	**22.** (b)	**23.** (b)	**24.** (b)	**25.** (b)
26. (b)				

TYPE - 2

01 Mark

Statement Based Questions

Q.1 A programmer is writing a Java program to determine if a given number is positive, negative, or zero. They have written the following incorrect statement:

```
if (number > 0)
{
  System.out.println("Positive");
}
else if (number < 0)
{
  System.out.println("Negative");
}
```

What is the correct way to handle the case where the number is zero?

A. Add

```
else if (number == 0)
{
  System.out.println("Zero");
}
```

after the second if.

B. Add

```
if (number == 0)
{
  System.out.println("Zero");
}
```

as a separate, independent if statement.

C. Add

```
else
{
  System.out.println("Zero");
}
```

after the second if.

D. Add

```
case 0: System.out.println("Zero");
```

within a switch statement.

(a) Both A and B (b) Only B
(c) Only C (d) Only D

Q.2 A computer science student is creating a menu-driven application and wants to use a switch statement to handle user choices. They have written the following incorrect code:

```
int choice = 2;
switch (choice)
{
  case 1:
    System.out.println("Option 1");
  case 2:
    System.out.println("Option 2");
  case 3:
    System.out.println("Option 3");
}
```

What is the correct way to prevent fall-through and ensure only "Option 2" is printed when choice is 2?

A. Remove all case labels.
B. Add break; after each case block.
C. Add default: at the end.
D. Change switch to if-else if statements.

(a) Only A (b) Only B
(c) Only C (d) Both D and C

Q.3 A computer teacher is writing a Java program to determine the grade based on a student's score. They have written the following incomplete statement:

```
if (score >= 90)
{
  System.out.println("A");
}
else if (score >= 80)
{
  System.out.println("B");
} // Missing logic for C, D, and F grades
```

What is the correct way to complete the code to handle the remaining grades (C, D, and F)?

A. Add multiple independent if statements.
B. Add nested if statements.
C. Add further else if and a final else for the 'F' grade.
D. Use a switch statement with ranges.

(a) Only A (b) Only B
(c) Only C (d) Only D

Q.4 A programmer is creating a Java program that requires the program to terminate when the user enters the value 0. They have written the following incorrect statement:

```
if(userInput == 0)
{
  return;
}
```

While return will exit the current method, it will not exit the entire program. What is the correct way to immediately terminate the Java program?

A. Use System.out.println(0);
B. Use break;
C. Use System.exit(0);
D. Use continue;

(a) Only A (b) Only B
(c) Only C (d) Only D

Q.5 A programmer is writing a menu-driven Java program using a switch statement. They want to ensure that if the user enters an invalid menu option, a default message is displayed. They have written the following incomplete code:

```
int option = 5;
switch (option)
{
  case 1:
    System.out.println("Option 1 selected.");
  case 2:
    System.out.println("Option 2 selected.");
  // Missing logic for invalid options
}
```

What is the correct way to add the logic to display a default message for invalid options?

A. Add
```
if (option > 2)
{
 System.out.println("Invalid option.");
}
```
B. Add
```
case default: System.out.println("Invalid option.");
```
C. Add
```
default: System.out.println("Invalid option.");
```
D. Add
```
else: System.out.println("Invalid option.");
```

(a) Only A (b) Only B
(c) Only C (d) Only D

Q.6 Consider the following statements related to the execution flow of a switch statement, which are jumbled. Choose the correct order of the steps involved:

A. The default block is executed.
B. The switch expression is evaluated.
C. The execution continues until a break statement or the end of the switch block is reached.
D. The matching case block is executed.

(a) B, D, C, A (b) B, A, C, D
(c) D, B, A, C (d) A, B, C, D

Q.7 Consider the following statements related to the use of if-else if ladder, which are jumbled. Choose the correct order of the steps involved:

A. The final else block is executed if no previous condition is true.

B. The first if condition is evaluated.

C. Subsequent else if conditions are evaluated in order until a true condition is found.

D. The block of code corresponding to the first true condition is executed.

(a) B, C, D, A (b) A, D, C, B
(c) D, A, B, C (d) C, B, A, D

Q.8 Consider the following statements related to the termination of a menu-driven Java program, which are jumbled. Choose the correct order of the steps involved:

A. The user enters the "exit" option.

B. The System.exit(0) method is called.

C. The program execution stops.

D. The program checks the user's input.

(a) A, D, B, C (b) D, A, B, C
(c) C, B, A, D (d) B, C, D, A

Q.9 Consider the following statements related to the behavior of break within a nested if statement, which are jumbled. Choose the correct order of the steps involved:

A. The innermost if condition is evaluated.

B. The break statement is encountered.

C. The execution jumps out of the innermost if block.

D. The outer block of code continues execution.

(a) A, B, C, D (b) B, A, D, C
(c) C, D, A, B (d) D, C, B, A

Answers

1. (c) **2.** (b) **3.** (c) **4.** (c) **5.** (c)
6. (a) **7.** (a) **8.** (b) **9.** (a)

TYPE - 3 01 Mark

Assertion-Reason Type Questions

Directions (Q. Nos. 1-8) The following questions are Assertion-Reason based questions. Choose the answer based on the code given below

(a) Both Assertion (A) and Reason (R) are true and Reason (R) is a correct explanation of Assertion (A).

(b) Both Assertion (A) and Reason (R) are true and Reason (R) is not a correct explanation of Assertion (A).

(c) Assertion (A) is true and Reason (R) is false.

(d) Assertion (A) is false and Reason (R) is true.

Q.1 Assertion (A) The if statement is used when only one condition needs to be checked.

Reason (R) The if-else statement is used when two conditions need to be checked.

Ans. (a) The if statement handles one condition, while if-else handles two conditions. Hence, Both Assertion (A) and Reason (R) are true and Reason (R) is a correct explanation of Assertion (A).

Q.2 Assertion (A) The else block in an if-else statement executes when the condition is true.

Reason (R) The else block executes when the condition is false.

Ans. (d) The else block executes only when the condition is false, not true. Hence, Assertion (A) is false and Reason (R) is true.

Q.3 Assertion (A) A nested if statement is an if statement inside another if statement.

Reason (R) Nested if statements are used to check conditions in a hierarchical manner.

Ans. (a) Nested if statements allow hierarchical condition checking. Hence, Both Assertion (A) and Reason (R) are true and Reason (R) is a correct explanation of Assertion (A).

Q.4 Assertion (A) Fall-through occurs when a switch case does not have a break statement.

Reason (R) Fall-through is the expected behavior in all switch statements.

Ans. (c) Fall-through occurs when break is omitted, but it's not the expected behavior. Hence, Assertion (A) is true and Reason (R) is false.

Q.5 Assertion (A) The System.exit(0) method stops the program without completing the remaining code.

Reason (R) The System.exit(0) method can be used to end a program successfully.

Ans. (a) System.exit(0) stops the program immediately and indicates successful completion. Hence, Both Assertion (A) and Reason (R) are true and Reason (R) is a correct explanation of Assertion (A).

Q.6 Assertion (A) An if-else-if ladder is used when there are multiple conditions to be checked in sequence.

Reason (R) An if-else-if ladder only checks the first condition.

Ans. (c) An if-else-if ladder checks multiple conditions, not just the first. Hence, Assertion (A) is true and Reason (R) is false.

Q.7 Assertion (A) The else block in an if-else statement is optional.

Reason (R) The else block is executed if the condition is false.

Ans. (b) The else block is optional, and executes when the if condition is false. Hence, Both Assertion (A) and Reason (R) are true and Reason (R) is not a correct explanation of Assertion (A).

Q.8 Assertion (A) Java supports multiple types for the switch expression.
Reason (R) The switch expression can handle only integer types.

Ans. (c) The switch expression can handle multiple types, not just integers. Hence, Assertion (A) is true and Reason (R) is false.

TYPE - 4

01 Mark

Odd One Out

Q.1 Choose the odd one.
(a) `if (x > 0) { System.out.println("Positive"); }`
(b) `switch(x) { case 1: System.out.println("One"); break; }`
(c) `while (x > 0) { x--; }`
(d) `if (x < 10) System.out.println("Less than 10");`

Ans. (c) while loop is a looping construct, not a conditional statement

Q.2 Choose the odd one.
(a) if-else (b) switch-case
(c) for loop (d) ternary operator (?:)

Ans. (c) for loop is not a conditional construct, it's an iteration construct

Q.3 Choose the odd one.
(a)
```
switch(x)
{
   case 1: System.out.println("One");
   case 2: System.out.println("Two");
}
```
(b)
```
switch(x)
{
   case 1: System.out.println("One");
   break;
   case 2: System.out.println("Two");
}
```
(c)
```
switch(x)
{
   case 1: System.out.println("One");
   case 2: System.out.println("Two");
   break;
}
```
(d)
```
switch(x)
{
   case 1: System.out.println("One");
   case 2: System.out.println("Two");
   default: System.out.println("Default");
}
```

Ans. (b) It includes break, preventing fall-through, while the others allow fall-through

Q.4 Choose the odd one.
(a) System.exit(0); (b) return;
(c) break; (d) continue;

Ans. (a) System.exit(0); terminates the entire program, while return, break, and continue only affect specific control flows

Q.5 Choose the odd one.
(a) System.exit(0);
(b) System.exit(1);
(c) System.exit(-1);
(d) System.out.println("Program Terminated");

Ans. (d) Printing a message does not terminate the program, while the others forcefully exit it

TYPE - 5

01 Mark

Very Short Answer Type Questions

Q.1 What are the different types of control statements in programming?

Ans. Sequential control, Selection control, Iteration control.

Q.2 What happens if we do not use a break statement in a switch block?

Ans. The program will continue executing the next case statements (fall-through) until a break or the end of the switch block is reached.

Q.3 What is the significance of the default case in a switch statement?

Ans. The default case executes when none of the case labels match the given expression.

Q.4 Mention two drawbacks of using a switch statement.

Ans. (a) It does not support conditions involving ranges.
(b) It cannot use case labels with variables or expressions.

Q.5 Rewrite this condition using a ternary operator:
`if (speed > 60) fine = 500; else fine = 200;`

Ans. `fine = (speed > 60) ? 500 : 200;`

Q.6 A student is promoted if they score 40 or more; otherwise, they fail. Write an if-else condition for this.

Ans.
```
if (marks >= 40)
   result = "Promoted";
else
   result = "Failed";
```

Q.7 A store offers discounts based on purchase amount:
Above → 5000 → 20% discount → 2000 to 5000 → 10% discount
Below → 2000 → No discount
Write an if structure for this condition.

Ans.
```
if (amount > 5000)
    discount = 20;
else if (amount >= 2000 && amount <= 5000)
    discount = 10;
else
    discount = 0;
```

Q.8 A company assigns job roles based on experience:
- More than 5 years → "Manager"
- 2 to 5 years → "Team Lead"
- Less than 2 years → "Intern"

Write an if-else structure for this.

Ans.
```
if (experience > 5)
    role = "Manager";
else if (experience >= 2 && experience <= 5)
    role = "Team Lead";
else
    role = "Intern";
```

Q.9 Mention one statement each to achieve:
(a) Bi-directional flow of control
(b) Multiple branching of control

Ans. (a) if-else statement
(b) switch statement

Q.10 Correct the following code.
```
int a=5, b=10;
int x = (a>b)>true:false;
```

Ans.
```
int a=5, b=10;
boolean x = (a>b) ? true:false;
```

TYPE - 6 — 2 Marks

Short Answer Type Questions

Q.1 Rewrite the following program segment using the if-else statement.
```
comm=(sale>15000) ? sale*5/100:0;
```

Ans. Program segment using the if-else statement
```
if(sale>15000)
{
    comm=(sale*5)/100;
}
else
{
    comm=0;
}
```

Q.2 Read the paragraph given below and answer the questions given below

Decision control statements are used to check for condition and execute the statements based on the condition. The two decision control statements in Java are if and switch, switch is also called as multiple branching statement.

An if statement within another if statement is termed as Nested if Statement.

(i) What are the two decision control statements in Java?
(a) if and switch (b) for and while
(c) ternary and logical

(ii) An if statement within another if statement is termed as
(a) Nested (b) Nested while
(c) Nested if

Ans (i) (a) if and switch
(ii) (c) Nested if

Q.3 Rewrite the following if statement, using the switch statement:
```
if (choice == 1)
  System.out.println("You selected One");
else if (choice == 2)
  System.out.println("You selected Two");
else if (choice == 3)
  System.out.println("You selected Three");
else if (choice == 4)
  System.out.println("You selected Four");
else if (choice == 5)
  System.out.println("You selected Five");
else if (choice == 6)
  System.out.println("You selected Six");
else
  System.out.println("Invalid choice");
```

Ans.
```
switch (choice)
{
  case 1:
    System.out.println("You selected One");
    break;
  case 2:
    System.out.println("You selected Two");
    break;
  case 3:
    System.out.println("You selected Three");
    break;
  case 4:
    System.out.println("You selected Four");
    break;
  case 5:
    System.out.println("You selected Five");
    break;
  case 6:
    System.out.println("You selected Six");
    break;
  default:
    System.out.println("Invalid choice");
}
```

Q.4 **Convert the following if-else-if construct into switch case**

```
if( var==1)
   System.out.println("good");
else if(var==2)
   System.out.println("better");
else if(var==3)
   System.out.println("best");
else
   System.out.println("invalid");
```

Ans. Program in Switch case

```
switch (var)
{
  case 1 :
     System.out. println("good");
     break;
  case 2:
     System.out.println("better");
     break;
  case 3:
     System.out.println("best");
     break;
  default:
     System.out.println("invalid");
}
```

Q.5 **What role does the default block play when all case labels in a switch fails to match the given value?**

Ans. The purpose of default in a switch statement, is that, if no case value matches the switch expression value, then the default clause is executed.

e.g.
```
int ch=10;
switch(ch)
{
  case1:
     System.out.println("Its one");
     break;
  case2:
     System.out.println("Its two");
     break;
  default:
     System.out.println("Not working");
}
```

Q.6 **Convert the following switch statement by using nested if statements:**

```
switch (choice)
{
  case 0:
  case 1:
     x = 111;
     y = 222;
     break;
  case 2:
     x = 333;
     y = 444;
     break;
  case 3:
     x = -11;
     y = -22;
     break;
  default:
     y = 555;
}
```

Ans.
```
if (choice == 0 || choice == 1)
{
 x = 111;
 y = 222;
}
else
{
 if (choice == 2)
 {
  x = 333;
  y = 444;
 }
 else
 {
  if (choice == 3)
  {
   x = -11;
   y = -22;
  }
  else
  {
   y = 555;
  }
 }
}
```

Q.7 **Correct the following code.**

```
char m="A";
Switch ("A");
{
 Case 'a';
   System.out.println("A");
   break;
 Case 'b';
   System.out.println("B");
   break;
 Default:
   System.out.println("Not a valid option");
}
```

Ans.
```
char m = 'A';
switch (m)
{
 case 'a':
  System.out.println("A");
  break;
 case 'b':
  System.out.println("B");
  break;
```

```
default:
  System.out.println("Not a valid option");
}
```

Q.8 Define the term fall through condition with reference to switch () case.

Ans Fall through is usually prevented with a break keyword at the end of the matching body, which exits execution of the switch block, but this can cause bugs due to unintentional fall through, if the programmer forgets to insert the break statement. e.g.

```
class Week
{
 public static void main (String[] args)
 {
   int wk = 4;
   switch (wk)
   {
     case 1: System.out.println("Sunday");
     case 2: System.out.println("Monday");
     case 3: System.out.println("Tuesday");
     case 4: System.out.println("Wednesday");
     case 5: System.out.println("Thursday");
     case 6: System.out.println("Friday");
     case 7: System.out.println("Saturday");
     break;
     default:
   }
 }
}
```

Q.9 Format the following if statement with proper indentation:

```
if (a == b) {if (b == c) a = 5; b = 10;} else c = 5;
```

Ans.

```
if (a == b)
{
  if (b == c)
    a = 5;
    b = 10;
}
else
  c = 5;
```

Q.10 The following is a segment of program

```
x = 1; y = 1;
  if (n > 0)
  {
    x = x + 1;
    y = y - 1;
  }
```

What will be the value of x and y, if n assumes a value

(i) 1 (ii) 0?

Ans. (i) If, n assume as a value 1

```
x = 1; y = 1;
if (n > 0)
{
  x = x + 1;
  y = y - 1;
}
```

Then, value of x = 2 and y = 0

(ii) If, n assume as a value 0

```
x = 1; y = 1;
if (n > 0)
{
  x = x + 1;
  y = y - 1;
}
```

Then, value of x = 1 and y = 1

Q.11 Write a switch statement to display the day of the week based on user input (1 for Monday, 2 for Tuesday, etc.).

Ans.

```
switch(day)
{
  case 1: System.out.println("Monday"); break;
  case 2: System.out.println("Tuesday"); break;
  case 3: System.out.println("Wednesday"); break;
  case 4: System.out.println("Thursday"); break;
  case 5: System.out.println("Friday"); break;
  case 6: System.out.println("Saturday"); break;
  case 7: System.out.println("Sunday"); break;
  default: System.out.println("Invalid day");
}
```

Q.12 Format the following if statement with indentation:

```
if (a > b) if (c < d) a = 10; else b = 20; else c = 30;
```

Ans.

```
if (a > b)
{
  if (c < d)
  {
    a = 10;
  }
  else
  {
    b = 20;
  }
}
else
{
  c = 30;
}
```

Q.13 Format the following if statement with indentation:

```
if (m != n) { if (p == q) m = 5; n = 6; } else p = 7;
```

Ans.
```
if (m != n)
{
  if (p == q)
  {
    m = 5;
  }
  n = 6;
}
else
{
  p = 7;
}
```

TYPE - 7 02 Marks

Differentiate

Q.1 if Statement and switch Statement

Ans.

if Statement	switch Statement
It works under the boolean literals.	It works under the integer/character literals.
It uses relational operator for check conditions.	It uses 'case' for check conditions.

Q.2 if-else Statement and switch Statement

Ans.

if-else Statement	switch Statement
if-else can evaluate a relational or logical expression.	switch can test only integer or char expressions. It tests only for the equality condition.
if-else statement encloses multiple statements inside curly braces { }.	switch statement never encloses multiple statements inside curly braces { }.
if-else is used to compare two or more variable.	switch case label value must be constant.

Q.3 if-else-if and switch case

Ans.

if-else-if	switch case
Range of values are checked.	Only one value is compared.
Supports both primitive and composite data types.	Supports only integer (byte, short, int, long), char.
Relational/Logical expressions can be checked.	Only equality can be checked.

Q.4 break and System.exit(0)

Ans.

break	System.exit(0)
break statement is used to jump out from the loop or switch-case.	System.exit(0) terminates the entire program.
break is a keyword.	System.exit(0) is a method provided by Java standard library.

TYPE - 8 2 Marks

Output Based Questions

Q.1 Predict the output of the following code snippet:
```
public class Main
{
  public static void main(String[] args)
  {
    int x = 15;
    if (x > 10)
    {
      if (x < 20)
      {
        System.out.println("In range");
      }
      else
      {
        System.out.println("Out of range (high)");
      }
    }
    else
    {
      System.out.println("Out of range (low)");
    }
  }
}
```
Ans. Output In range

Q.2 Predict the output of the following code snippet:
```
public class Main
{
  public static void main(String[] args)
  {
    int choice = 2;
    switch (choice)
    {
      case 1:
        System.out.println("Option 1");
      case 2:
        System.out.println("Option 2");
      case 3:
        System.out.println("Option 3");
      default:
        System.out.println("Invalid option");
    }
  }
}
```
Ans. Output

Option 2
Option 3
Invalid option

Q.3 Write the output of the following Java code snippets:

```
int x = 5;
(a) if (x > 0)
    {
      System.out.println("Positive");
    } else {
      System.out.println("Negative");
    }
(b) System.out.println(x == 5 ? "Yes" : "No");
```

Ans. (a) **Output**

Positive

(b) **Output**

Yes

Q.4 Write the output of the following Java code snippets:

```
int day = 3;
(a) switch (day) {
      case 1:
        System.out.println("Monday");
        break;
      case 3:
        System.out.println("Wednesday");
        break;
      default:
        System.out.println("Other");
    }
(b) if (day == 2) {
      System.out.println("Tuesday");
    } else {
      System.out.println("Not Tuesday");
    }
```

Ans. Output

(a) Wednesday

(b) Not Tuesday

TYPE - 9 — 15 Marks

Long Answer Type Questions

Q.1 Write a Java program to get a number from the user and print whether it is positive or negative.

Ans.

```
import java.util.Scanner;
class Main
{
  public static void main(String[] args)
  {
     Scanner in = new Scanner(System.in);
     System.out.print("Input number: ");
     int input = in.nextInt();
     if (input > 0)
     {
        System.out.println("Number is positive");
     }
     else if (input < 0)
     {
        System.out.println("Number is negative");
     }
     else
     {
        System.out.println("Number is zero");
     }
  }
}
```

Q.2 Write a Java program that reads a floating-point number and prints "zero" if the number is zero. Otherwise, print "positive" or "negative". Add "small" if the absolute value of the number is less than 1, or "large" if it exceeds 1,000,000.

Ans.

```
import java.util.Scanner;
class Main
{
  public static void main(String[] args)
  {
    Scanner in = new Scanner(System.in);
    System.out.print("Input value: ");
    double input = in.nextDouble();
    if (input > 0)
    {
      if (input < 1)
      {
        System.out.println("Positive small
                                   number");
      }
      else if (input > 1000000)
      {
        System.out.println("Positive large
                                   number");
      }
      else
      {
        System.out.println("Positive number");
      }
    }
    else if (input < 0)
    {
      if (Math.abs(input) < 1)
      {
        System.out.println("Negative small
                                   number");
      }
      else if (Math.abs(input) > 1000000)
```

```
        {
          System.out.println("Negative large
                                        number");
        }
        else
        {
          System.out.println("Negative number");
        }
      }
      else
      {
        System.out.println("Zero");
      }
    }
}
```

Q.3 Write a program to input basic salary of an employee and calculate its Gross salary according to following:
Basic Salary <= 10000 : HRA = 20%, DA = 80%
Basic Salary <= 20000 : HRA = 25%, DA = 90%
Basic Salary > 20000 : HRA = 30%, DA = 95%

Ans.
```
import java.util.Scanner;
class Main
{
  public static void main(String[] args)
  {
    Scanner input = new Scanner(System.in);
    System.out.print("Enter The Basic Salary :");
    int bs = input.nextInt();
    float hra,da,tot;
    if(bs<=10000)
    {
      hra = bs*0.2f;
      da = bs*0.8f;
    }
    else if(bs<=20000)
    {
      hra = bs*0.25f;
      da = bs*0.9f;
    }
    else
    {
      hra = bs*0.3f;
      da = bs*0.95f;
    }
    System.out.println("Gross Salary :
                                "+(bs+hra+da));
  }
}
```

Q.4 Write a program to input marks of five subjects Physics, Chemistry, Biology, Mathematics and Computer. Calculate percentage and grade according to following:
Percentage >= 90% : Grade A
Percentage >= 80% : Grade B
Percentage >= 70% : Grade C
Percentage >= 60% : Grade D
Percentage >= 40% : Grade E
Percentage < 40% : Grade F

Ans.
```
import java.util.Scanner;
class Main
{
  public static void main(String[] args)
  {
    Scanner input = new Scanner(System.in);
    System.out.println("Enter The Five Subject
                                    Marks :");
    int m1 = input.nextInt();
    int m2 = input.nextInt();
    int m3 = input.nextInt();
    int m4 = input.nextInt();
    int m5 = input.nextInt();
    int tot = m1+m2+m3+m4+m5;
    float per = tot/5;
    System.out.println("Total :"+tot);
    System.out.println("Percentage :"+per);
    if(per>=90)
      System.out.println("Grade A');
    else if(per>=80)
      System.out.println("Grade B');
    else if(per>=70)
      System.out.println("Grade C');
    else if(per>=60)
      System.out.println("Grade D');
    else if(per>=40)
      System.out.println("Grade E');
    else
      System.out.println("Grade F');
  }
}
```

Q.5 Write the program to print chosen month name with fall through switch.

Ans.
```
import java.util.Scanner;
  public class Main
  {
  public static void main(String[] args)
  {
    Scanner scanner = new Scanner(System.in);
    // Taking month number input from user
```

```
        System.out.print("Enter a month number
                                          (1-12): ");
        int month = scanner.nextInt();
        System.out.print("Month: ");
        switch (month)
        {
          case 1: System.out.println("January");
          case 2: System.out.println("February");
          case 3: System.out.println("March");
          case 4: System.out.println("April");
          case 5: System.out.println("May");
          case 6: System.out.println("June");
          case 7: System.out.println("July");
          case 8: System.out.println("August");
          case 9: System.out.println("September");
          case 10: System.out.println("October");
          case 11: System.out.println("November");
          case 12: System.out.println("December");
              break; // Break here to stop execution
          default: System.out.println("Invalid month
            number! Please enter a value between 1 and
                                                  12.");
        }
        scanner.close();
    }
}
```

Note Without break statements between cases, the execution falls through to all subsequent cases.

Q.6 **Write a java program that uses a switch statement to print the name of the month corresponding to a given integer value.**

Ans.

```
import java.util.Scanner;
public class MonthName
{
  public static void main(String[] args)
  {
    Scanner input = new Scanner(System.in);
    System.out.println("Please enter a month
                                   number (1-12):");
    int month = input.nextInt();
    String monthName;
    switch (month)
    {
      case 1:
        monthName = "January";
        break;
      case 2:
        monthName = "February";
        break;
      case 3:
        monthName = "March";
        break;
      case 4:
        monthName = "April";
        break;
      case 5:
        monthName = "May";
        break;
      case 6:
        monthName = "June";
        break;
      case 7:
        monthName = "July";
        break;
      case 8:
        monthName = "August";
        break;
      case 9:
        monthName = "September";
        break;
      case 10:
        monthName = "October";
        break;
      case 11:
        monthName = "November";
        break;
      case 12:
        monthName = "December";
        break;
      default:
        monthName = "Invalid month";
        break;
    }
    System.out.println("You entered " + monthName);
  }
}
```

Q.7 **Using the switch statement, write a menu driven program to perform following operations**

(i) To print the value of Z, where $Z = \frac{x^3 + 0.5x}{Y}$, where x ranges from – 10 to 10 with an increment of 2 and Y remains constant at 5.5.

(ii) To print the Floyds triangle with N rows
Example: If N = 5,
Output:

```
1
2   3
4   5   6
7   8   9   10
11  12  13  14  15
```

Ans.

```
import java.util.Scanner;
class Main
{
    public static void main(String args[])
```

```
    {
        Scanner in = new Scanner(System.in);
        System.out.println("Type 1 for Value
                                     of Z");
        System.out.println("Type 2 for Floyd's
                                     triangle");
        System.out.print("Enter your choice:");
        int choice = in.nextInt();
        switch (choice)
        {
            case 1:
            double Z, Y = 5.5;
            for (int x = -10; x <= 10; x+= 2)
            {
                Z=(Math.pow(x,3)+0.5 * x) / Y;
                System.out.println("Value of Z
                    when x is "+ x + " = " + Z);
            }
            break;
            case 2:
            System.out.print("Enter number of
                                     rows: ");
            int N = in.nextInt();
            int k = 1;
            for (int i = 1; i <= N; i++)
            {
                for (int j = 1; j <= i; j++)
                {
                    System.out.print(k + " ");
                    k++;
                }
                System.out.println();
            }
            break;
            default:
            System.out.println("Incorrect Choice");
            break;
        }
    }
}
```

Q.8 Write a Java program that takes a single character as input from the user and determines whether it is a vowel, a consonant, or not an alphabet. The program should print "Vowel" if the character is a vowel (uppercase or lowercase), "Consonant" if it is a consonant (uppercase or lowercase), and "Not an alphabet" if it is not an alphabetic character.

Ans.
```
import java.util.Scanner;
class Main
{
  public static void main(String[] args)
  {
    Scanner input = new Scanner(System.in);
    char ch;
    System.out.printf("Enter a Character : ");
    ch = input.next().charAt(0);
    if ((ch >= 'A' && ch <= 'Z') || (ch >= 'a' && ch
                                            <= 'z'))
    {
      switch (ch)
      {
        case 'A':
        case 'E':
        case 'I':
        case 'O':
        case 'U':
        case 'a':
        case 'e':
        case 'i':
        case 'o':
        case 'u':
          System.out.println("This is a Vowel");
          break;
        default:
          System.out.println("This is a
                                    Consonant");
          break;
      }
    }
    else
    {
      System.out.println("This is Not an
                                    alphabet");
    }
  }
}
```

08

ITERATIVE CONSTRUCTS IN JAVA

In previous chapter, we have discussed the selection statement. Now, we are going to introduce iteration and jump statements in this chapter.

Iteration Statements

The most basic method of looping in Java is iteration. The repetition of a block of statements either a fixed number of times or until a specific condition occurs is called iteration or looping.

A looping process includes the following four steps:

- **Initialization expression** The initialization of the loop variable take place under initialization expression. The initialization is executed only once, in the beginning of the loop.
- **Test expression** The test expression is an expression whose truth value decides whether the loop body will be executed or not. If the test expression evaluates to true, the loop body gets executed otherwise the loop is terminated.
- **Update expression** The update expression changes the value of the loop variable.
- **The body of the loop** The statements that are executed repeatedly form the body of the loop

Java provides three kinds of loops

- for loop (entry controlled loop)
- while loop (entry controlled loop)
- do-while loop (exit controlled loop)

for Loop

It is a short method of looping, which is commonly preferred by programmers. It tests the condition before entering in the loop body, if the condition evaluates to true, the given statements are executed else the loop will not execute.

Syntax
```
for (initialExpression; testExpression; updateExpression)
{  // body of the loop
}
```

Here,

1. The initialExpression initializes and/or declares variables and executes only once.
2. The condition is evaluated. If the condition is true, the body of the for loop is executed.
3. The updateExpression updates the value of initialExpression.
4. The condition is evaluated again. The process continues until the condition is false.

e.g. Java Program to demonstrate the example of for loop which prints table of 1.

```
public class ForExample
{
   public static void main(String[] args)
   {  //Code of Java for loop
      for(int i=1;i<=10;i++)
      {
         System.out.println(i);
      }
   }
}
```

while Loop

While loop checks the condition first before entering in a loop. If the condition evaluates to true, the statements given inside the while loop get executed.

Syntax
```
while (testExpression)
{  // body of loop
}
```

Here,

1. A while loop evaluates the testExpression inside the parenthesis ().
2. If the testExpression evaluates to true, the code inside the while loop is executed.
3. The testExpression is evaluated again.
4. This process continues until the testExpression is false.
5. When the testExpression evaluates to false, the loop stops.

e.g. Java Program to demonstrate the example of while loop which prints table of 1.

```
public class WhileExample
{
   public static void main(String[] args)
   {
      int i=1;
      while(i<=10)
      {
         System.out.println(i);
         i++;
      }
   }
}
```

do-while Loop

This loop ensures that the complete loop is executed atleast once, then it checks whether the given condition is true or false. If the condition is true then the loop will continue but if the condition is false, the loop will be terminated.

Syntax
```
do
{
   // body of loop
} while(testExpression);
```

Here,

1. The body of the loop is executed at first. Then the testExpression is evaluated.
2. If the testExpression evaluates to true, the body of the loop inside the do statement is executed again.
3. The testExpression is evaluated once again.
4. If the testExpression evaluates to true, the body of the loop inside the do statement is executed again.
5. This process continues until the testExpression evaluates to false. Then the loop stops.

e.g. Java Program to demonstrate the example of do-while loop which prints table of 1.

```
public class DoWhileExample
{
   public static void main(String[] args)
   {
      int i=1;
      do
      {
         System.out.println(i);
         i++;
      }while(i<=10);
   }
}
```

Difference between for loop-while loop-do-while loop

Difference	for Loop	while Loop	do-while Loop
Introduction	for loop in Java iterates a given set of statements multiple times.	The Java while loop executes a set of instructions until a boolean condition is met.	The do-while loop executes a set of statements at least once, even if the condition is not met. After the first execution, it repeats the iteration until the boolean condition is met.
Best time to use	Use it when you know the exact number of times to execute the part of the program.	Use it when you don't know how many times you want the iteration to repeat.	Use it when you don't know how many times you want the iteration to repeat, but it should execute at least one time.

Syntax	`for(init; condition; icr/dcr){`
	`//statements to be repeated`
	`}`
		`while(condition){`
		`//statements to be repeated`
		`}`
			`do{`
			`//statements to be repeated`
			`}while(condition);`

Example	`for(int x=0; x<=5; x++){`
	`System.out.println(x);`
	`}`
		`int x=0;`
		`while(x<=5){`
		`System.out.println(x);`
		`x++;`
		`}`
			`int x=0;`
			`do{`
			`System.out.println(x);`
			`x++;`
			`}while(x<=5);`

Finite and Infinite Loops

A **finite loop** is a loop that runs a specific number of times and then stops. It is commonly used when you know the exact number of iterations needed.

- **Finite for Loop** The for loop runs for a defined number of iterations.
- **Finite while Loop** A while loop runs until a condition becomes false.
- **Finite do-while Loop** A do-while loop runs at least once before checking the condition.

An **infinite loop** is a loop that never stops unless manually interrupted. These loops are useful for long-running processes like servers, game loops, and event listeners.

- **Infinite for Loop** A for loop without a condition runs forever or a loop that always evaluates to be true.
- **Infinite while Loop** A while loop that always evaluates true runs infinitely.
- **Infinite do-while Loop** A do-while loop that always evaluates true also runs infinitely.

Delay in Loops

A delay loop in Java is a programming technique used to introduce a pause or delay in the program's execution. It can serve various purposes, such as controlling the speed of a loop, waiting for a specific condition to be satisfied, or adding a timed interval in the program flow.

e.g.
```
for (int i = 1; i < 100; i++);
                             ↑
delay loop (loop without a body)
```

Multiple Counter Variables

In a loop, typically one counter variable is used to control the number of iterations, but Java allows you to use multiple counter variables to manage different parameters or conditions simultaneously. You can initialize and update multiple counter variables in the loop header.

Initializing Multiple Counter Variables

Multiple counter variables are initialized within the loop's initialization section. You can separate them by a comma.

e.g.
```
for (int i = 0, j = 10; i < 5; i++, j--)
{
  System.out.println("i = " + i + ", j = " + j);
}
```

Updating Multiple Counter Variables

Update multiple variables in the increment/update section of the loop. This allows you to control the progression of each variable separately.

e.g.
```
for (int i = 0, j = 100; i < 5; i++, j -= 10)
{
    System.out.println("i = " + i + ", j = " + j);
}
```

Jump

These are used to transfer control to other parts of the program. These statements can be used to modify the behaviour of conditional and iterative statements. Jump statements allow you to exit a loop, start the next iteration of a loop or explicitly transfer program control to a specified location in your program.

Some jump statements are as follows:

break Statement

This statement is generally used to break the loop or switch statement.

It has three uses:

- It terminates a statement sequence in a switch statement.
- It can be used to exit a loop.
- It can be used as a 'civilised' form of goto statement.

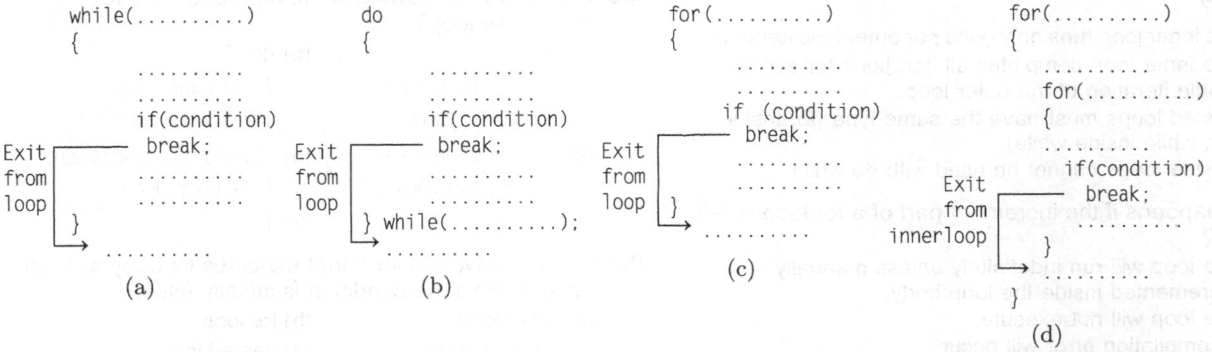

By using break, you can force immediate termination of a loop by passing the conditional expression and any remaining code in the body of the loop. The break statement should be used to cancel a loop only when some sort of special situation occurs.

continue Statement

In Java, continue statement is used to skip the part of loop. Unlike break statement, it does not terminate the loop, instead it skips the remaining part of the loop and controls go back to check the condition again.

continue statement performs below mentioned actions:

- In while and do-while loops, a continue statement causes control to be transferred directly to the conditional expression that controls the loop. i.e. to the next iteration.
- With the break statement, continue may specify a label to describe which enclosing loop to continue.

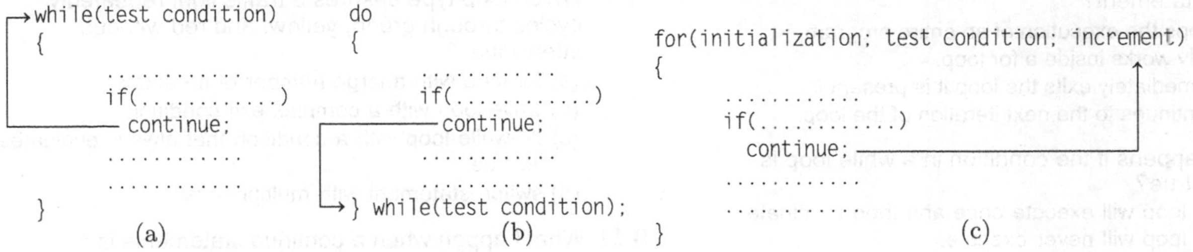

- It is a jumping statement and is used as keyword.
- It skips the loop and re-executes loop with new condition.
- In for loop, continue statement takes control to 'increment' step. i.e. After continue 'i++' will be get executed.

EXAM ORIENTED QUESTIONS

TYPE - 1 — 01 Mark

Multiple Choice Questions

Q.1 What will be the effect of using a return statement inside a loop?

(a) It will terminate only the current iteration of the loop.
(b) It will exit the entire method, stopping all further execution.
(c) It will throw a compilation error.
(d) It will behave the same as a break statement.

Q.2 Which of the following statements about nested loops is true?

(a) The inner loop runs only once per outer loop iteration.
(b) The inner loop completes all iterations for every single iteration of the outer loop.
(c) Nested loops must have the same type (for inside for, while inside while).
(d) Nested loops cannot be used with do-while.

Q.3 What happens if the increment part of a for loop is left empty?

(a) The loop will run indefinitely unless manually incremented inside the loop body.
(b) The loop will not execute.
(c) A compilation error will occur.
(d) Java automatically increments the loop variable.

Q.4 What is the key difference between a while loop and a do-while loop?

(a) A while loop always executes at least once, while a do-while loop may not.
(b) A do-while loop always executes at least once, while a while loop may not.
(c) A while loop uses a counter, but a do-while loop does not.
(d) There is no difference between the two.

Q.5 Which of the following statements is true about the break statement?

(a) It stops the execution of an entire program.
(b) It only works inside a for loop.
(c) It immediately exits the loop it is present in.
(d) It continues to the next iteration of the loop.

Q.6 What happens if the condition in a while loop is always true?

(a) The loop will execute once and then terminate.
(b) The loop will never execute.
(c) The loop will execute indefinitely, causing an infinite loop.
(d) The program will crash immediately.

Q.7

The conveyor belt stops when a specific number of items have passed.

This scenario best represents which type of loop?

(a) for loop (b) while loop
(c) do-while loop (d) Infinite loop

Q.8 Which of the following is the correct syntax for a do-while loop?

(a)
```
do
{ // Loop body
} (condition);
```
(b)
```
do
{ // Loop body
} while (condition);
```
(c)
```
while (condition)
{ // Loop body
} do;
```
(d)
```
do while (condition)
{ // Loop body
};
```

Q.9 Name the type of loop that executes its body at least once, even if the condition is initially false.

(a) while loop (b) for loop
(c) do-while loop (d) nested loop

Q.10

Which loop type ensures a traffic light repeatedly cycles through green, yellow, and red without interruption?

(a) for loop with a large number of iterations
(b) while loop with a complex exit condition
(c) do-while loop with a condition that always evaluates to true
(d) switch statement with multiple cases

Q.11 What happen when a continue statements is encountered inside a loop?

(a) It terminates the loop.
(b) It restarts the loop from the beginning.

(c) It skips the remaining code in the current iteration and jumps to the next iteration.
(d) It stops the program.

Q.12 Which loop should you use when the number of iterations is unknown?

(a) for loop (b) while loop
(c) do-while loop (d) Both (b) and (c)

Q.13 What will happen if the condition in a do-while loop is false during the first iteration?

(a) The loop will not execute at all.
(b) The loop will execute once and then terminate.
(c) The loop will execute indefinitely.
(d) The program will crash.

Q.14 Name the category of loops where the condition is evaluated before executing the loop body, ensuring it may not run at all.

(a) Entry-controlled loop (b) Exit-controlled loop
(c) Post-test loop (d) Infinite loop

Q.15 What is the output of the following code?

```
for (int i = 0; i < 10; i++)
{
  if (i % 3 == 0)
  {
    continue;
  }
  System.out.print(i + " ");
}
```

(a) 0 1 2 3 4 5 6 7 8 9 (b) 1 2 4 5 7 8
(c) 0 3 6 9 (d) 1 2 4 5 7 8

Q.16 What is the output of the following code?

```
int i = 1;
do
{
  System.out.print(i + " ");
  i += 3;
} while (i <= 10);
```

(a) 1 4 7 10 (b) 1 2 3 4 5
(c) 1 4 7 (d) 1 4 7 10 13

Q.17 What will be the output of this while loop?

```
int i = 1;
while (i < 10)
{
  System.out.print(i + " ");
  i *= 2;
}
```

(a) 1 2 4 8 (b) 1 3 5 7 9
(c) 1 2 3 4 5 (d) Infinite loop

Q.18 What will be the final value of x after executing this loop?

```
int x = 1;
for (int i = 1; i <= 5; i++)
{
  x *= i;
}
System.out.println(x);
```

(a) 5 (b) 15
(c) 120 (d) 25

Q.19 Give the output of the following

```
int v = 5;
while (--v >= 0)
{
  System.out.print(v);
}
```

(a) 43210 (b) 54321
(c) 543210 (d) 4321

Q.20 Name the loop control statement that can be used to exit not just a loop, but also switch statements.

(a) continue (b) return
(c) jump (d) break

Q.21 Name the loop control statement that allows skipping the remaining statements in the current iteration and jumps to the next cycle of the loop.

(a) break (b) return
(c) jump (d) continue

Q.22 Name the type of loop that continuously executes without termination due to an always-true condition or missing an exit condition.

(a) delay loop (b) finite loop
(c) while loop (d) Infinite loop

Q.23

The person wants to stop searching as soon as they find the book. Which control flow statement would be most appropriate to use within the loop?

(a) continue (b) break
(c) return (d) throw

Q.24 Name the type of loop in Java that allows multiple counter variables to be declared, initialized, and updated within its loop header.

(a) while loop (b) do-while loop
(c) nested loop (d) for loop

Q.25 Name the component of a for loop that executes once at the start, before the loop condition is checked.

(a) condition (b) increment
(c) initialization (d) loop body

Q.26

To achieve the one-second delay between each number in the countdown, which of the following techniques would likely be used?

(a) Nested loops
(b) A sleep() or delay() function within the loop
(c) A very fast for loop
(d) Multiple counter variables

Q.27 Name the loop type where the loop body is executed at least once before checking the condition, ensuring minimum execution.

(a) entry-controlled loop (b) pretest loop
(c) delay loop (d) Exit-controlled loop

Q.28

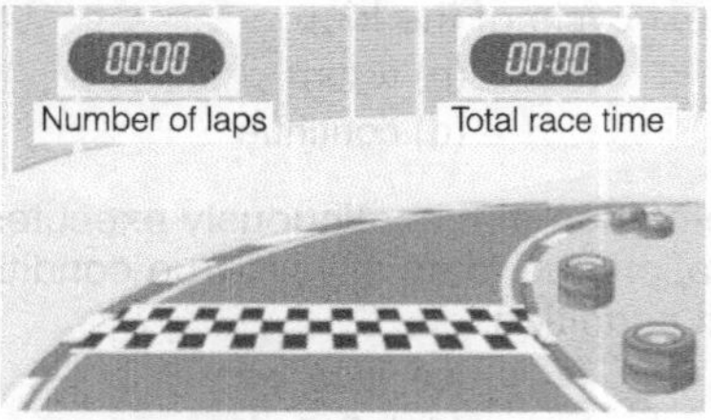

Why is it necessary to use multiple counter variables in this scenario?

(a) To increase the speed of the loop
(b) To track independent but related values within the loop
(c) To ensure the loop executes only once
(d) To create a more complex loop structure

Q.29 Name the type of loop best suited for situations where the number of iterations is predetermined before execution begins.

(a) while loop (b) do-while loop
(c) nested loop (d) for loop

Q.30

The process repeats until a specific number of sheets are baked.

This scenario best represents which type of loop?

(a) while loop (b) do-while loop
(c) for loop (d) Infinite loop

Answers

1. (b)	**2.** (b)	**3.** (a)	**4.** (b)	**5.** (c)
6. (c)	**7.** (b)	**8.** (b)	**9.** (c)	**10.** (c)
11. (c)	**12.** (d)	**13.** (b)	**14.** (a)	**15.** (d)
16. (a)	**17.** (a)	**18.** (c)	**19.** (a)	**20.** (d)
21. (d)	**22.** (d)	**23.** (b)	**24.** (d)	**25.** (c)
26. (b)	**27.** (d)	**28.** (c)	**29.** (d)	**30.** (c)

TYPE - 2

01 Mark

Statement Based Questions

Q.1 A data analyst is tasked with processing a series of daily sales records. They need to analyze the data and perform certain calculations on each day's sales. Which of the following statements about using loops in this scenario are true?

A. A loop is essential to iterate through each day's sales record and perform the required calculations.
B. Using a while loop would be ideal if the analyst knows the exact number of days in advance.
C. A for loop is most appropriate when the analyst knows the number of days they need to process.
D. A do-while loop guarantees that the calculations will be performed at least once, even if there are no sales records.

(a) Only A and C (b) Only B and D
(c) Only A, C, and D (d) All of these

Q.2 Consider the following loop-related code snippets. Which of these are correctly written for or while loops?

A. `for (int i = 0; i < 10; i++) { ... }`
B. `while (condition) { ... }`
C. `for (int i = 0, j = 10; i < 5, j > 5; i++, j--) { ... }`
D. `while; { ... }`

(a) Only A and B (b) Only C and D
(c) Only A, B, and C (d) All of these

Q.3 Which of the following code snippets demonstrate a valid do-while loop and the use of jump statements?

A. `do { ... } while (condition);`
B. `while (condition) { ... }`
C. `for (int i = 0; i < 10; i++) { break; }`
D. `do { continue; } while (condition);`

(a) Only A and B (b) Only A, C, and D
(c) Only B and C (d) All of these

Q.4 Which of the following code snippets demonstrate valid loop variations or inter-conversions?

A. `for (int i = 0, j = 10; i < 5; i++, j--) { ... }`
B. `int i = 0; while (i < 5) { ... i++; }`

C. `do { ... } while (false);`

D. `for (int i = 5; i < 0; i--) { ... }`

(a) Only A and B (b) Only A, B, and C
(c) Only B and D (d) All of these

Q.5 Consider the following steps involved in the execution of a while loop with a break statement. Choose the correct order of the steps:

A. The condition of the while loop is evaluated.
B. The break statement is encountered.
C. The loop body is executed.
D. The loop terminates.

(a) A, C, B, D (b) C, A, B, D
(c) A, B, C, D (d) B, A, C, D

Q.6 Consider the following steps involved in converting a for loop to a while loop. Choose the correct order of the steps:

A. Initialize the loop counter variable outside the while loop.
B. Copy the for loop's condition into the while loop's condition.
C. Copy the for loop's update statement into the while loop's body.
D. Write the while loop's header and body.

(a) B, A, C, D (b) A, B, D, C
(c) A, D, B, C (d) D, A, C, B

Q.7 Consider the following steps involved in using multiple counter variables in a for loop. Choose the correct order of the steps:

A. Declare and initialize the multiple counter variables in the for loop's initialization.
B. Write the loop's condition using the counter variables.
C. Write the loop's body.
D. Update the counter variables in the for loop's update statement.

(a) A, B, C, D (b) B, A, D, C
(c) C, A, D, B (d) D, C, B, A

Answers

1. (c) 2. (c) 3. (b) 4. (d) 5. (a)
6. (b) 7. (a)

TYPE - 3 — 01 Mark

Assertion-Reason Type Questions

Directions (Q. Nos. 1-10) The following questions are Assertion-Reason based questions. Choose the answer based on the code given below

(a) Both Assertion (A) and Reason (R) are true and Reason (R) is a correct explanation of Assertion (A).
(b) Both Assertion (A) and Reason (R) are true and Reason (R) is not a correct explanation of Assertion (A).
(c) Assertion (A) is true and Reason (R) is false.
(d) Assertion (A) is false and Reason (R) is true.

Q.1 Assertion (A) The for loop is an entry-controlled loop.

Reason (R) In a for loop, the condition is checked before the execution of the loop body.

Ans. (a) The for loop is an entry-controlled loop, meaning the condition is checked before executing the loop body, and Reason (R) explains this behavior correctly. Hence, Both A and R are true and R is the correct explanation for A.

Q.2 Assertion (A) The do-while loop is an exit-controlled loop.

Reason (R) In a do-while loop, the condition is evaluated after the loop body executes.

Ans. (a) The do-while loop is an exit-controlled loop because the loop body is executed at least once before checking the condition, which makes Reason (R) the correct explanation for Assertion (A). Hence, Both A and R are true and R is the correct explanation for A.

Q.3 Assertion (A) The break statement terminates the entire loop.

Reason (R) When the break statement is executed, the program control moves to the statement immediately after the loop.

Ans. (a) The break statement exits the loop prematurely, and the control moves outside the loop, as Reason (R) correctly explains. Hence, Both A and R are true and R is the correct explanation for A.

Q.4 Assertion (A) The continue statement skips the current iteration and moves to the next iteration.

Reason (R) The continue statement stops the execution of the current iteration and proceeds to the next iteration.

Ans. (a) The continue statement skips the remaining code in the current iteration and moves to the next iteration, which matches Reason (R). Hence, Both A and R are true and R is the correct explanation for A.

Q.5 Assertion (A) A while loop can be converted into a for loop.

Reason (R) Both while and for loops are entry-controlled and can be interconverted with proper initialization and update.

Ans. (b) While both while and for loops are entry-controlled, the conversion is based on managing the initialization, condition, and update in a single for statement. However, the Reason does not explain the full mechanics of converting between them. Hence, Both A and R are true and R is not the correct explanation for A.

Q.6 Assertion (A) An infinite loop has no termination condition.

Reason (R) Infinite loops run indefinitely because the termination condition is never met.

Ans. (a) Infinite loops lack a condition that can stop them, so they run indefinitely. Hence, Both A and R are true and R is the correct explanation for A.

Q.7 Assertion (A) Multiple counter variables can be used in a for loop.

Reason (R) In a for loop, multiple variables can be initialized and updated using commas.

Ans. (a) Java allows multiple counters in a for loop by using commas for initialization and update, making Reason (R) the correct explanation for Assertion (A). Hence, Both A and R are true and R is the correct explanation for A.

Q.7 Assertion (A) The do-while loop guarantees at least one execution of the loop body.

Reason (R) The condition in a do-while loop is evaluated after the loop body executes.

Ans. (a) The do-while loop guarantees the execution of the loop body at least once, and this behavior is explained correctly by Reason (R). Hence, Both A and R are true and R is the correct explanation for A.

Q.9 Assertion (A) A finite loop has a well-defined stopping condition.

Reason (R) Finite loops terminate after a specific number of iterations.

Ans. (b) Finite loops have a well-defined stopping condition, but they may not always be related to a "specific number of iterations" — the condition could be a logical expression that eventually evaluates to false. Hence, Both A and R are true and R is not the correct explanation for A.

Q.10 Assertion (A) The continue statement can be used in nested loops.

Reason (R) The continue statement only affects the innermost loop in which it is placed.

Ans. (a) The continue statement skips the current iteration of the innermost loop, and Reason (R) provides the correct explanation for Assertion (A). Hence, Both A and R are true and R is the correct explanation for A.

TYPE - 4

01 Mark

Odd One Out

Q.1 Find the Odd One Out

(a) for loop (b) while loop
(c) do-while loop (d) switch-case

Ans. (d) switch-case (switch-case is a decision-making statement, whereas the others are looping constructs used for iteration.)

Q.2 Find the Odd One Out

(a) Entry-controlled loop (b) Exit-controlled loop
(c) Infinite loop (d) Recursion

Ans. (d) Recursion (Recursion is a function-based approach to iteration, whereas the other options represent different types of looping constructs)

Q.3 Find the Odd One Out

(a) break (b) continue
(c) return (d) += operator

Ans. (d) += operator (The first three (break, continue, return) are control flow statements, whereas += is an arithmetic assignment operator used for updating values.)

Q.4 Find the Odd One Out

(a) Initialization (b) Condition
(c) Increment (d) Function Call

Ans. (d) Function Call (The first three are essential parts of a loop, whereas a function call is not directly related to loop execution.)

Q.5 Find the Odd One Out

(a) for (; ;) (b) while (true)
(c) do { } while (true); (d) if-else

Ans. (d) if-else (The first three are infinite loops, whereas if-else is a conditional statement that does not iterate.)

Q.6 Find the Odd One Out

(a) i++ (b) i-- (c) ++i (d) break

Ans. (d) break (The first three are increment/decrement operators, whereas break is a control statement used to exit a loop.)

TYPE - 5

01 Mark

Very Short Answer Type Questions

Q.1 How does using multiple counter variables in a for loop affect performance?

Ans. It can reduce redundant loops, improving efficiency when tracking multiple values.

Q.2 What will happen if you place a semicolon (;) immediately after the condition in a while loop?

Ans. It creates an empty loop, causing infinite execution if the condition is always true.

Q.3 Can a for loop run indefinitely without using a condition? If yes, how?

Ans. Yes, a for loop can run indefinitely by omitting all expressions:

```
for (;;)
{
  System.out.println("Infinite Loop");
}
```

Q.4 **How does Java handle loop termination internally in terms of bytecode execution?**

Ans. Java uses conditional branch instructions (goto, if_icmp, ifeq, etc.) in its bytecode to determine when to jump out of a loop.

Q.5 **What is the major difference between while(true) and for(;;) in terms of execution?**

Ans. There is no difference at runtime; both generate an infinite loop. However, for(;;) is more compact and idiomatic for infinite loops.

Q.6 **Can a while loop execute zero times? If yes, under what condition?**

Ans. Yes, if the loop condition is false initially, the while loop will never execute.

Q.7 **Identify the issue in the following loop and correct it:**

```
int i = 0;
while (i < 5)
   System.out.println(i);
   i++;
```

Ans. Error: The i++ statement is outside the loop due to missing {}.

Corrected Code

```
int i = 0;
while (i < 5)
{
   System.out.println(i);
   i++;
}
```

Q.8 **What is the difference between return and break inside a loop?**

Ans. break exits the loop, but execution continues with the next statement outside the loop.

return exits the entire method, stopping further execution.

TYPE - 6 (2 Marks)

Short Answer Type Questions

Q.1 **Explain how multiple counter variables can be used in a for loop with an example.**

Ans. In Java, a for loop can have multiple counter variables initialized and updated together using commas.

Example:

```
for (int i = 1, j = 10; i <= 5 && j >= 5; i++, j--)
{
   System.out.println("i: " + i + ", j: " + j);
}
```

Here, i increases while j decreases in each iteration.

Q.2 **Can a for loop work without an initialization, condition, or update statement? Justify with an example.**

Ans. Yes, a for loop can work without any of its three components, resulting in an infinite loop:

```
for (;;)
{
   System.out.println("Infinite Loop");
}
```

The loop runs indefinitely because no condition is provided to terminate it.

Only an explicit break statement or an external condition (like user input) can stop it.

Q.3 **In which scenarios is a while loop more efficient than a for loop, and why?**

Ans. A while loop is more efficient when the number of iterations is unknown at runtime because it only checks a logical condition rather than relying on a counter.

It is preferred for waiting mechanisms (e.g., waiting for user input, reading from a file, checking network responses) where termination depends on an external event rather than a fixed iteration count.

Q.4 **Predict and explain the output of the following do-while loop:**

```
int x = 5;
do {
   System.out.println("Value of x: " + x);
   x--;
} while (x > 5);
```

Ans. **Output**

Value of x: 5

Explanation

- The do-while loop executes at least once, regardless of the condition.
- Even though x > 5 is false initially, the loop body executes once, printing "Value of x: 5", before terminating.

Q.5 **What are some real-world applications of the do-while loop, and why is it preferred in those cases?**

Ans.

- **User Input Validation** Ensures a valid input is entered at least once before rechecking conditions.
- **Menu-driven Programs** Used in console-based applications where a menu should appear at least once before checking for exit conditions.
- **Retry Mechanisms** Used in network requests or database connections that need at least one attempt before checking for failure.
- **File Reading** Ensures a file is read at least once before verifying if there's more data to process.

Q.6 What happens if a break statement is used inside a for loop that contains multiple counter variables?

Ans. The break statement exits the loop entirely, stopping updates for all counter variables, even if only one condition required termination.

Example

```
for (int i = 0, j = 10; i <= 5 && j >= 5; i++, j--)
{
  if (i == 3) break;
  System.out.println("i: " + i + ", j: " + j);
}
```

Output

i: 0, j: 10
i: 1, j: 9
i: 2, j: 8

The loop terminates when i == 3, skipping all further iterations.

Q.7 Analyze the given program segment and answer the following questions.?

```
for (int m = 5; m <= 20; m += 5)
{
  if (m % 3 == 0)
    break;
  else if (m % 5 == 0)
    System.out.println(m);
  continue;
}
```

(i) Write the output of the program segment.

(ii) How many times does the body of the loop get executed?

Ans. (i) **Output**

5
10

(ii) **Execution Count**: Three times the body of the loop will be executed.

Q.8 What is an infinite loop? Write an infinite loop statement.

Ans. An infinite loop is one in which the iteration never stops. This is because the condition output is always true; the loop continues an infinite number of times. e.g., entry-controlled loop.

```
int a=0;
for(a=10; a>0; a++)
{
  System.out.println("The value of a="+a);
}
```

In the above example, the 'for' loop will check condition first and as the initial values of a (i.e. 10) is greater than 0 so it will execute once.

Next time, the loop will increase the value of a by 1 and the condition will again evaluated. This process will be repeated again and again and the loop will execute infinite times.

TYPE - 7   2 Marks

Differentiate

Q.1 For Loop and While Loop

Ans.

For Loop	While Loop
It is used when the number of iterations is known.	It is used when the number of iterations is unknown.
Initialization, condition, and increment are part of the loop header.	Only the condition is in the header; initialization and increment happen separately.
It is more suitable for counter-controlled loops.	It is more suitable for condition-based loops.
Example: for (int i = 0; i < 5; i++)	Example: while (i < 5) { i++; }

Q.2 Break and Continue

Ans.

Break	Continue
It terminates the loop immediately.	It skips the current iteration and moves to the next iteration.
It is used when an immediate exit from the loop is required.	It is used to skip certain values while continuing the loop.

Q.3 Entry-Controlled Loop and Exit-Controlled Loop

Ans.

Entry-Controlled Loop	Exit-Controlled Loop
Condition is checked before executing the loop body.	Condition is checked after executing the loop body.
If the condition is false initially, the loop body does not execute.	The loop body executes at least once before checking the condition.
Examples: for loop, while loop	Example: do-while loop

Q.4 Finite Loop and Infinite Loop

Ans.

Finite Loop	Infinite Loop
It executes for a fixed number of iterations.	It runs indefinitely unless explicitly terminated.
It has a well-defined termination condition.	It lacks a proper termination condition or updates incorrectly.

Q.5 Do-while Loop and While Loop

Ans.

Do-while Loop	While Loop
It executes the loop body at least once.	It may not execute at all if the condition is false initially.
Condition is checked after executing the loop body.	Condition is checked before executing the loop body.
It is used when at least one iteration is required.	It is used when iterations depend on an initial condition.

TYPE - 8   2 Marks

Output Based Questions

Q.1 Predict the output of the following code snippet:

```
public class LoopExample {
   public static void main(String[] args) {
      int count = 0;
      while (count < 10) {
         count += 2;
         if (count == 6) {
            break;
         }
         System.out.print(count + " ");
      }
   }
}
```

Ans. Output

2 4

Q.2 Predict the output of the following code snippet:

```
public class LoopExample
{
   public static void main(String[] args)
   {
      int num = 5;
      do
      {
         System.out.print(num + " ");
         num--;
      } while (num > 0);
   }
}
```

Ans. Output

5 4 3 2 1

Q.3 Write the output of the following Java code snippets:

```
for (int j = 5; j > 0; j--) {
(a) if (j == 3)
    {
       continue;
    }
    System.out.print(j + " ");
    }
(b) if (j == 0)
    {
       System.out.println("\nLoop finished with j
                                            = 0");
    }
    else
    {
       System.out.println("\nLoop did not finish
                                     with j = 0");
    }
```

Ans. (a) **Output**

5 4 2 1

(b) **Output**

Loop finished with j = 0

Q.4 Write the output of the following Java code snippets:

```
int num = 2;
(a) do
    {
       System.out.print(num + " ");
       num += 2;
    } while (num < 8);
(b) if (num == 8)
    {
       System.out.println("\nLoop finished with
                                        num = 8");
    }
    else
    {
       System.out.println("\nLoop did not finish
                                   with num = 8");
    }
```

Ans. (a) **Output**

2 4 6

(b) **Output**

Loop finished with num = 8

Q.5 Determine the number of iterations and the final value of sum after the following code snippet executes.

```
int i = 5;
int sum = 0;
while (i > 0)
{
   sum += i;
   i -= 2;
}
System.out.println("Iterations: " +
                             /* Insert answer here */);
System.out.println("Final sum: " +
                             /* Insert answer here */);
```

Ans. Output

Iterations: 3

Final sum: 9

Q.6 How many times will the loop execute, and what will be the output of the following code?

```
int count = 1;
do
{
   System.out.println("Value: " + count);
   count *= 2;
} while (count < 10);
```

```
System.out.println("Loop executed " +
    /* Insert answer here */ + " times.");
```

Ans. Output

Value: 1

Value: 2

Value: 4

Value: 8

Loop executed 4 times.

TYPE - 9 (2 Marks)

Convert the Code

Q.1 Convert the following while loop into an equivalent for loop.

```
int num = 1;
while (num <= 10)
{
    System.out.print(num + " ");
    num += 2;
}
```

Ans. Converted for loop:

```
for (int num = 1; num <= 10; num += 2)
{
    System.out.print(num + " ");
}
```

Q.2 Convert the following for loop into an equivalent do-while loop.

```
int a = 10;
int b = 1;
for (int i = 0; i < 5; i++)
{
    b = a - b;
    if (b < 0)
    {
        b = -b;
    }
    System.out.println("Iteration " + i + ": b = " + b);
}
```

Ans. Converted do-while loop:

```
int a = 10;
int b = 1;
int i = 0;
do {
    b = a - b;
    if (b < 0)
    {
        b = -b;
    }
    System.out.println("Iteration " + i + ": b = " + b);
    i++;
} while (i < 5);
```

Q.3 Convert the following do-while loop into an equivalent while loop.

```
int x = 1;
int y = 10;
boolean condition = true;
do
{
    x += 2;
    y -= 1;
    if (x > y)
    {
        condition = false;
    }
    System.out.println("x: " + x + ", y: " + y);
} while (condition);
```

Ans. Converted while loop:

```
int x = 1;
int y = 10;
boolean condition = true;
while (condition)
{
    x += 2;
    y -= 1;
    if (x > y)
    {
        condition = false;
    }
    System.out.println("x: " + x + ", y: " + y);
}
```

Q.4 Convert the following for loop into a while loop.

```
int n = 4;
int result = 1;
for (int i = 1; i <= n; i++)
{
    result *= i * 2;
    System.out.println("Iteration " + i + ": result
                                   = " + result);
}
```

Ans. Converted while loop:

```
int n = 4;
int result = 1;
int i = 1;
while (i <= n)
{
    result *= i * 2;
    System.out.println("Iteration " + i + ": result
                                   = " + result);
    i++;
}
```

Q.5 Convert the following do-while loop into a for loop.

```
int i = 1;
int d = 5;
do
```

```
{
   d = d * 2;
   System.out.println(d);
   i++;
} while (i <= 5);
```

Ans.
```
for (int i = 1, d = 5; i <= 5; i++)
{
   d = d * 2;
   System.out.println(d);
}
```

TYPE - 10 15 Mark

Long Answer Type Questions

Q.1 Write a program in Java to check whether a number is prime.

Ans.
```
import java.util.Scanner;
public class PrimeCheck
{
   public static void main(String[] args)
   {
      Scanner sc = new Scanner(System.in);
      System.out.print("Enter a number: ");
      int num = sc.nextInt();
      boolean isPrime = true;
      if (num <= 1)
      {
         isPrime = false;
      }
      else
      {
         for (int i = 2; i <= num / 2; i++)
         {
            if (num % i == 0)
            {
               isPrime = false;
               break;
            }
         }
      }
      if (isPrime)
      {
         System.out.println(num + " is a prime
                                        number.");
      }
      else
      {
         System.out.println(num + " is not a prime
                                        number.");
      }
      sc.close();
   }
}
```

Q.2 Write a program in Java to print Fibonacci Series.

Ans.
```
import java.util.Scanner;
public class FibonacciSeries
{
   public static void main(String[] args)
   {
      Scanner sc = new Scanner(System.in);
      System.out.print("Enter the number of terms: ");
      int n = sc.nextInt();
      int first = 0, second = 1, next;
      System.out.print("Fibonacci Series: "
                         + first + ", " + second);
      int count = 2; // First two numbers are
                                 already printed
      while (count < n)
      {
         next = first + second;
         System.out.print(", " + next);
         first = second;
         second = next;
         count++;
      }
      sc.close();
   }
}
```

Q.3 Write a program in Java to print numbers in reverse order.

Ans.
```
import java.util.Scanner;
public class ReverseNumbers
{
   public static void main(String[] args)
   {
      Scanner sc = new Scanner(System.in);
      System.out.print("Enter a positive number: ");
      int num = sc.nextInt();
      System.out.println("Numbers in reverse order:");
      do
      {
         System.out.println(num);
         num--;
      } while (num > 0);
      sc.close();
   }
}
```

Q.4 Write a program in Java to print even and odd Numbers separately.

Ans.
```
import java.util.Scanner;
public class EvenOddSeparation
{
   public static void main(String[] args)
```

```java
    {
        Scanner sc = new Scanner(System.in);
        System.out.print("Enter the range (1 to N): ");
        int n = sc.nextInt();
        System.out.println("Even Numbers:");
        for (int i = 1; i <= n; i++)
        {
          if (i % 2 != 0) continue;
          System.out.print(i + " ");
        }
        System.out.println("\nOdd Numbers:");
        for (int i = 1; i <= n; i++)
        {
          if (i % 2 == 0) continue;
          System.out.print(i + " ");
        }
         sc.close();
    }
}
```

Q.5 **Write a program in Java to find the sum of digits of a number.**

Ans.
```java
import java.util.Scanner;
public class SumOfDigits
{
    public static void main(String[] args)
    {
        Scanner sc = new Scanner(System.in);
        System.out.print("Enter a number: ");
        int num = sc.nextInt();
        int sum = 0;
        while (num > 0)
        {
          sum += num % 10;
          num /= 10;
        }
        System.out.println("Sum of digits: " + sum);
        sc.close();
    }
}
```

Q.6 **Write a program in Java to find the factorial of a number.**

Ans.
```java
import java.util.Scanner;
public class ForLoopFactorial
{
    public static void main(String[] args)
    {
        Scanner scanner = new Scanner(System.in);
        System.out.print("Enter a number to find
                                  its factorial: ");
        int num = scanner.nextInt();
        long factorial = 1;
        for (int i = 1; i <= num; i++)
        {
          factorial *= i;
        }
        System.out.println("The factorial of "
                                  + num + " is " + factorial);
    }
}
```

Q.7 **Write a program in Java to check whether a numbered is palindrome or not.**

Ans.
```java
import java.util.Scanner;
public class DoWhilePalindrome
{
    public static void main(String[] args)
    {
        Scanner scanner = new Scanner(System.in);
        System.out.print("Enter a number to check
                                  if it's a palindrome: ");
        int num = scanner.nextInt();
        int originalNum = num;
        int reversedNum = 0;
        do
        {
          int digit = num % 10;
          reversedNum = reversedNum * 10 + digit;
          num /= 10;
        } while (num != 0);
        if (originalNum == reversedNum)
        {
          System.out.println(originalNum + " is a
                                  Palindrome.");
        }
        else
        {
          System.out.println(originalNum + " is not a
                                  Palindrome.");
        }
    }
}
```

Q.8 **Write a program to input any 5 numbers (including positive and negative). Perform the following tasks:**
(a) Count the positive numbers
(c) Sum of positive numbers
(b) Count the negative numbers
(d) Sum of negative numbers

Ans.
```java
import java.util.Scanner;
public class ProgIntegers
{
    public static void main(String args[])
    {
        Scanner in = new Scanner(System.in);
```

```java
        int pSum = 0, pCount = 0, nSum = 0, nCount = 0;
        System.out.println("Enter 5 numbers:");
        for (int i = 1; i <= 5; i++)
         {
           int n = in.nextInt();
           if (n >= 0)
           {
              pSum += n;
              pCount++;
           }
           else
           {
             nSum += n;
             nCount++;
           }
        }
        System.out.println("Positive Count = " + pCount);
        System.out.println("Positive Sum = " + pSum);
        System.out.println("Negative Count = " + nCount);
        System.out.println("Negative Sum = " + nSum);
        in.close();
    }
}
```

Q.9 Write a program to enter any 5 numbers and check whether they are divisible by 5 or not. If divisible then perform the following tasks:

(a) Display all the numbers ending with the digit 5.

(b) Count those numbers ending with 0 (zero).

Ans.

```java
import java.util.Scanner;
public class DivisibleByFive
{
   public static void main(String[] args)
   {
      Scanner in = new Scanner(System.in);
      int countZero = 0;
      int countFive = 0;
      int[] numbers = new int[5];
      System.out.println("Enter 5 numbers:");
      for (int i = 0; i < 5; i++)
       {
         numbers[i] = in.nextInt();
       }
      for (int num : numbers)
       {
         if (num % 5 == 0)
          {
           if (num % 10 == 5)
            {
              System.out.println(num + " ends
                                        with 5.");
              countFive++;
            }
           if (num % 10 == 0)
            {
              countZero++;
            }
          }
       }
      System.out.println("Count of numbers ending
                                   with 0: " + countZero);
      in.close();
   }
}
```

Q.10 Write a program to input a number and display the new number after reversing the digits of the original number. The program also displays the absolute difference between the original number and the reversed number.

Sample Input: 194

Sample Output: 491

Absolute Difference- 297

Ans.

```java
import java.util.Scanner;
public class ReverseNumber
{
  public static void main(String args[])
  {
    Scanner in = new Scanner(System.in);
    System.out.print("Enter a number: ");
    int originalNumber = in.nextInt();
    int reversedNumber = 0;
    int tempNumber = originalNumber;
    while (tempNumber != 0)
    {
      int digit = tempNumber % 10;
      reversedNumber = reversedNumber * 10 + digit;
      tempNumber = tempNumber / 10;
    }
    int absoluteDifference =
        Math.abs(originalNumber - reversedNumber);
    System.out.println("Reversed Number: "
                               + reversedNumber);
    System.out.println("Absolute Difference: "
                               + absoluteDifference);
    in.close();
  }
}
```

09

NESTED LOOP

A nested loop in Java is a loop inside another loop. The inner loop executes completely for each iteration of the outer loop. This structure is often used in problems involving multidimensional data, pattern printing, and matrix operations.

Structure of Nested Loop

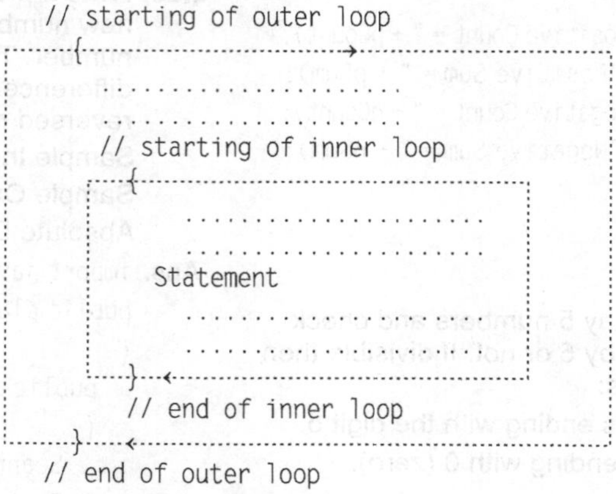

Types of Nested Loops

- Nested for loop
- Nested while loop
- Nested do while loop

In this chapter , we will discuss only nested for loop.

Nested for Loop

When a for loop is used within another for loop, is called a nested for loop.

Syntax

```
for (initialization; condition; increment/decrement)
{
   //Outer loop code
   for (initialization; condition; increment/decrement)
   {
      // Inner loop code
   }
   //Outer loop continuation
}
```

e.g.

```
public class NestedForLoopExample
{
   public static void main(String[] args)
   {
      int rows = 4;  // Number of rows
      int columns = 5;  // Number of columns
      // Outer loop (for rows)
```

REVISION NOTES

```
        for (int i = 1; i <= rows; i++)
        {
          // Inner loop (for columns)
          for (int j = 1; j <= columns; j++)
           {
             System.out.print("* "); // Print star
           }
          System.out.println(); // Move to the next line after one row is printed
        }
      }
    }
```

Output

```
* * * * *
* * * * *
* * * * *
* * * * *
```

break Statement in a Nested Loop

This statement is used for unusual termination of a block .As soon as, the break statement is invoked, the control will come out of the block by ignoring rest of the statements. The break statement can be used in the inner loop as well as in the outer loop.

Use of break Statement in the Outer Loop

The example illustrates the use of break statement in the outer loop:

```
int i,j;
 for(i=1;i<=5;i++)
 {
   for(j=1;j<=3;j++)
   {
     System.out.println(i*j);
   }
   if(i> 2)
   break;
  System.out.println("****");
}
Exits the outer loop
```

Use of break Statement in the Inner Loop

This example illustrates the use of break in the inner loop.

```
int i,j;
for(i=1;i<=5;i++)
{
  for(j=1;j<=3;j++)
  {
    System.out.println(i*j);
    if(i*j> 8)
    break;
  }
Exits the inner loop
}
```

Labelled break Statement

Sometimes, it may happen that the requirement of the user is fulfilled during the iteration of the inner loop and statements in the outer loop should not be executed further. Labelled break statement will be helpful to serve this purpose. The termination of outer loop from the block of inner loop can be done by using keyword 'break' along with a label (say, 'outer') as in the illustration shown below:

```
int i,j;
outer:
for(i=1;i<=5;i++)
{
  for(j=1;j<=3;j++)
  {
    System.out.println(i*j);
   if(j ==2)
   break outer;
  }
}
Exits the outer loop
```

continue Statement in Nested Loop

Like break statement, you can also use 'continue' statement in the nested loop to get your task done. As soon as, the control reaches to 'continue', it takes the control to the next iteration by ignoring rest of the statements.

continue Statement used in Inner Loop

Here, you can notice when the control reaches 'continue', it immediately takes the control to the next iteration of the inner loop by ignoring remaining statements of the inner block.

In the example shown below, the 'continue' statement is used in the inner loop.

```
int i,j;
for(i=1;i<=5;i++)
{
   for(j=1;j<=3;j++)
   {
      if(i*j > 10)
      continue;
       System.out.print(i*j+" ");
   }
}
```

continue Statement used in Outer Loop

When 'continue' is used in the outer loop then the control returns to the next iteration by ignoring rest part of the statements. An example is illustrated below to show the use of 'continue' statement in the outer loop.

```
int i,j;
for(i=1;i<=5;i++)
 {
   if(i== 2)
   continue;
   for(j=1;j<=3;j++)
   {
     System.out.print(i*j+" ");
   }
}
```

Labelled continue Statement

Labelled continue is a situation where you can skip the iterations of the inner loop. This task can be done by using the keyword 'continue outer' in the inner loop by ignoring the rest of the statements.

```
int i,j;
outer:
for(i=1;i<=5;i++)
{
   for(j=1;j<=3;j++)
   {
      if(i%2==0)
      continue outer;
    System.out.print(i*j+" ");
  }
}
```

Program based on Nested Loops

Write a program to produce a rectangular pattern

```
public class NestedLoopExample
{
   public static void main(String[] args)
    {
      for (int i = 1; i <= 5; i++)
        { // Outer loop (controls rows)
          for (int j = 1; j <= 5; j++)
          { // Inner loop (controls columns)
              System.out.print("* ");
          }
          System.out.println();
          // Moves to the next line after inner loop
        }
    }
}
```

Output

```
* * * * *
* * * * *
* * * * *
* * * * *
* * * * *
```

Write a program to produce a right-angled triangle pattern

```
public class TrianglePattern
{
   public static void main(String[] args)
    {
      for (int i = 1; i <= 5; i++)
        { // Outer loop (rows)
          for (int j = 1; j <= i; j++)
          { // Inner loop (columns)
              System.out.print("* ");
          }
          System.out.println();
        }
    }
}
```

Output

```
*
* *
* * *
* * * *
* * * * *
```

Series involving single variable

A single-variable series is a sequence of numbers or terms that follow a defined pattern, where each term is represented using a single variable.

Examples:

Arithmetic Series (Linear Growth)

Formula: $an=a+(n-1)d$

Code

```
public class ArithmeticSeries
{
    public static void main(String args[])
    {
        int a = 2, d = 3, n = 10;
        for (int i = 0; i < n; i++)
        {
            System.out.print(a + (i * d) + " ");
        }
    }
}
```

Output 2 5 8 11 14 17 20 23 26 29

Geometric Series (Exponential Growth)

Formula: $an=a\times r(n-1)$

Code

```
public class GeometricSeries
{
    public static void main(String args[])
    {
        int a = 2, r = 3, n = 10;
        for (int i = 0; i < n; i++)
        {
            System.out.print(a * (int)Math.pow(r, i) + " ");
        }
    }
}
```

Output 2 6 18 54 162 486 1458 4374 13122 39366

Factorial Series

Formula: $n=n\times(n-1)\times(n-2)\times...\times1$

Code

```
public class FactorialSeries
{
    public static void main(String args[])
    {
        int n = 10; // Number of terms
        int fact = 1;
        for (int i = 1; i <= n; i++)
        {
            fact *= i;
            System.out.print(fact + " ");
        }
    }
}
```

Output: 1 2 6 24 120 720 5040 40320 362880 3628800

EXAM ORIENTED QUESTIONS

TYPE - 1 (01 Mark)

Multiple Choice Questions

Q.1 What is the main drawback of using nested loops in Java?
(a) They reduce the readability of the code
(b) They always produce incorrect output
(c) They decrease code reusability
(d) They increase time complexity significantly

Q.2 Which statement best describes the execution of nested loops?
(a) The inner loop executes only once per outer loop iteration
(b) The outer loop executes completely before the inner loop starts
(c) The inner loop executes completely for each iteration of the outer loop
(d) The inner loop executes a fixed number of times regardless of the outer loop

Q.3 What will be the output of the following nested loop?

```
for (int i = 1; i <= 3; i++)
{
   for (int j = 1; j <= 3; j++)
   {
         System.out.print(i * j + " ");
   }
   System.out.println();
}
```

(a) 1 2 3 2 4 6 3 6 9
(b) 1 2 3
2 4 6
3 6 9
(c) 1 1 1
2 2 2
3 3 3
(d) 1 2 3 4 5 6 7 8 9

Q.4

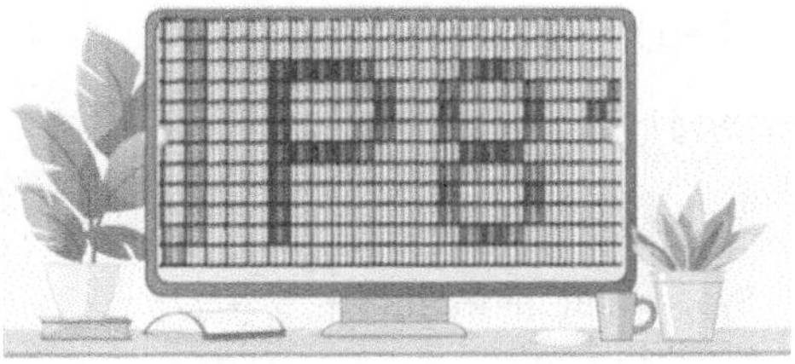

This scenario, where each pixel in a rectangular grid is processed sequentially, best represents which programming construct?
(a) A single for loop
(b) Nested for loops
(c) A while loop
(d) A do-while loop

Q.5 Why are nested loops useful in programming?
(a) To execute the outer loop repeatedly
(b) To handle multi-dimensional data structures like matrices
(c) To optimize the execution time of a single loop
(d) To reduce the number of loop iterations

Q.6

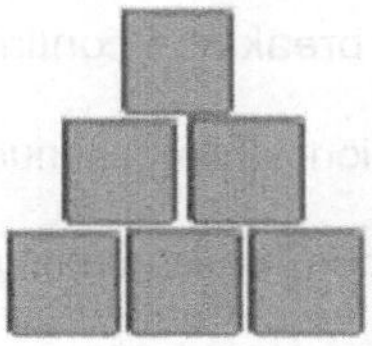

The process of building this triangular stack, where the number of blocks per row depends on the row number, best illustrates the use of:
(a) A simple if statement
(b) A single for loop
(c) Nested for loops
(d) A switch statement

Q.7

The task of generating a multiplication table, where each cell's value is the product of two numbers, is best achieved using:
(a) A single for loop
(b) Nested for loops
(c) A while loop
(d) A do-while loop

Q.8 What is the total number of times "Hello" will be printed in the following nested loop?

```
for (int i = 1; i <= 3; i++)
{
   for (int j = 1; j <= 2; j++)
   {
      System.out.println("Hello");
   }
}
```

(a) 2
(b) 3
(c) 5
(d) 6

Q.9 Which of the following loops is used to repeat the body of the inner loop completely for each iteration of the outer loop?
(a) for loop (b) while loop
(c) do-while loop (d) All of these

Q.10 If the continue statement is used in the outer loop of a nested loop, what happens?
(a) It terminates the outer loop
(b) It skips the iteration of the outer loop and moves to the next iteration
(c) It skips the iteration of the inner loop
(d) It terminates the inner loop only

Q.11 What is the difference between break and continue in nested loops?
(a) break skips the current iteration, while continue stops the entire loop
(b) break terminates the entire loop, while continue skips the remaining code of the current iteration
(c) continue is used only in the outer loop, while break is used in the inner loop
(d) Both are the same in their function

Q.12 What happens when a break statement is encountered in an inner loop?

```
for (int i = 1; i <= 3; i++)
{
   for (int j = 1; j <= 3; j++)
   {
      if (j == 2) break;
      System.out.print(i + " " + j + " ");
   }
}
```

(a) The outer loop stops
(b) Only the inner loop stops when j == 2
(c) The entire program terminates
(d) It has no effect

Q.13 Which of the following is not a valid nested loop structure in Java?
(a) for loop inside while loop
(b) while loop inside for loop
(c) do-while loop inside for loop
(d) break inside the outer loop

Q.14

The act of stopping the search through this 2D inventory as soon as the item is located best represents the use of:
(a) A continue statement (b) A break statement
(c) A return statement (d) A System.exit(0) call

Answers

1. (d)	**2.** (c)	**3.** (b)	**4.** (b)	**5.** (b)
6. (c)	**7.** (b)	**8.** (d)	**9.** (d)	**10.** (b)
11. (b)	**12.** (b)	**13.** (d)	**14.** (b)	

TYPE - 2

01 Mark

Statement Based Questions

Q.1 A Student is creating a pattern. They want to print a 2x3 rectangle of asterisks. Which of the following code snippets will achieve this?

```
for (int i = 0; i < 2; i++)
{
   for (int j = 0; j < 3; j++)
   {
     System.out.print("*");
   }
   System.out.println();
}
```

A. A line of 6 asterisks.
B. A 2x3 rectangle of asterisks.
C. A 3x2 rectangle of asterisks.
D. A triangle of asterisks.
(a) A (b) B
(c) C (d) D

Q.2 A coder is calculating a simple sum. They want to calculate the sum of the numbers from 1 to 3. Which of the following is the correct result?

```
int sum = 0;
for (int i = 1; i <= 3; i++)
{
   sum += i;
}
System.out.println(sum);
```

A. 3 B. 6 C. 9 D. 12
(a) A (b) B (c) C (d) D

Q.3 A developer is using nested for loops with a break statement. They want to find the first pair of numbers (i, j) where i * j > 2. Which of the following will achieve this?

```
for (int i = 1; i <= 2; i++)
{
   for (int j = 1; j <= 2; j++)
   {
      if (i * j > 2)
      {
         System.out.println(i + " " + j);
         break;
      }
   }
}
```

A. 1 1 B. 1 2 C. 2 1 D. 2 2
(a) A (b) B (c) C (d) D

Q.4 Consider the following steps involved in printing a rectangular pattern of asterisks using nested for loops. Choose the correct order of the steps:

A. The outer loop iterates through the rows.

B. The inner loop prints asterisks for each column.

C. The outer loop initializes the row counter.

D. The inner loop moves to the next line.

(a) A, C, D, B (b) C, A, B, D

(c) B, D, A, C (d) D, C, B, A

Q.5 Consider the following steps involved in calculating the sum of a series (1 + 2 + 3 + ... + n) using a single for loop. Choose the correct order of the steps:

A. The loop iterates from 1 to n.

B. The loop initializes the counter variable to 1.

C. The current value of the loop counter is added to the sum.

D. The final sum is displayed.

(a) C, D, A, B (b) A, C, D, B

(c) B, A, C, D (d) D, C, B, A

Answers

1. (b) **2.** (b) **3.** (c) **4.** (b) **5.** (c)

TYPE - 3

01 Mark

Assertion-Reason Type Questions

Directions (Q. Nos. 1-5) The following questions are Assertion-Reason based questions. Choose the answer based on the code given below

(a) Both Assertion (A) and Reason (R) are true and Reason (R) is a correct explanation of Assertion (A).

(b) Both Assertion (A) and Reason (R) are true and Reason (R) is not a correct explanation of Assertion (A).

(c) Assertion (A) is true and Reason (R) is false.

(d) Assertion (A) is false and Reason (R) is true.

Q.1 Assertion (A) In a nested loop, the inner loop completes all its iterations for each iteration of the outer loop.

Reason (R) The outer loop is responsible for controlling the number of times the inner loop runs, but the inner loop executes fully before returning control to the outer loop.

Ans. (a) Both Assertion (A) and Reason (R) are true, and Reason (R) is the correct explanation for Assertion (A).

Q.2 Assertion (A) The break statement in a nested loop terminates both the inner and outer loops immediately.

Reason (R) The break statement only terminates the loop in which it is placed.

Ans. (c) The break statement in a nested loop only terminates the loop in which it is placed, not both loops. Hence, Assertion (A) is false and Reason (R) is true.

Q.3 Assertion (A) The break statement in a nested loop terminates both the inner and outer loops immediately.

Reason (R) The break statement only terminates the loop in which it is placed.

Ans. (d) Assertion (A) is false and Reason (R) is true.

Q.4 Assertion (A) In a nested loop, the inner loop will run a fixed number of times regardless of the outer loop's iteration.

Reason (R) The number of iterations of the inner loop is controlled independently of the outer loop.

Ans. (d) Assertion (A) is false and Reason (R) is true.

Q.5 Assertion (A) If the break statement is used inside the inner loop of a nested loop, it only terminates the inner loop and not the outer loop.

Reason (R) The break statement only terminates the loop in which it is directly placed.

Ans. (a) Both Assertion (A) and Reason (R) are true, and Reason (R) is the correct explanation for Assertion (A).

TYPE - 4

01 Mark

Odd One Out

Q.1 Choose the odd one out:

(a) for (int i = 0; i < 5; i++) { ... }

(b) while (condition) { ... }

(c) do { ... } while (condition);

(d) repeat { ... }

Ans. (d) repeat { ... } (In Java, there is no repeat loop construct. The other three (for, while, and do-while) are valid loop structures. The repeat loop is not a part of Java's syntax.)

Q.2 Choose the odd one out:

(a) break

(b) continue

(c) exit

(d) return

Ans. (c) exit (In Java, break, continue, and return are used to control the flow within loops or methods. exit is not a valid control statement in Java; the correct method to terminate a program is System.exit(), but it is not used in the context of loop control.)

Q.3 Choose the odd one out:
(a) do { ...} while (condition);
(b) for (int i = 0; i < 5; i++) { }
(c) while (condition) { }
(d) if (condition) { }

Ans. (d) if (condition) { } (The if statement is a conditional construct, not a loop. The other options represent loop constructs: a variable initialization for loops, a for loop, and a while loop.)

Q.4 Choose the odd one out:
(a) for (int i = 0; i < 10; i++)
(b) for (int i = 0; i < 10; i--)
(c) for (int i = 10; i > 0; i--)
(d) for (int i = 0; i < 10; i++) { i = 5; }

Ans. (b) for (int i = 0; i < 10; i--) (In this case, i-- will result in an infinite loop. While the other loops have proper increment or conditions to exit, the i-- will keep decrementing and never reach a point to stop the loop.)

Q.5 Choose the odd one out:
(a) for (int i = 0; i < 5; i++)
(b) while (condition) { }
(c) do { ... } while (condition);
(d) switch (condition) { }

Ans. (d) switch (condition) { } (A switch statement is used for branching and selecting one out of multiple options, not for repeating a block of code. The other three (for, while, and do-while) are loop constructs used to repeat a block of code.)

TYPE - 5 — 01 Mark

Very Short Answer Type Questions

Q.1 What is a nested loop, and how does it differ from a single loop?

Ans. A loop inside another loop, the inner loop runs fully for each outer loop iteration.

Q.2 Given below a loop:

```
for(i=1;i<=6;i++)
    for(j=1;j<=6;j++)
        System.out.println("Arihant");
```

How many times will the string " Arihant" printed?

Ans. 36 times.

Q.3 What is the effect of using continue in the outer loop of a nested loop?

Ans. It skips the rest of the current outer loop iteration and starts the next one.

Q.4 In a nested loop, which loop controls the overall execution count?

Ans. The outer loop controls the total number of executions.

Q.5 Why is the inner loop crucial in a nested loop structure?

Ans. It allows repeated execution within each iteration of the outer loop.

Q.6 Can different types of loops be combined in a nested loop structure?

Ans. Yes, for, while, and do-while can be nested within each other.

Q.7 Given the loop

```
for(i=1;i<=6;i++)
    for(j=1;j<=i;j++)
        System.out.println("Arihant");
```

What will be the value of j after both the loops close?

Ans. 7

Q.8 What is the impact of placing a break in the outer loop of a nested loop?

Ans. It stops both the outer and inner loops completely.

Q.9 What happens when multiple continue statements are used in a nested loop?

Ans. Each affects its respective loop; inner continue skips inner iteration, outer continue skips outer iteration.

Q.10 How is the inner loop initialized in a nested loop, and how often does it reset?

Ans. It reinitializes every time the outer loop iterates.

TYPE - 6 — 02 Marks

Short Answer Type Questions

Q.1 How do nested loops contribute to solving multi-dimensional problems?

Ans. Nested loops allow iteration over multi-dimensional data structures like matrices, graphs, and tables, making them essential for processing large datasets.

Q.2 How does the continue statement behave differently when placed inside the inner loop versus the outer loop?

Ans. **Inside the inner loop** Skips the remaining code in the inner loop and moves to the next iteration of the inner loop.

Inside the outer loop Skips the rest of the outer loop iteration and starts the next iteration, effectively skipping the entire inner loop for that cycle.

Q.3 Correct the error in the following code so that the program works as expected.

```
for (int i = 1; i <= 3; i++)
{
```

```
    for (int j = 1; j <= 2; j++)
    {
      if (i == 2)
        break;
      System.out.print(j + " ");
    }
  }
```

Ans.

```
for (int i = 1; i <= 3; i++)
{
  for (int j = 1; j <= 2; j++)
  {
    if (i == 2)
      continue; // Corrected: Use continue
                              instead of break
    System.out.print(j + " ");
  }
}
```

Q.4 How do initialization and termination conditions of the inner loop affect the overall execution of a nested loop?

Ans. The inner loop reinitializes for each outer loop iteration and executes fully before the outer loop increments. If not properly defined, it can cause infinite loops or unexpected behavior.

Q.5 What happens if a nested loop has an inner loop with an incorrect or missing termination condition?

Ans. The inner loop may run infinitely, preventing the outer loop from progressing, leading to an unresponsive or crashing program.

Q.6 Explain the role of multiple counter variables in nested loops.

Ans. Multiple counter variables help track the iterations of each loop separately, allowing controlled execution of multi-dimensional structures like grids, matrices, and patterns.

Q.7 What are some common use cases for nested loops in real-world applications?

Ans.
- Matrix operations (e.g., addition, multiplication)
- Sorting algorithms (e.g., Bubble Sort, Selection Sort)
- Pattern printing
- Graph traversal (e.g., BFS, DFS)
- Processing nested lists/tables

Q.8 How can you optimize a nested loop to improve efficiency?

Ans.
- Minimize iterations by reducing unnecessary checks.
- Use break wisely to exit early.
- Avoid redundant calculations inside loops.
- Consider alternative algorithms (e.g., recursion, hashing).

Q.9 What happens if the inner loop condition depends on the outer loop variable?

Ans. The inner loop's execution count varies dynamically based on the outer loop, leading to non-uniform iterations (e.g., triangular patterns).

Q.10 Identify and correct the issue in the following nested loop:

```
for (int i = 1; i <= 2; i++)
{
  for (int j = 1; j <= 3; j++)
  {
    if (j == 2)
      continue;
    if (i == 2)
      break;
    System.out.print(i + " " + j + " ");
  }
}
```

Ans. Error: The break inside the inner loop for i == 2 prevents it from executing fully, which may not be intended.

Correction

```
for (int i = 1; i <= 2; i++)
{
  for (int j = 1; j <= 3; j++)
  {
    if (j == 2)
      continue; // Skip iteration when j == 2
    if (i == 2 && j == 3)
      break; // Stop when i = 2 and j = 3
    System.out.print(i + " " + j + " ");
  }
}
```

Q.11 How does the execution of a nested loop differ when using do-while instead of for or while?

Ans. A do-while nested loop executes at least once before checking the condition, unlike for and while, which may not execute if the condition is false initially.

Q.12 What is the impact of using a return statement inside a nested loop?

Ans. A return inside any loop completely terminates the method, stopping all further execution of both loops and returning control to the calling function.

TYPE - 6 (02 Marks)

Output Based Questions

Q.1 Predict output of the following code:

```
int a, b;
for (a = 5; a >= 1; a--)
{
  for (b = 1; b <= a; b++)
```

```
    {
        System.out.print("*");
    }
    System.out.println();
}
```

Ans.
```
*****
****
***
**
*
```

Q.2 Predict output of the following code:

```
int m, n;
for (m = 1; m <= 3; m++)
{
    for (n = 1; n <= m; n++)
    {
        System.out.print(m + n);
    }
    System.out.println();
}
```

Ans.
```
2
34
456
```

Q.3 Predict output of the following code:

```
int p, q;
for (p = 1; p <= 3; p++)
{
    for (q = 3; q >= p; q--)
    {
        System.out.print(q);
    }
    System.out.println();
}
```

Ans.
```
321
32
3
```

Q.4 Predict output of the following code:

```
int x, y;
for (x = 1; x <= 4; x++)
{
    for (y = 1; y <= x; y++)
    {
        if (x % 2 == 0)
        {
            System.out.print("*");
        }
        else
        {
            System.out.print("#");
        }
    }
    System.out.println();
}
```

Ans.
```
#
**
###
****
```

TYPE - 9 15 Marks

Long Answer Type Questions

Q.1 Write a program in Java to print a rectangle of stars (*) with 4 rows and 5 columns.

Ans.
```
public class RectangularPattern
{
    public static void main(String[] args)
    {
        for (int i = 1; i <= 4; i++)
        { // Outer loop for rows
            for (int j = 1; j <= 5; j++)
            {  // Inner loop for columns
                System.out.print("* ");
                // Print stars on the same line
            }
            System.out.println();
            // Move to the next line after each row
        }
    }
}
```

Q.2 Write a program in Java to print a right-angled triangle of stars.

Ans.
```
public class RightAngledTriangle
{
    public static void main(String[] args)
    {
        for (int i = 1; i <= 5; i++)
        {
            // Outer loop for rows
            for (int j = 1; j <= i; j++)
            {
                // Inner loop for columns
                System.out.print("* ");
                // Print stars on the same line
            }
            System.out.println();
            // Move to the next line after each row
        }
    }
}
```

Q.3 **Write a program in Java to print a right-angled triangle with numbers increasing in each row.**

Ans.
```
public class NumberTriangle
{
   public static void main(String[] args)
   {
      int num = 1;
         // Initialize the number to be printed
      for (int i = 1; i <= 4; i++)
      {
         // Outer loop for rows
         for (int j = 1; j <= i; j++)
         {
            // Inner loop for columns
            System.out.print(num + " ");
            // Print the number
          num++; // Increment the number
         }
         System.out.println();
            // Move to the next line after each row
      }
   }
}
```

Q.4 **Write a program in Java to print a multiplication table for numbers 1 to 3.**

Ans.
```
public class MultiplicationTable
{
   public static void main(String[] args)
   {
      fcr (int i = 1; i <= 3; i++) { // Outer loop
                             for the first multiplier
         for (int j = 1; j <= 10; j++)
         { // Inner loop for the second multiplier
           System.out.println(i + " x " + j + " = "
                                         + (i * j));
         }
         System.out.println();
          // Add an empty line between tables
      }
   }
}
```

Q.5 **Write a program in Java to print a triangle pattern using alphabets.**

Ans.
```
public class AlphabetTriangle
{
   public static void main(String[] args)
   {
      for (int i = 1; i <= 5; i++)
       { // Outer loop for rows
         char ch = 'A'; // Start with 'A' for each row
         for (int j = 1; j <= i; j++)
          { // Inner loop for columns
            System.out.print(ch + " ");
              // Print the character
            ch++; // Move to the next character
         }
         System.out.println();
           // Move to the next line after each row
       }
    }
}
```

Q.6 **Write a program in Java to print a Fibonacci series in a triangle.**

Ans.
```
public class FibonacciTriangle
{
   public static void main(String[] args)
   {
      int a = 0, b = 1;
      for (int i = 1; i <= 5; i++)
      {
         // Outer loop for rows
         for (int j = 1; j <= i; j++)
         { // Inner loop for columns
            System.out.print(a + " ");
            int next = a + b;
            // Calculate next Fibonacci number
          a = b;
          b = next;
      }
      System.out.println();
       // Move to the next line after each row
     }
   }
}
```

Q.7 **Write a program in Java to print a series Involving a Single Variable in a triangular format.**

Ans.
```
public class NumberTriangle
{
   public static void main(String[] args)
   {
      int number = 1; // Start from 1
      for (int i = 1; i <= 4; i++)
       { // Outer loop for rows
         for (int j = 1; j <= i; j++)
          { // Inner loop for columns
            System.out.print(number + " ");
          // Print the current number
            number++;
```

```
            // Increment the number
            }
            System.out.println();
            // Move to the next line
        }
    }
}
```

Q.8 Write a program in Java to exit both loops when a condition is met

Ans.
```
public class BreakNestedLoops
{
    public static void main(String[] args)
    {
        outer: // Label for the outer loop
        for (int i = 1; i <= 5; i++)
        {
            for (int j = 1; j <= 5; j++)
            {
                if (i == 3 && j == 3)
                {
                    System.out.println("Breaking out
                        of loops at i = " + i + ", j = " + j);
                    break outer; // Exit both loops
                }
                System.out.println("i = " + i + ", j = " + j);
            }
        }
    }
}
```

Q.9 Write a program in Java to print a multiplication table of 3 and stopping after 5 Multiplications

Ans.
```
public class MultiplicationTable
{
    public static void main(String[] args)
    {
        int count = 0;
        for (int i = 1; i <= 10; i++)
        {
            System.out.println("3 x " + i + " = " + (3 * i));
            count++;
            if (count == 5)
            {
                System.out.println("Stopping after 5
                                        multiple of 3.");
                break; // Stop after 5 numbers
            }
        }
    }
}
```

Q.10 Write a program in Java to print right-angled triangle with Skipped Rows(Skip rows with even numbers using continue.)

Ans.
```
public class TriangleWithSkip
{
    public static void main(String[] args)
    {
        for (int i = 1; i <= 5; i++)
        {
            if (i % 2 == 0)
            {
                System.out.println("Skipping row " + i);
                continue; // Skip even rows
            }
            for (int j = 1; j <= i; j++)
            {
                System.out.print("* ");
            }
            System.out.println();
        }
    }
}
```

Q.11 Write a program to input a number and check whether it is <Magic Number> or not. Display the message accordingly.

Ans.
```
import java.util.Scanner;
public class ProgMagicNum
{
    public static void main(String args[])
    {
        Scanner in = new Scanner(System.in);
        System.out.print("Enter a number to check: ");
        int num = in.nextInt();
        in.close();
        int n = num;
        while (n > 9)
        {
            int sum = 0;
            while (n != 0)
            {
                int d = n % 10;
                sum += d;
                n /= 10;
            }
            n = sum;
        }
        if (n == 1)
            System.out.println(num + " is a Magic
                                        Number.");
        else
```

```
            System.out.println(num + " is NOT a
                                      Magic Number.");
        }
    }
```

Q.12 Write a program to compute and display the sum of the following series:
S = (1 + 2) / (1 " 2) + (1 + 2 + 3) / (1 " 2 " 3) + -------- + (1 + 2 + 3 + ----- + n) / (1 " 2 " 3 " ----- " n)

Ans.
```
import java.util.Scanner;
public class ProgSeries
{
    public static void main(String args[])
    {
        Scarner in = new Scanner(System.in);
        System.out.print("Enter n: ");
        int n = in.nextInt(); // Fixed: in.nextIntt() ?
                                           in.nextInt()
        in.close();
        double sum = 0.0;
        for (int i = 1; i <= n; i++)
        {
            double num = 0.0, den = 1.0;
            for (int j = 1; j <= i; j++)
            {
                num += j;
                den *= j;
            }
            sum += (num / den);
        }
        System.out.println("Sum = " + sum);
    }
}
```

Q.13 Write a program to display all prime palindrome numbers between 10 and 1000.

Ans.
```
public class ProgPrimePalindrome
{
    public static void main(String[] args)
    {
        int count = 0;
        for (int i = 10; i <= 1000; i++)
        {
            if (isPalindrome(i) && isPrime(i))
            {
                System.out.print(i + " ");
                count++;
                if (count == 10)
                {
                    System.out.println();
                    count = 0;
                }
            }
        }
    }
    // Method to check if a number is a palindrome
    public static boolean isPalindrome(int num)
    {
        int revNum = 0, temp = num;
        while (temp != 0)
        {
            int digit = temp % 10;
            revNum = revNum * 10 + digit;
            temp /= 10;
        }
        return revNum == num;
    }
    // Method to check if a number is prime
    public static boolean isPrime(int num)
    {
        if (num < 2) return false;
        for (int i = 2; i <= num / 2; i++)
        {
            if (num % i == 0)
            {
                return false;
            }
        }
        return true;
    }
}
```

10

COMPUTING AND ETHICS

Ethical Issues in Computing

Ethical issues in computing refer to the moral challenges and dilemmas that come with using computers, software, and digital technology. As technology grows, new concerns arise, affecting people, businesses, and society. Some key ethical issues include privacy, security, the digital divide, intellectual property, and the responsible use of artificial intelligence (AI).

These ethical concerns cover many aspects of how technology is developed, used, and shared. Since computing is now a major part of daily life, it is important to ensure that technology helps society while reducing harm.

Intellectual Property Rights (IPR)

Intellectual Property Rights (IPR) are legal protections given to people or organizations for their inventions, creative works, and original ideas. These rights allow creators to control and benefit from their work while stopping others from using it without permission.

IPR helps encourage new ideas, creativity, and economic growth by rewarding inventors, artists, and businesses for their efforts in research and development.

Types of Intellectual Property Rights

Copyright

- Copyright protects original creative works like books, music, films, software, and paintings, giving creators exclusive rights to use, copy, and share their work.
- It lasts for the creator's lifetime plus 50-100 years, ensuring long-term protection under national laws.

Patents

- Patents protect new inventions, processes, or technical solutions, giving the holder exclusive rights to produce, sell, or license them for about 20 years.
- Inventors must provide a detailed description of their invention, which is made public in patent databases in exchange for exclusive rights.

Trademarks

- Trademarks protect brand names, logos, symbols, and slogans, helping businesses establish a unique identity.
- They prevent others from copying a brand's identity and can be renewed indefinitely if actively used.

Trade Secrets

- Protects confidential business information that gives a company an advantage (e.g., secret formulas, business strategies).
- Unlike patents, trade secrets are not registered but must be kept secret using contracts and security measures.

Industrial Design Rights

- Industrial design rights protect the appearance and shape of a product, ensuring its unique design is legally safeguarded.
- These rights prevent others from copying the product's design without permission.

Protection of an Individual's Right to Privacy

The right to privacy is a fundamental human right that protects people from unwanted interference in their personal lives. In today's digital world, where personal data is frequently collected, stored, and shared, protecting privacy has become an important ethical and legal issue. Safeguarding privacy ensures that individuals can control their personal information and protect their dignity, security, and freedom.

Key Aspects of Privacy Protection

- **Personal Data Protection** Personal data includes information that can identify an individual, like name, address, or online activity. Laws like the GDPR require organizations to handle data safely and lawfully, with consent from individuals.
- **Online and Digital Privacy** Digital footprints from social media and online shopping raise concerns about privacy and data breaches. Platforms like Facebook and Google offer privacy settings so users can control who sees their information.
- **Financial and Medical Privacy** Financial privacy protects banking and transaction details, while medical privacy ensures sensitive health data stays secure. Laws like HIPAA protect medical records from unauthorized access.
- **Workplace and Employee Privacy** Employers may monitor emails and online activity for security, but too much surveillance can breach privacy rights. Companies must inform employees about their monitoring practices.
- **Government Surveillance and Privacy** Governments collect data for security reasons, but concerns grow when surveillance becomes excessive, threatening individual freedoms. Programs like PRISM have sparked debates about privacy vs. security.

Challenges and Threats to Privacy

- **Data Breaches and Hacking** Cybercriminals steal personal data, leading to identity theft and financial loss. For example, the 2017 Equifax breach exposed millions of Social Security numbers.
- **Social Media and Oversharing** People often share too much personal information online, making them vulnerable to fraud and cyberstalking. For example, sharing real-time locations can attract criminals.
- **AI and Facial Recognition Technology** AI surveillance can track people without their consent, raising ethical concerns. Some cities have banned facial recognition to protect privacy.
- **Lack of Awareness and Legal Protections** Many people don't read privacy policies or fully understand how their data is used. Some countries also lack strong privacy laws, making individuals more vulnerable to exploitation.

Data Protection on the Internet

Data protection on the internet means keeping personal and sensitive information safe from unauthorized access, theft, or misuse. With the widespread use of digital platforms, securing data is crucial for individuals, businesses, and governments.

Key Aspects of Data Protection

- **Personal Data Security** Personal data, like names, addresses, and financial details, must be protected to prevent identity theft and fraud. Using strong passwords and multi-factor authentication helps secure online accounts.
- **Encryption and Secure Communication** Encryption turns data into a code that only authorized users can read. HTTPS and encrypted messaging apps like WhatsApp ensure safe communication and prevent data interception.
- **Protection Against Cyber Threats** Cyber threats like phishing, malware, and MITM attacks can steal or damage data. Avoiding suspicious links and using updated antivirus software helps protect against these threats.
- **Data Privacy Policies and Regulations** Laws like GDPR and CCPA ensure companies handle personal data responsibly. Websites often ask for cookie consent to comply with data protection regulations.
- **Cloud Data Protection** Cloud services store data but need encryption, access control, and backups. Two-factor authentication (2FA) boosts security for cloud accounts.
- **Social Media and Data Protection** Social media platforms collect user data, so it's important to review privacy settings. Disabling location tracking prevents location-based tracking.

Best Practices for Data Protection

- **Use Strong and Unique Passwords** Avoid simple passwords and use password managers to create strong, secure passwords.

- **Enable Two-Factor Authentication (2FA)** Add an extra layer of protection to your online accounts for better security.
- **Be Cautious of Public Wi-Fi** Public Wi-Fi is often insecure, so use a VPN to browse safely.
- **Keep Software and Devices Updated** Regularly update systems and software to fix security vulnerabilities.

Protection Against Spam

Spam refers to unwanted messages sent in bulk, often through email, social media, or messaging apps. These can be harmless ads or dangerous phishing attempts and malware. Protecting yourself from spam is important for online security, privacy, and keeping your digital space clean.

Types of Spam

- **Email Spam** Unwanted emails that may contain ads, phishing scams, or harmful attachments. Example: Emails claiming you've won a lottery and asking for personal details.
- **Social Media Spam** Fake accounts or bots posting links or scams in comments or DMs. Example: Instagram messages from unknown accounts claiming you won a giveaway.
- **Messaging App Spam** Spam messages on apps like WhatsApp or SMS, often with phishing links. Example: A text pretending to be from a bank, asking for login information.
- **Search Engine Spam (SEO Spam)** Websites using unethical tactics to manipulate search engine results. Example: Clicking on a search result that redirects to an unsafe site.
- **Robocalls and Spam Calls** Automated or fake calls pretending to be from legitimate organizations. Example: A call pretending to be from tax authorities, demanding immediate payment.

How to Protect Yourself from Spam

- **Use Spam Filters** Email services like Gmail and Outlook have built-in filters to detect and move spam emails. Check your spam folder regularly to ensure no important emails were misclassified.
- **Avoid Sharing Your Email Publicly** Spammers often collect emails from public sites and forums. Use a secondary email for sign-ups and subscriptions.
- **Do Not Click on Suspicious Links** Hover over links to check where they lead before clicking. Spam links often lead to phishing or malware sites.
- **Use a Strong and Unique Email Address** Use hard-to-guess usernames to prevent spammers from targeting your email.
- **Use Anti-Spam Software and Extensions** Install software or browser extensions to block spam websites.

Software Piracy

Software piracy is the illegal copying, sharing, or using of software without permission. It's a type of intellectual property theft that harms both developers and users, causing financial losses and security risks from using pirated software.

Types of Software Piracy

- **End-User Piracy** Happens when individuals or businesses install more copies of software than the license allows.

  Example A company buys one copy of Microsoft Office but installs it on multiple computers without the proper license.
- **Counterfeit Software** Involves making and selling fake versions of software that look real.

  Example Buying a fake version of Windows from an unauthorized seller, often with fake packaging.
- **Internet Piracy** The illegal downloading or sharing of software through websites, torrents, or file-sharing platforms.

  Example Downloading a cracked version of Adobe Photoshop from an unauthorized site.
- **Hard-Disk Loading** Retailers install unlicensed software on computers before selling them to attract buyers without raising costs.

  Example A store sells a laptop preloaded with pirated versions of Windows and Microsoft Office.
- **Client-Server Overuse** Happens when businesses let more users than the license allows access software on a network.

  Example A company with a 10-user license allows 50 employees to use the software.

How to Prevent Software Piracy

- **Use Licensed Software** Always buy software from authorized sellers and use official product keys.
  Example Purchase Microsoft Office from the official Microsoft Store.
- **Implement Digital Rights Management (DRM)** DRM technology prevents unauthorized copying and sharing of software.
  Example Some video games require online activation to stop piracy.
- **Use Open-Source or Free Software** Choose legal alternatives to pirated software.
  Example Use LibreOffice instead of pirated Microsoft Office.
- **Educate Users About Software Ethics** Teach people the importance of respecting intellectual property in schools and businesses.
  Example Train employees to use legally purchased software.
- **Report Piracy** Companies offer rewards for reporting software piracy.
  Example The Business Software Alliance (BSA) investigates piracy and takes legal action.

Cybercrime

Cybercrime refers to illegal activities done using computers, networks, or the internet, such as hacking, identity theft, fraud, and cyberbullying. As technology improves, cybercriminals use more advanced methods, making cybersecurity a top priority worldwide.

Types of Cybercrime

- **Hacking** Hacking refers to the unauthorized access of computer systems with the intent to steal, alter, or delete data.
  Example A hacker gaining access to a bank's database and transferring funds without permission.
- **Identity Theft** Identity theft involves the illegal acquisition of personal information to commit fraudulent activities.
  Example Using stolen credit card details to make unauthorized online purchases.
- **Phishing** Phishing is the practice of sending fraudulent emails or creating fake websites to deceive individuals into providing sensitive information.
  Example A phishing email impersonating a bank, requesting account information.
- **Ransomware Attacks** Ransomware attacks involve encrypting or locking files on a computer or network and demanding payment for their release.
  Example The 2017 WannaCry ransomware attack, which affected thousands of organizations worldwide.
- **Online Fraud and Scams** Online fraud and scams refer to deceptive schemes carried out over the internet to steal money or personal information.
  Example A fake online store that accepts payment but fails to deliver products.
- **Cyberbullying and Harassment** Cyberbullying and harassment involve the use of the internet to intimidate, threaten, or harm individuals.
  Example Posting harmful or defamatory messages on social media to damage someone's reputation.
- **Distributed Denial-of-Service (DDoS) Attacks** A Distributed Denial-of-Service (DDoS) attack occurs when multiple systems are used to flood a website or network, making it inaccessible.
  Example Disrupting online banking services by overwhelming their servers with excessive traffic.
- **Cyber Terrorism** Cyber terrorism is the use of technology to carry out attacks on government systems or critical infrastructure with the intent to cause widespread harm or fear.
  Example Hacking into a nation's power grid to cause widespread blackouts.

How to Prevent Cybercrime

- **Use Strong Passwords and Multi-Factor Authentication (MFA)** Create strong, complex passwords and enable MFA for added protection.
  Example Using a password manager to store unique, secure passwords.
- **Avoid Suspicious Links and Emails** Do not click on unverified links or download attachments from unknown sources.

Example Check the sender's email address before opening messages.

- **Keep Software and Antivirus Updated** Regular updates fix security flaws and prevent malware.

  Example Set up automatic updates for your operating system and antivirus software.
- **Secure Wi-Fi Networks** Use encryption and avoid using public Wi-Fi for sensitive activities.

  Example Use a VPN to protect your data when accessing public Wi-Fi.
- **Report Cybercrime** Report incidents to the authorities for further investigation.

  Example Report phishing attempts to agencies like the FBI's IC3.

Hacking

Hacking is the act of gaining unauthorized access to computer systems, networks, or digital devices to steal, change, or manipulate data. While hacking is usually linked to cybercrime, it can also be ethical when done for security testing and protection. Hackers use different methods and tools to find and take advantage of weaknesses in software, hardware, or human behavior.

Types of Hacking

- **Ethical Hacking (White-Hat Hacking)** This is done by security professionals who have permission to test and improve cybersecurity defenses. It helps companies find weaknesses before malicious hackers can exploit them.
- **Black-Hat Hacking (Malicious Hacking)** This type of hacking is carried out by cybercriminals who break into systems for financial gain, data theft, or to cause damage.
- **Grey-Hat Hacking** A mix of ethical and malicious hacking; hackers break into systems without permission but do not intend to cause harm. They might report vulnerabilities to companies but may demand payment for their findings.
- **Script Kiddies** Inexperienced hackers who use pre-made tools without understanding how they work. They often attack systems for fun or to gain recognition, not for financial gain.
- **Hacktivism** Hacking done as a form of political or social activism. Targets often include government websites, corporations, or media outlets.
- **State-Sponsored Hacking** Governments hire hackers to conduct cyber espionage, sabotage, or attacks on other countries. This is often used for intelligence gathering, election interference, or disabling enemy infrastructure.

How to Prevent Hacking

- **Use Strong Passwords and Multi-Factor Authentication (MFA)** Avoid weak passwords and add extra security measures like SMS or authentication apps.

  Example Use a password manager to create and securely store unique passwords.
- **Keep Software and Security Systems Updated** Install updates and patches to fix security holes.

  Example Regularly update Windows to prevent malware infections.
- **Use Firewalls and Antivirus Software** Firewalls block unauthorized access, while antivirus software detects and removes malware.

  Example Enable Windows Defender to protect against cyber threats.
- **Regularly Back Up Important Data** Store backups of important files to prevent data loss.

  Example Back up important business documents to cloud storage like Google Drive in case of ransomware.
- **Educate Users on Cybersecurity Best Practices** Train employees and individuals to recognize and avoid cyber threats.

  Example Run cybersecurity awareness programs in workplaces and schools.

Note *Cracking refers to the act of breaking or bypassing security measures on software, systems, or networks, typically for malicious purposes. This can involve activities like:*

- ***Cracking Software*** *Removing copy protection or licensing restrictions on software (e.g., bypassing a product key or activation process) to use it illegally or for free.*
- ***Password Cracking*** *Attempting to guess or decrypt a password to gain unauthorized access to a system or account.*
- ***Cracking Network Security*** *Breaking into networks or systems by exploiting vulnerabilities in order to steal data or disrupt operations.*

Protection Against Malicious Intent and Malicious Code

Malicious intent refers to actions that harm systems, networks, or users, while malicious code (malware) includes viruses, worms, Trojans, ransomware, and spyware designed to disrupt operations, steal data, or damage systems. Protecting against these threats is crucial as cybercriminals continuously find new vulnerabilities to exploit.

- **Viruses** Self-replicating programs that attach to files and spread when the file is opened.
  Example A virus infecting a USB drive and spreading to multiple computers.
- **Worms** Standalone programs that spread across networks without needing user interaction.
  Example A worm infecting a corporate network by exploiting security weaknesses.
- **Trojans** Malicious software disguised as a legitimate program to trick users into installing it.
  Example A fake antivirus program that steals passwords.
- **Ransomware** Encrypts files and demands payment for their decryption.
  Example A hacker locking a company's database and demanding cryptocurrency for decryption.
- **Spyware** Secretly monitors user activity and steals sensitive data.
  Example A keylogger recording passwords and banking details.
- **Adware** Unwanted software that displays excessive ads and redirects users to harmful websites.
  Example A browser extension showing fake pop-up ads.
- **Rootkits** Gives hackers deep access to a system, allowing them to hide their presence.
  Example A rootkit allowing a hacker to control a victim's computer remotely.
- **Botnets** A network of infected computers controlled remotely to launch cyberattacks.
  Example A hacker using thousands of compromised computers to carry out a DDoS attack.

Consequences of Malicious Code

- **Data Theft and Privacy Violations** Malware can steal personal and financial data.
  Example Credit card details being sold on the dark web.
- **Financial Losses** Individuals and businesses lose money from fraud, ransom, and repairs.
  Example A company paying millions to recover data after a ransomware attack.
- **System Damage and Downtime** Malware can corrupt files, crash networks, or slow down systems.
  Example A hospital's computer system failing due to an attack.
- **Reputational Damage** Businesses lose customer trust after security breaches.
  Example A bank losing clients after a hacking incident.
- **National Security Risks** Cyberattacks can target critical infrastructure and government systems.
  Example Hackers disrupting power grids and communication networks.

Protection Against Malicious Code

- **Install and Update Security Software** Use antivirus, anti-malware, and firewalls to block threats.
  Example Windows Defender protecting against infections.
- **Keep Systems Updated** Apply security patches to fix vulnerabilities.
  Example Regular updates to Windows to prevent exploits.
- **Educate Users on Cybersecurity** Awareness helps users avoid scams and malware.
  Example Companies training employees to recognize phishing attempts.
- **Monitor Networks for Suspicious Activity** Detect and respond to unauthorized access attempts.
  Example Security software detecting and responding to suspicious activities.
- **Enable Application Whitelisting** Only allow approved programs to run on systems.
  Example Preventing employees from installing unknown software.
- **Report Cyber Threats** Reporting threats to authorities helps take action against cybercriminals.
  Example Reporting a phishing attempt to cybersecurity agencies.

Good Etiquette and Ethical Practices in Computing

In the digital world, good etiquette and ethical practices are essential, just as they are in face-to-face interactions. These practices ensure respect, fairness, and security in communication, online transactions, and software usage, protecting privacy, maintaining trust, and upholding the integrity of systems and data.

Importance of Good Etiquette in Computing

- **Respect for Others' Time and Resources** Avoid wasting time with unnecessary emails or tasks. Be clear and to the point.

  Example Combine multiple emails into one well-organized message for colleagues.
- **Thoughtful Online Communication** Be polite and professional online, avoiding sarcasm or offensive language.

  Example Disagreeing respectfully in online discussions without using insults.
- **Acknowledging Others' Work and Ideas** Always give credit for others' ideas, work, or code.

  Example Properly cite the source when using someone else's code snippet.
- **Confidentiality and Privacy** Respect others' privacy and handle sensitive information with care.

  Example Do not forward confidential emails or reports without permission.
- **Avoiding Overuse of Resources** Be considerate of shared resources and avoid overloading systems.

  Example Avoid streaming videos or downloading large files on work networks unless necessary.

Ethical Practices in Computing

- **Respect for Intellectual Property** Do not use or share pirated or unlicensed software.

  Example Make sure to use properly licensed software or opt for open-source alternatives.
- **Promoting Fair Access** It ensure that everyone has equal access to technology.

  Example Develop software with features like screen readers or voice commands for accessibility.
- **Data Protection and Security** Protect sensitive data using encryption, strong passwords, and privacy policies.

  Example Encrypt confidential data to prevent unauthorized access in case of a breach.
- **Avoiding Harmful or Malicious Activities** Avoid engaging in hacking, cyberbullying, or spreading malware.

  Example Never share pirated content or malware-infected files online.
- **Adherence to Legal and Organizational Standards** Follow laws and company guidelines on cybersecurity, privacy, and intellectual property.

  Example Companies enforce rules about acceptable use of networks and devices.

EXAM ORIENTED QUESTIONS

TYPE – 1 01 Mark

Multiple Choice Questions

Q.1 Which of the following is NOT recognized as a form of intellectual property protection?
(a) Trademark (b) Patent
(c) Trade Secret (d) Data Breach

Q.2 What is the main function of a patent in intellectual property law?
(a) To protect creative expressions
(b) To protect inventions and technical processes
(c) To prevent unauthorized use of trade secrets
(d) To safeguard artistic works

Q.3

Collecting a user's address without explicit consent violates which ethical principle?
(a) Software piracy
(b) Protection of individual's right to privacy
(c) Cybercrime
(d) Protection against malicious intent

Q.4

Sending unsolicited bulk emails to a large number of recipients is known as:
(a) Hacking (b) Spamming
(c) Malicious coding (d) Ethical marketing

Q.5 Which legislation in the U.S. ensures the confidentiality and security of medical records?
(a) General Data Protection Regulation (GDPR)
(b) Health Insurance Portability and Accountability Act (HIPAA)
(c) California Consumer Privacy Act (CCPA)
(d) Digital Millennium Copyright Act (DMCA)

Q.6 What is the most significant ethical concern surrounding the use of facial recognition technology?
(a) The cost of implementation
(b) The potential for misuse in tracking individuals without consent
(c) The lack of accuracy in detecting faces
(d) Difficulty in gaining widespread adoption

Q.7 Which of the following is a typical consequence for organizations affected by malicious code?
(a) Increased software functionality
(b) Financial losses and data theft
(c) Better security updates
(d) Reduced risk of malware

Q.8

Distributing a computer virus designed to harm other users' systems demonstrates:
(a) Intellectual property rights
(b) Protection against spam
(c) Malicious intent and malicious code
(d) Data protection

Q.9 What is the primary objective of ethical hacking?
(a) To exploit vulnerabilities for malicious purposes
(b) To enhance security measures and identify weaknesses
(c) To sell data to the highest bidder
(d) To introduce malware into a system for testing

Q.10 Which of the following is classified as a malicious software that locks files and demands payment for their release?
(a) Trojan Horse (b) Worm
(c) Ransomware (d) Virus

Q.11 Which action best helps protect against phishing scams?
(a) Regularly updating antivirus software
(b) Using a secure connection via VPN
(c) Clicking links only from verified sources
(d) Avoiding email attachments from unknown sources

Q.12 Which of the following is an example of good ethical computing behavior?
(a) Sharing confidential files without authorization
(b) Appropriating software without licenses
(c) Giving credit to others for their work and ideas
(d) Using excessive network resources

Q.13 What is the role of encryption in protecting digital data?
(a) To allow public access to private data
(b) To secure data by converting it into an unreadable format
(c) To enable easy sharing of sensitive information
(d) To back up data in the cloud for quick access

Q.14

Creating and spreading false information online, especially if it causes harm, is considered:
(a) Good cyber etiquette
(b) Ethical data sharing
(c) Malicious intent
(d) Copyright infringement

Q.15 Which of the following types of intellectual property is protected by copyright law?
(a) Company's trademark
(b) A newly developed business logo
(c) An original song or manuscript
(d) A product's design and appearance

Q.16 Which of the following best distinguishes ethical hacking from black-hat hacking?
(a) Ethical hackers exploit system weaknesses for profit, while black-hat hackers do so to improve security
(b) Ethical hackers have authorization for their actions, whereas black-hat hackers engage in illegal activities
(c) Black-hat hackers work with the permission of the system owner, while ethical hackers work without it
(d) Ethical hackers damage data, while black-hat hackers protect it

Q.17 How does ransomware differ from spyware in its actions?
(a) Ransomware collects personal data covertly, while spyware demands payment for file access
(b) Spyware locks files, while ransomware encrypts them for ransom
(c) Ransomware monitors system activity, while spyware spreads across networks autonomously
(d) Spyware steals personal information in real-time, while ransomware requires user interaction to function

Q.18 What is the key objective of the General Data Protection Regulation (GDPR)?
(a) To ensure the protection of U.S. health data
(b) To safeguard personal data privacy within the European Union
(c) To protect against global cyberattacks
(d) To regulate the storage of financial data

Q.19 Which statement accurately describes the difference between viruses and worms?
(a) Viruses require user interaction to spread, while worms can spread independently without user action
(b) Worms spread only via email, while viruses are transferred through websites
(c) Viruses self-replicate across systems, while worms attach themselves to files
(d) Both viruses and worms require direct user installation to infect systems

Q.20

Using public Wi-Fi for sensitive transactions without a VPN or secure connection violates what principle of good ethical practice?
(a) Data protection on the internet.
(b) Software piracy protection.
(c) Anti-spam measures.
(d) Intellectual property rights.

Answers

1. (d)	**2.** (b)	**3.** (b)	**4.** (b)	**5.** (b)
6. (b)	**7.** (b)	**8.** (c)	**9.** (b)	**10.** (c)
11. (d)	**12.** (c)	**13.** (b)	**14.** (c)	**15.** (c)
16. (b)	**17.** (a)	**18.** (b)	**19.** (a)	**20.** (a)

TYPE - 2

01 Mark

Statement Based Questions

Q.1 A company collects personal data from its users for targeted advertising. Which ethical principle is most directly related to ensuring this data is handled responsibly?

A. Intellectual property rights
B. Protection of individual's right to privacy
C. Protection against spam
D. Software piracy

(a) Only A (b) Only B
(c) Only C (d) Both B and D

Q.2 A software developer creates a program that bypasses security measures to access restricted data. Which ethical issue is primarily involved?

A. Protection of individual's right to privacy
B. Software piracy
C. Hacking
D. Protection against spam

(a) Only A (b) Only B
(c) Only C (d) Both B and D

Q.3 Distributing copyrighted software without purchasing a license is a violation of which ethical principle?

A. Protection against malicious intent
B. Intellectual property rights
C. Data protection on the internet
D. Protection of individual's right to privacy

(a) Only A (b) Only B
(c) Only C (d) Both A and C

Q.4 Sending unsolicited bulk emails to a large number of recipients is associated with which ethical issue?

A. Cybercrime
B. Protection against spam
C. Hacking
D. Protection of individual's right to privacy

(a) Only A (b) Only B
(c) Only C (d) Both B and D

Q.5 Creating and spreading computer viruses designed to damage systems is a direct violation of which ethical principle?

A. Software piracy
B. Protection against malicious intent and malicious code
C. Data protection on the internet
D. Intellectual property rights

(a) Only A (b) Only B
(c) Only C (d) Both B and D

Q.6 Consider the following steps involved in handling a data breach. Arrange them in the correct order:

A. Notify affected individuals and relevant authorities.
B. Identify the source and extent of the breach.
C. Implement measures to prevent future breaches.
D. Secure compromised systems and data.

(a) A, B, C, D (b) B, D, A, C
(c) D, A, B, C (d) C, B, D, A

Q.7 Arrange the following stages of addressing software piracy in a company:

A. Implement a software asset management system.
B. Conduct an audit to identify unlicensed software.
C. Educate employees on software licensing policies.
D. Remove or replace unlicensed software.

(a) A, B, C, D (b) B, D, A, C
(c) C, A, D, B (d) D, C, B, A

Q.8 Arrange the following stages of addressing a cybercrime incident:

A. Preserve evidence and document the incident.
B. Report the incident to law enforcement.
C. Investigate the cause and extent of the attack.
D. Restore systems and data from backups.

(a) A, C, B, D (b) B, D, A, C
(c) C, A, D, B (d) D, B, C, A

Answers

1. (b)	2. (c)	3. (b)	4. (b)	5. (b)
6. (b)	7. (b)	8. (a)		

TYPE - 3

01 Mark

Assertion-Reason Type Questions

Directions (Q. Nos. 1-5) The following questions are Assertion-Reason based questions. Choose the answer based on the code given below

(a) Both Assertion (A) and Reason (R) are true and Reason (R) is a correct explanation of Assertion (A).
(b) Both Assertion (A) and Reason (R) are true and Reason (R) is not a correct explanation of Assertion (A).
(c) Assertion (A) is true and Reason (R) is false.
(d) Assertion (A) is false and Reason (R) is true.

Q.1 **Assertion (A)** Intellectual Property Rights (IPR) provide a legal framework for creators to benefit from their work.

Reason (R) IPR protects inventions, ensuring creators receive exclusive rights over their intellectual property.

Ans. (a) IPR grants legal protection, allowing creators to control and benefit from their inventions, thus encouraging innovation. Hence, Both A and R are true, and R is the correct explanation for A.

Q.2 Assertion (A) Ethical hacking is legal when conducted with the system owner's consent.

Reason (R) Ethical hackers perform tests to find vulnerabilities with permission to improve security.

Ans. (a) Ethical hackers are authorized to test systems for security flaws to prevent potential threats, ensuring systems are secure. Hence, Both A and R are true, and R is the correct explanation for A.

Q.3 Assertion (A) Data breaches often result in financial and reputational damage to businesses.

Reason (R) Exposed personal information can be misused, leading to fraud and lawsuits.

Ans. (b) While data breaches lead to financial losses and reputational harm, the reason isn't just misuse of information, but also the loss of trust and legal obligations businesses face. Hence, Both A and R are true, but R is not the correct explanation for A.

Q.4 Assertion (A) Software piracy is harmful and illegal, leading to significant consequences for both developers and users.

Reason (R) Pirated software may introduce security vulnerabilities and lack necessary updates.

Ans. (a) Pirated software often lacks essential updates and security patches, putting users at risk for cyberattacks, while also violating intellectual property rights. Hence, Both A and R are true, and R is the correct explanation for A.

Q.5 Assertion (A) Encryption is essential for maintaining data confidentiality and security during transmission.

Reason (R) Encryption changes data into unreadable code to prevent unauthorized access.

Ans. (b) While encryption is essential for data security, the reason is not solely for making data unreadable, but also for ensuring privacy during transit and preventing unauthorized tampering. Hence, Both A and R are true, but R is not the correct explanation for A.

TYPE - 4 — 01 Mark

Odd One Out

Q.1 Choose the odd one out:

(a) Encryption (b) Backups

(c) Phishing (d) Two-factor authentication (2FA)

Ans. (c) Phishing

Q.2 Choose the odd one out:

(a) Hacking (b) Identity theft

(c) Phishing (d) Copyright infringement

Ans. (d) Copyright infringement

Q.3 Choose the odd one out:

(a) Patents (b) Copyright

(c) Trademark (d) Rootkit

Ans. (d) Rootkit

Q.4 Choose the odd one out:

(a) Data breach (b) Spam

(c) Cybersecurity (d) Phishing

Ans. (c) Cybersecurity

Q.5 Choose the odd one out:

(a) Intellectual Property Theft

(b) Malware

(c) End-user Piracy

(d) Trade Secret Theft

Ans. (b) Malware

TYPE - 5 — 01 Mark

Very Short Answer Type Questions

Q.1 What is the duration of protection granted by copyright in most countries for creative works?

Ans. Copyright lasts for the creator's lifetime plus 50-100 years, depending on the country's laws.

Q.2 Which type of intellectual property right is granted for new inventions and gives exclusive rights for about 20 years?

Ans. A patent grants exclusive rights to inventions and processes for about 20 years.

Q.3 What term describes the unauthorized access to a computer system to gain control or steal information?

Ans. Hacking refers to unauthorized access to systems to steal or manipulate data.

Q.4 Which law protects the privacy of sensitive medical information and imposes strict security measures for health data?

Ans. HIPAA ensures the confidentiality and security of medical records in the U.S.

Q.5 What is the main function of Digital Rights Management (DRM) technology?

Ans. DRM prevents unauthorized copying and distribution of software or digital content.

Q.6 Which term refers to software that secretly monitors user activity, often for malicious purposes like stealing personal data?

Ans. Spyware is malicious software designed to monitor and steal user data.

Q.7 Which privacy law gives individuals the right to be informed about how their data is being used and to control its collection?

Ans. GDPR grants individuals rights over their personal data in the European Union.

Q.8 What is the primary purpose of using encryption in data protection?

Ans. Encryption converts data into a coded format to protect it from unauthorized access.

Q.9 What is the term for malicious programs that spread across networks, often without user interaction, to exploit vulnerabilities?

Ans. Worms are self-replicating programs that spread across networks without user interaction.

Q.10 What is the main ethical issue related to the use of facial recognition technology in surveillance?

Ans. Facial recognition technology raises privacy concerns as it tracks individuals without consent.

TYPE - 6

02 Marks

Short Answer Type Questions

Q.1 Explain the key aspects of privacy protection and how they help safeguard personal information.

Ans. Key aspects include personal data protection (ensuring data security and consent-based collection), online and digital privacy (controlling social media and browsing activity), financial and medical privacy (securing banking and health data), workplace privacy (limiting excessive employee surveillance), and government surveillance regulations (balancing national security with individual rights).

Q.2 Discuss the Legal and Security Consequences of Malicious Code for Individuals and Businesses.

Ans. Malicious code causes data theft, financial losses, and system damage, leading to downtime and disruptions in businesses and hospitals.

It results in reputational damage, making customers lose trust in companies. Additionally, national security risks emerge when cyberattacks target critical infrastructure like power grids and government networks.

Q.3 What advanced strategies can individuals and organizations implement for robust data protection on the internet?

Ans. Strategies include multi-layered authentication (biometrics, security keys), end-to-end encryption (for emails and cloud storage), firewalls and intrusion detection systems, regular security audits, zero-trust security models, and cyber hygiene training to prevent social engineering attacks.

Q.4 Compare and contrast different types of malicious code and their potential impacts on cybersecurity.

Ans. Viruses attach to files and spread via execution, worms self-replicate across networks, Trojans disguise as legitimate software to gain access, ransomware encrypts files for ransom, spyware secretly collects user data, rootkits provide unauthorized backdoor access, and botnets control multiple infected systems for large-scale attacks.

Q.5 What ethical dilemmas arise in computing, particularly regarding AI, data privacy, and digital accessibility?

Ans. Ethical dilemmas include AI bias and fairness (discriminatory algorithms in hiring or law enforcement), privacy concerns (mass surveillance, data breaches), intellectual property issues (AI-generated content ownership), digital divide (ensuring fair technology access), and cybersecurity ethics (responsibility in ethical hacking and encryption policies).

Q.6 What is an Antivirus? Name Different Types of Antivirus Software?

Ans. An antivirus software is a computer program designed to scan, detect, prevent, and remove viruses, worms, trojans, spyware, and other malicious software from a system.

It helps protect computers from cyber threats by identifying and neutralizing harmful files.

Functions of Antivirus Software:

Antivirus software performs its task using two primary techniques:

1. **Virus Dictionary-Based Detection** Scans files and compares them against a database of known viruses.
2. **Behavior-Based Detection** Monitors programs for suspicious activities that indicate potential malware infections.

Q.7 Evaluate the significance of cloud security measures in preventing data breaches and unauthorized access.

Ans. Cloud security relies on data encryption, access controls, multi-factor authentication, regular penetration testing, automated threat detection, and data redundancy strategies to prevent breaches, insider threats, and unauthorized access to sensitive data.

Q.8 How are trade secrets different from patents, and how are they protected?

Ans. Trade secrets keep business information private without needing registration, while patents must be publicly disclosed. They are protected using contracts, security rules, and limited access.

Q.9 How do ransomware attacks harm businesses and national security?

Ans. Ransomware locks important files and demands payment to unlock them, causing financial losses and work delays.

It can also disrupt essential services like government systems, hospitals, and power grids.

Q.10 Why is ethical hacking allowed, but black-hat hacking is illegal?

Ans. Ethical hacking is done with permission to improve security, while black-hat hacking is unauthorized and illegal because it harms systems, steals data, and breaks cybersecurity laws.

Q.11 Consider a social media platform that collects user data for targeted advertising.

(a) Explain how this platform's data collection practices can potentially violate the principle of "protection of individual's right to privacy."

(b) Describe how users of this platform can take steps to protect their privacy in this context.

Ans. (a) **Violation of Privacy Rights** The platform collects personal data, potentially including sensitive information, without clear consent or adequate safeguards. This compromises users' right to privacy, violating principles like data protection and informed consent.

(b) **Protecting Privacy** Users can protect their privacy by adjusting privacy settings, limiting shared information, using pseudonyms, and utilizing privacy-focused tools like VPNs or anonymous browsing.

Q.12 Imagine a software company that distributes a trial version of its software with limited features, but some users crack the software to use it without purchasing a license.

(a) Explain how this action violates "intellectual property rights."

(b) Describe the potential consequences for both the users and the software company.

Ans. (a) **Violation of Intellectual Property Rights** Cracking software to bypass licensing restrictions breaks the software company's intellectual property rights, as it involves using the software without permission or payment.

(b) **Consequences** Users may face fines or legal charges. The company could lose money, damage its reputation, and face higher security risks due to unauthorized access.

Q.13 A group of hackers develops and deploys a ransomware attack that encrypts critical data on a hospital's servers.

(a) Explain how this action constitutes "cybercrime" and "protection against malicious intent and malicious code."

(b) Describe the ethical responsibilities of security professionals in preventing and responding to such attacks.

Ans. (a) **Cybercrime and Protection against Malicious Intent** The ransomware attack is a type of cybercrime that intentionally disrupts a legitimate organization's operations. It breaks cybersecurity laws and shows harmful intent by damaging important systems.

(b) **Ethical Responsibilities of Security Professionals** Security professionals need to actively protect systems, respond quickly to problems, and use strong defenses like encryption, backups, and training to prevent attacks.

Q.14 Consider an email service that automatically filters out spam messages based on content and sender information.

(a) Explain how this service contributes to "protection against spam."

(b) Describe the potential ethical considerations related to the accuracy and transparency of spam filtering algorithms.

Ans. (a) **Protection against Spam** Spam filters block unwanted messages, protecting users from irrelevant or harmful content like phishing or malware. It improves the efficiency and security of communication platforms.

(b) **Ethical Considerations** Spam filters may occasionally misclassify legitimate emails as spam (false positives). Developers must ensure the accuracy of algorithms, disclose filtering criteria, and provide users with transparency and control over the filtering process.

Q.15 A website allows users to post anonymous comments without any moderation or oversight.

(a) Explain how this practice can lead to violations of "good etiquette and ethical practices" online.

(b) Describe the role of website administrators or moderators in promoting ethical online behavior and preventing abuse.

Ans. (a) **Violation of Good Etiquette** Allowing anonymous comments without oversight can lead to abusive language, trolling, or spreading misinformation. It encourages unethical online behavior by hiding the identity of users.

(b) **Role of Moderators** Website administrators must implement moderation tools, enforce community guidelines, and promote respectful discourse. By reviewing comments and implementing reporting mechanisms.

TYPE - 7 — 02 Marks

Differentiate

Q.1 Copyright and Trademark

Ans.

Copyright	Trademark
It protects original literary, artistic, and creative works (e.g., books, music, films).	It protects brand names, logos, and symbols that identify goods or services (e.g., Nike logo, Coca-Cola brand).
It grants exclusive rights to creators of original content, ensuring control over reproduction and distribution.	It helps distinguish goods or services in the marketplace, preventing confusion among consumers.

Q.2 Ethical Hacking and Black-Hat Hacking

Ans.

Ethical Hacking	Black-Hat Hacking
It performed with permission to identity and fix vulnerabilities in systems, helping improve security.	It conducts illegally to steal data, cause harm, or gain unauthorized access to systems.
It aims to protect systems and networks by testing them for weaknesses in a legal and controlled manner.	It often exploits security flaws for malicious purposes, such as financial gain or creating disruption.

Q.3 Ransomware and Spyware

Ans.

Ransomware	Spyware
It encrypts files and demands payment for decryption, often extorting money from the victim.	It secretly monitors user activity, capturing sensitive data like passwords and browsing history.
It can lock the user out of their files or system until the ransom is paid.	It operates covertly, usually without the user's knowledge, to gather information for malicious purposes.

Q.4 GDPR and HIPAA

Ans.

GDPR	HIPAA
A data protection law applicable in the European Union that focuses on personal data privacy.	A U.S. law that protects medical records and health information, ensuring confidentiality.
It aims to give individuals more control over their personal data, requiring organizations to be transparent about data usage.	It requires health organizations to secure patient data and enforce strict access control to medical records.

Q.5 Virus and Worm

Ans.

Virus	Worm
It equires user interaction to spread (e.g., opening an infected file or email).	It spreads automatically across networks, exploiting system vulnerabilities without needing user interaction.
It often attaches itself to files or programs and spreads when those files are shared.	It can replicate itself, causing widespread damage and network congestion.

Sample Question Paper

SAMPLE QUESTION PAPER
COMPUTER APPLICATIONS

General Instructions

Maximum Marks : 100

Time allowed : Two hours

Answers to this paper must be written on the paper provided separately.

You will not be allowed to write during the first 15 minutes.

This time is to be spent in reading the question paper.

The time given at the head of this paper is the time allowed for writing the answers.

This paper is divided into two sections.

Attempt all questions from **Section A** and any four questions from **Section B**.

The intended marks for questions or parts of questions are given in brackets [ ].

SECTION A

(Attempt all questions from this Section)

Question 1 **[20]**

Choose the correct answers to the questions from the given options.

(Do not copy the question, write the correct answers only.)

(i)

Name the OOP principle shown above.

(a) Polymorphism (b) Inheritance (c) Encapsulation (d) Abstraction

(ii) Which of the following statements about the Java compilation process is incorrect?

(a) Java source code is written in .java files.

(b) Bytecode is platform-dependent and cannot run on any machine.

(c) The JVM converts bytecode into machine-specific object code.

(d) The Java compiler (javac) generates .class files from .java files.

(iii) Which of the following is not a feature of Java?

(a) Platform independence. (b) Object-oriented programming.

(c) Direct memory management using pointers. (d) Built-in security features.

(iv) What is the primary role of the Java Virtual Machine (JVM)?
(a) To write Java source code.
(b) To compile Java source code into bytecode.
(c) To execute Java bytecode and provide platform independence.
(d) To debug Java programs.

(v) A class "Car" has attributes like model, color, and speed, and methods like startEngine() and accelerate(). Which OOP principle does this best illustrate?
(a) Inheritance
(b) Encapsulation
(c) Polymorphism
(d) Abstraction

(vi) In an e-commerce system, you have a class called "Product" with attributes like name, price, and description and methods like addToCart() and displayDetails(). You create several "Product" objects. What is the primary purpose of creating multiple objects of the "Product" class?
(a) To define the structure and behavior of all products.
(b) To represent different individual products in the system.
(c) To store all the product information in a single entity.
(d) To create a relationship between different product categories.

(vii) A software company releases a new video game with a "try before you buy" option, allowing users to play a limited version before purchasing the full game. This is an example of:
(a) Software piracy
(b) Ethical software distribution
(c) Copyright infringement
(d) None of the above

(viii) What is the result of the following code snippet?

```
double d = 10.5;
int i = (int) d;
```

(a) i will be 10.5
(b) i will be 10
(c) i will be 11
(d) The code will result in a compilation error.

(ix) Which of the following is NOT a primitive data type in Java?
(a) int
(b) String
(c) boolean
(d) double

(x) A company uses AI-powered facial recognition software to track customer behavior in their store without informing the customers. This raises ethical concerns primarily related to:
(a) Intellectual property rights
(b) Privacy violation
(c) Cybercrime
(d) Software piracy

(xi) Which type of malware encrypts files and demands a ransom for their release?
(a) Virus
(b) Worm
(c) Trojan
(d) Ransomware

(xii) Consider the following program segment in which the statements are jumbled. Choose the correct order of statements to print numbers 1 to 5 using a while loop.

```
System.out.println(i);    → 1
while(i <= 5)             → 2
int i = 1;                → 3
i++;                      → 4
```

(a) 2, 1, 4, 3
(b) 3, 2, 1, 4
(c) 3, 1, 2, 4
(d) 1, 3, 2, 4

(xiii) You are designing a system for a zoo. You have classes like "Animal," "Mammal," "Bird," "Lion," and "Eagle." Which OOP principle would be most helpful in representing the relationships between these classes and minimizing code duplication?
(a) Polymorphism
(b) Inheritance
(c) Abstraction
(d) Encapsulation

(xiv) What is the difference between next() and nextLine() methods of the Scanner class? (Understanding)

(a) next() reads an entire line, while nextLine() reads only the next word.

(b) next() reads the next word, while nextLine() reads an entire line.

(c) next() reads an integer, while nextLine() reads a string.

(d) next() and nextLine() are the same.

(xv) What is the term for unwanted messages sent in bulk, often via email or social media?

(a) Malware (b) Spam

(c) Phishing (d) Hacking

(xvi) **Assertion (A)** Ethical hacking plays an important role in cybersecurity.

Reason (R) Ethical hackers identify vulnerabilities in systems before malicious hackers can exploit them.

(a) Both A and R are true, and R is the correct explanation for A.

(b) Both A and R are true, but R is not the correct explanation for A.

(c) A is true, but R is false.

(d) A is false, but R is true.

(xvii) You have a class called "Dog." You create two objects from this class named "Buddy" and "Max." Which of the following is true?

(a) Buddy and Max will have the same attributes and methods.

(b) Buddy and Max will have the same attribute values but different methods.

(c) Buddy and Max will have different attributes but the same methods.

(d) Buddy and Max will have different attributes and different methods.

(xviii) Which method of the Math class returns the square root of a number? (Recall)

(a) sqrt() (b) pow()

(c) cbrt() (d) random()

(xix) You want to generate a random integer between 1 and 10 (inclusive). Which of the following approaches is closest to correct?

(a) (int)(Math.random() * 10) (b) (int)(Math.random() * 10) + 1

(c) Math.random() * 10 + 1 (d) (int)(Math.random() * 11) + 1

(xx) **Assertion (A)** Spam is merely an annoyance and poses no real threat.

Reason (R) Spam messages can contain phishing links, malware, and other harmful content that can compromise your security.

(a) Both A and R are true, and R is the correct explanation for A.

(b) Both A and R are true, but R is not the correct explanation for A.

(c) A is true, but R is false.

(d) A is false, but R is true.

Question 2.

(i) Rewrite the following code using a nested if statement: **[2]**

```
if (age > 18)
{
  System.out.println("Adult");
} else if (age == 18)
{
  System.out.println("Just became an adult");
}
```

(ii) Predict the output of the following Java program: **[2]**

```
class Test
{
  public static void main(String[] args)
  {
    int x = 5, y = 7;
```

SAMPLE QUESTION PAPER

```
        y += ++x - y-- + --x;
        System.out.println("x = " + x);
        System.out.println("y = " + y);
    }
}
```

What will be the final values of x and y?

(iii) The following Java program contains errors. Identify and correct them. **[2]**

```
import java.util.Scanner;
class Example
{
    public static void main(String args)
    {
        Scanner sc = new Scanner(System);
        int a;
        System.out.println("Enter a number: ");
        a = sc.nextInt;
        System.out.println("You entered: " + a);
    }
}
```

(iv) What is software piracy, and why is it considered unethical? **[2]**

(v) Change the for loop into while loop for the given code. **[2]**

```
class LoopExample
{
    public static void main(String[] args)
    {
        for (int i = 1; i <= 5; i++)
        {
            System.out.println("Iteration: " + i);
        }
    }
}
```

(vi) How does data protection on the internet help safeguard an individual's privacy? **[2]**

(vii) Write the differences between break and continue. **[2]**

(viii) Consider the following Java code using the java.lang.Math package. Predict the output of the program: **[2]**

```
class MathExample
{
    public static void main(String[] args)
    {
        double a = 4.5, b = 2.3;
        System.out.println("pow(a, b): " + Math.pow(a, b));
        System.out.println("sqrt(a): " + Math.sqrt(a));
        System.out.println("cbrt(a): " + Math.cbrt(a));
        System.out.println("ceil(a): " + Math.ceil(a));
        System.out.println("floor(a): " + Math.floor(a));
        System.out.println("round(a): " + Math.round(a));
        System.out.println("abs(-a): " + Math.abs(-a));
```

```java
            System.out.println("max(a, b): " + Math.max(a, b));
            System.out.println("min(a, b): " + Math.min(a, b));
            System.out.println("random(): " + Math.random());
        }
    }
```

(ix) Consider the following Java code snippet and answer the questions given below: **[2]**

```java
int a = 10, b = 20, c = 30;
if (a < b && b < c)
{
   System.out.println("Condition 1 is true");
}
else
{
   System.out.println("Condition 1 is false");
}
if (a + b > c)
{
   System.out.println("Condition 2 is true");
}
else
{
   System.out.println("Condition 2 is false");
}
```

(a) What will be the output for Condition 1?

(b) What will be the output for Condition 2?

(x) A developer writes a Java program on a Windows machine using a simple text editor. The developer then compiles the program and generates a .class file containing byte code. This byte code is uploaded to a website, where it is executed by users on different machines, including Linux and Mac systems. **[2]**

Answer the following questions:

(a) How does the use of the Java Virtual Machine (JVM) make this program platform-independent?

(a) What is the role of byte code in ensuring that the Java program can run on different platforms?

SECTION - B

(Answer any four questions from this Section.)

The answers in this section should consist of the programs in either BlueJ environment or any program environment with java as the base.

Each program should be written using variable description/mnemonic codes so that the logic of the program is clearly depicted Flowcharts and algorithms are not required.

Question 3. **[15]**

Write a program in Java to identify whether thee entered number is an Armstrong Number or not.

(An Armstrong number (or narcissistic number) is a number that is equal to the sum of its own digits each raised to the power of the number of digits. Example: 153 is an Armstrong number because $1^3 + 5^3 + 3^3 = 153$.)

Question 4. **[15]**

Create a Calculator in java using switch-case which finds the Sum, Difference, Product and Quotient.

Question 5. **[15]**

Write a program in Java to output the given inverted right-angled triangle pattern of stars (*).

```
*   *   *   *
    *   *   *
        *   *
            *
```

Question 6. **[15]**

Write a program in Java to identify whether the entered number is a Spy Number or not.

*(A Spy number is a number where the sum of its digits is equal to the product of its digits. Example: 1124 is a Spy number because 1 + 1 + 2 + 4 = 8 and 1 * 1 * 2 * 4 = 8.)*

Question 7. **[15]**

Write a program in Java to calculate the HCF and LCM of two numbers.

(HCF is the greatest divisor that two numbers share.
LCM is the smallest number that both numbers divide into evenly.)

Question 8. **[15]**

Write a program in Java to identify whether thee entered number is a Niven Number or not.

(A Niven number (also known as a Harshad number) is a number that is divisible by the sum of its digits.Example: 18 is a Niven number because 18 is divisible by 1 + 8 = 9.)

Answers

1. (i) (b) Inheritance

   (ii) (b) Bytecode is platform-dependent and cannot run on any machine.

   (iii) (c) Direct memory management using pointers.

   (iv) (c) To execute Java bytecode and provide platform independence.

   (v) (b) Encapsulation

   (vi) (b) To represent different individual products in the system.

   (vii) (b) Ethical software distribution

   (viii) (b) i will be 10

   (ix) (b) String

   (x) (b) Privacy violation.

   (xi) (d) Ransomware

   (xii) (b) 3, 2, 1, 4

   (xiii) (b) Inheritance

   (xiv) (b) next() reads the next word, while nextLine() reads an entire line.

   (xv) (b) Spam

   (xvi) (a) Both A and R are true, and R is the correct explanation for A.

   (xvii) (c) Buddy and Max will have different attributes but the same methods.

   (xviii) (a) sqrt()

   (xix) (d) Math.random() generates a number between 0.0 (inclusive) and 1.0 (exclusive). Multiplying by 11 gives you a range from 0.0 to 11.0 (exclusive). Casting to int truncates the decimal part, resulting in values from 0 to 10. Adding 1 shifts the range to 1 to 11. However, you want up to 10 so the best is d.

   (xx) (d) A is false, but R is true.

2. (i)
```
if (age >= 18)
{
  if (age == 18)
  {
    System.out.println("Just became an adult");
  }
  else
  {
    System.out.println("Adult");
  }
}
```

   (ii) Initial values: x = 5, y = 11

   Expression Breakdown:

   ++x (Pre-increment x)

   x becomes 6, so ++x = 6.

   --x (Pre-decrement x)

x is decremented back to 5, so --x = 5.
y-- (Post-decrement y)
First, y = 7 is used in the expression, and then y is decremented to 6.
Substituting values in the expression:

$$y \mathrel{+}= 6 - 7 + 5;$$
$$y \mathrel{+}= 4$$

or $y = y + 4 = 6 + 4 = 10$

Final values: x = 5, y = 10

Output

x = 5
y = 10

(iii)
```
import java.util.Scanner;
class Example
{
   public static void main(String[] args)
   {
      Scanner sc = new Scanner(System.in);
      int a;
      System.out.println("Enter a number: ");
      a = sc.nextInt();
      System.out.println("You entered: " + a);
   }
}
```

(iv) Software piracy refers to the illegal copying, distribution, or unauthorized use of software without proper licensing. It violates intellectual property rights, leading to financial losses for software developers and companies. Pirated software often lacks official updates and support, making it vulnerable to security threats like malware and viruses. It also discourages innovation and fair competition in the technology industry.

Software piracy is considered unethical because it violates intellectual property rights, depriving developers and companies of their rightful earnings. It discourages innovation by reducing incentives for developers to create new and improved software. Pirated software often lacks security updates, leading to higher risks of malware and cyber threats.

(v)
```
class LoopExample
{
   public static void main(String[] args)
   {
      int i = 1; // Initialization
      while (i <= 5)
      { // Condition
         System.out.println("Iteration: " + i);
         i++; // Increment
      }
   }
}
```

(vi) Data protection on the internet helps safeguard an individual's privacy by ensuring that personal data is securely stored and transmitted. It limits access to sensitive information to authorized individuals only. By implementing encryption, personal data is protected from unauthorized interception during online transactions. Strong passwords and multi-factor authentication add extra layers of security to online accounts. Furthermore, privacy policies dictate how data is collected, used, and shared, offering individuals more control over their information. Ultimately, data protection helps prevent issues like identity theft, financial fraud, and unauthorized data collection.

(vii) The differences between break and continue in Java are:

Feature	break	continue
Purpose	Exits the loop completely.	Skips the current iteration and moves to the next one.
Effect	Terminates the loop or switch statement.	Skips the remaining code in the loop body and moves to the next iteration.
Usage	Used when we want to stop loop execution based on a condition.	Used when we want to skip certain iterations but continue looping.
Applicable In	for, while, do-while, and switch statements.	for, while, and do-while loops.
Example in a for loop	`for (int i = 1; i <= 5; i++) { if (i == 3) break; System.out.println(i); }`	`for (int i = 1; i <= 5; i++) { if (i == 3) continue; System.out.println(i); }`

(viii) The output of the program would be:

```
pow(a, b): 31.79719290
    // 4.5 raised to the power of 2.3
sqrt(a): 2.1213203435596424
    // Square root of 4.5
cbrt(a): 1.6506291914393887
    // Cube root of 4.5
ceil(a): 5.0
    // Round up 4.5 to the next integer
floor(a): 4.0
    // Round down 4.5 to the nearest integer
round(a): 5
    // Round 4.5 to the nearest whole number
abs(-a): 4.5
    // Absolute value of -4.5
max(a, b): 4.5
    // Maximum of 4.5 and 2.3
min(a, b): 2.3
    // Minimum of 4.5 and 2.3
random(): 0.12345678912345678
    // A random value between 0.0 and 1.0 (will vary each time)
```

(ix) (a) For Condition 1:

The condition checks if a < b && b < c.

a = 10, b = 20, and c = 30

Since 10 < 20 and 20 < 30, the condition is true.

Therefore, the output will be:

Condition 1 is true

(b) For Condition 2:

The condition checks if a + b > c.

a + b = 10 + 20 = 30

Since 30 is not greater than 30, the condition is false.

Therefore, the output will be:

Condition 2 is false

(x) (a) ***JVM and Platform Independence*** *The Java Virtual Machine (JVM) provides an abstraction layer between the compiled byte code and the underlying operating system. Since the JVM exists for all major platforms, it allows the same byte code to be executed on any platform (Windows, Linux, Mac, etc.) without modification, making Java platform-independent.*

(b) ***Role of Byte Code*** *Byte code is a universal, machine-independent format generated after compiling the Java source code. It can be executed on any system that has the appropriate JVM, ensuring the program is portable across platforms. This allows the program to run on different machines, regardless of the underlying hardware or operating system.*

3.

```
import java.util.Scanner;
public class ArmstrongNumber
{
    public static void main(String[] args)
    {
        Scanner sc = new Scanner(System.in);
        // Get user input
        System.out.print("Enter a number: ");
        int num = sc.nextInt();
        int originalNum = num;
        int sum = 0;
        int numberOfDigits = String.valueOf(num).length();
        // Calculate the sum of the digits raised to the power of the number of digits
        while (num != 0)
        {
            int digit = num % 10;
            sum += Math.pow(digit, numberOfDigits);
            num /= 10;
        }
        // Check if the number is an Armstrong number
        if (sum == originalNum)
        {
            System.out.println(originalNum + " is an Armstrong number.");
        }
        else
        {
            System.out.println(originalNum + " is not an Armstrong number.");
        }
        sc.close();
    }
}
```

4.

```
import java.util.Scanner;
public class Calculator
{
    public static void main(String[] args)
    {
        Scanner sc = new Scanner(System.in);
        System.out.print("Enter first number: ");
        double num1 = sc.nextDouble();
        System.out.print("Enter second number: ");
        double num2 = sc.nextDouble();
        // Operation choice
        System.out.println("Choose operation: +, -, *, /");
        char operator = sc.next().charAt(0);
        double result;
        switch (operator)
        {
            case '+':
                result = num1 + num2;
                System.out.println("Sum = " + result);
```

```
            break;
        case '-':
            result = num1 - num2;
            System.out.println("Difference = " + result);
            break;
        case '*':
            result = num1 * num2;
            System.out.println("Product = " + result);
            break;
        case '/':
            if (num2 != 0)
            {
                result = num1 / num2;
                System.out.println("Quotient = " + result);
            } else {
                System.out.println("Error: Division by zero!");
            }
            break;
        default:
            System.out.println("Invalid operator!");
        }
        sc.close();
    }
}
```

5.

```
import java.util.Scanner;
public class InvertedRightAngleTriangle
{
    public static void main(String[] args)
    {
        Scanner sc = new Scanner(System.in);
        // Input: Number of rows
        System.out.print("Enter the number of rows: ");
        int rows = sc.nextInt();
        // Nested loop for printing the inverted triangle
        for (int i = rows; i >= 1; i--)
        {
            for (int j = 1; j <= i; j++)
            {
                System.out.print("*");
                // Print the star
            }
            System.out.println();
            // Move to the next line after each row
        }
        sc.close();
    }
}
```

6.

```
import java.util.Scanner;
public class SpyNumber
{
    public static void main(String[] args)
    {
        Scanner sc = new Scanner(System.in);
        // Get user input
        System.out.print("Enter a number: ");
```

```java
        int num = sc.nextInt();
        int sum = 0;
        int product = 1;
        // Calculate the sum and product of the digits
        int originalNum = num;
        while (num != 0)
        {
            int digit = num % 10;
            sum += digit;
            product *= digit;
            num /= 10;
        }
        // Check if the number is a Spy number
        if (sum == product)
        {
            System.out.println(originalNum + " is a Spy number.");
        }
        else
        {
            System.out.println(originalNum + " is not a Spy number.");
        }
        sc.close();
    }
}
```

7.

```java
import java.util.Scanner;
public class LCMHCF
{
    public static void main(String[] args)
    {
        Scanner sc = new Scanner(System.in);
        // Input from the user
        System.out.print("Enter the first number: ");
        int num1 = sc.nextInt();
        System.out.print("Enter the second number: ");
        int num2 = sc.nextInt();
        // Calculate HCF using Euclidean Algorithm
        int a = num1, b = num2;
        while (b != 0)
        {
            int temp = b;
            b = a % b;
            a = temp;
        }
        int hcf = a; // HCF is now stored in 'a'
        // Calculate LCM using the formula LCM(a, b) = (a * b) / HCF(a, b)
        int lcm = (num1 * num2) / hcf;
        // Display the results
        System.out.println("HCF of " + num1 + " and " + num2 + " is: " + hcf);
        System.out.println("LCM of " + num1 + " and " + num2 + " is: " + lcm);
        sc.close();
    }
}
```

8.

```java
import java.util.Scanner;
public class NivenNumber
{
   public static void main(String[] args)
   {
      Scanner sc = new Scanner(System.in);
      // Get user input
      System.out.print("Enter a number: ");
      int num = sc.nextInt();
      int sum = 0;
      int originalNum = num;
      // Calculate the sum of digits
      while (num != 0)
      {
         int digit = num % 10;
         sum += digit;
         num /= 10;
      }
      // Check if the number is divisible by the sum of its digits
      if (originalNum % sum == 0)
      {
         System.out.println(originalNum + " is a Niven number.");
      }
      else
      {
         System.out.println(originalNum + " is not a Niven number.");
      }
      sc.close();
   }
}
```

